Assessing Information Needs in the Age of the Digital Consumer

Assessing Information Needs in the Age of the Digital Consumer

Third Edition

David Nicholas and Eti Herman

 Routledge
Taylor & Francis Group

LONDON AND NEW YORK

3rd edition
Routledge
Albert House, 1–4 Singer Street, London, EC2A 4BQ, United Kingdom
Routledge is an imprint of the Taylor & Francis Group, an **informa** business

© Routledge 2009

ISBN 978-1-85743-487-3 (pbk)
ISBN 978-0-203-85579-9 (ebk)

Development Editor: Michael Salzman
Copy Editor: Alison Neale
Proofreader: Kate Kirkpatrick

Typeset in 10 on 12 pt Times New Roman by
Taylor & Francis Books

Printed and bound in Great Britain by
TJ International Ltd, Padstow, Cornwall

Contents

The authors

Eti Herman is a faculty member in the Information and Library Studies Programme at the University of Haifa, Israel. She is also a member of the UCL CIBER Research Group and serves on the editorial boards of Aslib Proceedings and the Israeli journal Meidaat. Her research and teaching interests are in the areas of information needs, information behaviour and scholarly communication. She is currently exploring the stereotypic characterisations of today's young information consumers.

David Nicholas is Head of the Department of Information Studies, University College London. He is also Director of the CIBER Research Group. Current interests lie in the impact of the Internet on key strategic groups, scholarly publishing and web log analysis. Other interests include information needs analysis and bibliometrics.

Introduction

Aiming at seeing to it that everyone obtains the rich rewards available in today's information-centred realities, this book sets out to help ensure that the myriad changing and pressing information needs people have are actually met by the unbelievable cornucopia of information resources surrounding us 24/7 in the office, home, coffee bar, place of recreation and train. A timely undertaking indeed, for there is good deal of evidence to suggest that in the 'Information Wild West' in which we find ourselves, there is a growing risk of information systems running wild – and running free of the information seeker. For, ironically enough, whilst the information that flows continuously through society now should be its lifeblood, people's understanding, appreciation and evaluation of it seems to have become materially poorer. In fact, members of today's information society, happily exercising their new-found options in the internet-redefined and vastly widened virtual information space, seem to manifest a dumbing down in their information-seeking and reading behaviour. This not in the least because the very act of switching the information tap on to everyone inevitably took the information professional out of the information equation. To coin a phrase, everyone has become a librarian, but, unfortunately, few people know how to behave like a librarian; instead they behave like e-shoppers.

This book constitutes a small step towards avoiding the disaster looming on our horizons in result of this behaviour. It does this in two ways. Firstly, by providing information professionals and information service providers with a framework for information needs analysis, which, based as it is on the insights gained from research projects involving hundreds of thousands of people, is firmly grounded in theory, but, nevertheless, highly practical. Thus, the framework, enabling as it does the ongoing assessment of people's information needs, should help information mediators to provide better services and greater support to their customers. Secondly, by spreading professional thinking and practices to today's new librarians, the digital consumers, which should ensure that they (and their families and communities) are better placed to meet their information needs on their own.

Since the last edition of this book the digital transition has moved at such a pace that we had to consider at the outset at whom this book is actually aimed. This is because the potential audience for the book has expanded hugely in size and character. Librarians, the professional group for whom the book was originally intended, are still a key audience. In fact, for them knowledge of information needs has become even more crucial, because without it the digital transition will see them decoupled from their increasingly digital and anonymous users, which would amount to professional suicide (something we will look into in more detail later). However, the professional audience for the book has grown substantially because the internet has been busy blowing-up and re-drawing the boundaries between professional groups. The once-neat demarcation lines that existed between librarians, archivists, records managers, journalists and publishers have become obscured as information consumers (and professions) use their recently found freedom to relocate themselves and their activities in the virtual information space. Most notably, publishers now build and operate digital libraries and librarians now get involved in publishing via open access journals and institutional repositories. Thus, more professions are concerned with information needs, and some of them are relatively new to it. It is in recognition of this that we have changed our vocabulary throughout, referring to information professionals, rather than just librarians.

Perhaps even more significantly, the digital transition has led to the general public (end-users in the old parlance) being involved in matters once the exclusive preserve of the librarian or archivist. Indeed, in many respects, everyone is a librarian or archivist now: we all search for information ourselves, have at our beck and call vast amounts of data, are responsible for the organization and archiving of information and even search for it on the behalf of others, as is the case with parents and carers. It follows, then, that everyone will have to sort out their own information needs (and those of their family and friends, too), if they are to really benefit from the information abundance available to them. It might be that information professionals will be able to help them here by teaching information needs analysis as part of digital and information literacy classes. In any case, the likes of the amateur scholar, student, academic, concerned parent, home worker and informed patient might find it useful to dip into particular parts of the book, especially the section on the information needs analysis framework, where we explain how individuals' information needs might be articulated to ensure positive information outcomes. While the section is lengthy in its explanation of the various characteristics of need, this does not mean that employing the framework on a daily basis is a long and laborious task, for it is just the initial understanding that takes the time. Thus, once the form of analysis has been mastered, then the various aspects shrink into a headings check list that can be mentally brought out for the strategic search.

Altogether, there are six sections to the book. The first section explains why information needs assessments are so important both for information professionals and, on a different level, for individual information consumers. The second section defines and maps out the terrain, delineating the whole information process. The various stages of the information-seeking and finding process – from need to use or consumption – are ordered and described. The key terms that are associated with the study of information consumption are defined and discussed, not to be pedantic, but to clarify what is being studied. Section three – in many ways the core section, lays out the essential characteristics of information need. The 11 characteristics, which combine together to form a comprehensive evaluatory framework, are identified and described: subject, function, nature, intellectual level, viewpoint, quantity, quality/authority, date/currency, speed of delivery, place of publication/origin, and processing and packaging. Section four examines the factors involved in people's decisions to start gathering data in response to a problem, perceived as calling for additional information, and the ways and means they choose for the purpose. Section five is somewhat different in nature from the earlier ones. It provides a review of the available data collection methods, not in any attempt to give instant 'how to do it yourself' instructions for those wishing to conduct needs/consumer studies, but in order to provide a basic understanding for anyone interested in the significance of a particular information needs exploration. The book ends with a call to information professionals to fulfil their part in providing for the enfranchisement in information terms of today's enthusiastic digital consumer.

1 Why undertake information needs assessments?

The user-oriented holistic approach to the development of information systems and services has been strongly advocated by the vast majority of information studies researchers for quite some time now (for extensive reviews of the literature on the subject see Dervin and Nilan, 1986; Hewins, 1990; Pettigrew et al., 2001). Indeed, according to Stefl-Mabry et al. (2003, 441) 'user-centred design has become an established goal of much of the work in information science'. Practice, however, seems to lag (far) behind theory where the actual set up, evaluation and auditing of information provision systems are concerned. As Pettigrew et al. (2001) point out, the realisation that information systems and services should be designed to support information behaviour and that the design of such systems should be based on our understanding of this behaviour, has not often led to the forging of a direct link from the study of information needs and behaviour to information provision specifications or practice. Thus, information professionals may be forever paying what is really not much more than lip service to the 'user', but while space-age information systems grace our desk tops, information centres and libraries, we still do not use suitably modern and effective management methods to ensure that these systems are providing their customers with what they need and want. To say that information systems are largely free from consumer evaluation and are seldom challenged with user needs or usage data, would be to exaggerate, but not by very much. Rarely are high-quality data fed into the design, evaluation and running of information systems, like intranets, libraries and websites.

It is hardly surprising, then, to find that people in the information professions, alert as they are to the technical changes that have taken place in the virtual information space, are nevertheless going about their business as if nothing really fundamental has happened to their clients, the users-cum-consumers. Indeed, contrary to what is plainly there for all to see, they seem to believe that the digital information consumers of today are no different from the 'library patrons' or 'readers' of yore. However, as we have noted elsewhere (Nicholas et al., 2008b), these days information professionals are confronted with an entirely different breed of information seekers, looking for information, yes, but also for goods, services, new experiences, titillation, excitement and entertainment. Moreover, they can do their information seeking unbelievably easily and expediently through a plethora of devices and platforms at their disposal 24 hours a day, seven days a week. Indeed, as our whole experience of the virtual scholar clearly indicates, for today's information consumer convenience and user satisfaction will triumph, even over content, any day of the week (Nicholas et al., 2008b). What is more, as CIBER's 'Google Generation' project amply proves, today's digital consumers benchmark their online experiences against more immersive environments like Amazon or Facebook (Williams et al., 2008). It is a foregone conclusion, then, that virtual library spaces need to be involving, easy to use and simple. Why, then, are so many of the sites produced by information professionals and publishers as complex and austere as they are? Why can't library catalogues be like Amazon, with sample pages, trust metrics, referral metrics, user feedback and colour? Why do they not speak to the user? We need to remember: if the traditional purveyor of information is not there (at best) or gets in the way of communication (at worst), consumers will simply abandon what to them is a sinking ship – after all, they can go their own way! This key aspect of the digital revolution applies to all members of the communication and information food chain, and ignoring it brings about a real risk of libraries becoming decoupled from the user. We will take up this point again further on, but first, why this patent disregard of the user?

The whys and wherefores of the ongoing neglect of information needs

Would anyone actually doubt that libraries, archives, information units and databases are there solely to service the needs of their clients? Would anyone really accuse information professionals of not being wholly aware that this is the gist of their mission? There are, however, six factors that add up to a general neglect of the user:

1 Believe it or not, there are still many (quite well-known) information professionals who feel that it is not necessary to consult the client in what they consider to be professional matters.
2 Information professionals tend to be preoccupied with information systems and not the users of these systems.
3 The professions, especially librarianship, are plagued by insular attitudes and poor communication skills, something that does not lead to a close relationship with the consumer.
4 It is by no means easy to get hold of the necessary needs data.
5 The expenditure of resources involved in the obtaining of needs data is not thought to be justified in these hard budgetary times.
6 There is an absence of a standard, commonly understood framework for the assessment of information needs – something, which, it has to be said, lets information professionals off the hook.

There is little point in conducting information needs assessments (trust us)

It is hard to credit, but there is a school of thought that believes there is very little point in consulting the users: people do not know what their needs are; they do not know what they are talking about; why ask them; far better to trust professional judgement. Just listen to this: 'there is something rather absurd in being constantly enjoined to meet the needs of the user, when needs have been probed the outcomes have been worse rather than better' (Shinebourne, 1980). Shinebourne is not alone, either: some quite eminent (more recent) Library and Information Science (LIS) researchers have also been questioning the value of user-centred design, development and implementation at the individual and system levels (Rosenbaum et al., 2003; Stefl-Mabry et al., 2003). Thus, Rosenbaum et al. (2003, 429) may freely admit that 'much has been gained intellectually and culturally from the emphasis on the user, from improvements in the design and use of information and communication technologies (ITCs) to enhancements in library services for patrons', but they still wonder as to the 'cash value' of the concept of the user (not something Google wonders about, of course). Has it reached a point of marginal or diminishing returns in LIS research, to the point that we may be actually witnessing 'the death of the user in LIS'? After all, they go on to say, the outcome of user-centred design can hardly be tooted as a success story: 'many ITCs do not work well for their intended audiences and there is a rich history of costly information systems failures in corporate, educational and governmental organizations.'

Instead, proponents of this approach often argue that since we are the experts, we should simply trust our professional judgement to get it right, and then it is just a question of convincing the users of it. True, people no longer dare say 'we know better what is good for you' in so many words (it would be politically incorrect), just as today's physicians refrain from voicing such patronising attitudes (at least in the presence of their patients), but these stances, perhaps worded more carefully, are still endemic in our profession. Thus, for example, Stefl-Mabry et al. (2003, 441), exploring 'the extent to which there is real substance behind the rhetoric of user-centeredness in our research and practice', set out to answer questions such as 'What do you fail to learn when you rely solely on users for input on decisions?', or 'When do users not know what is best for them?' They even speculate if 'we have uncovered significant knowledge of users since the advent of the user-centred approach'. Cronin (1981, 38; 46), too, despite claiming that 'user studies are on the whole a jolly good idea', has his reservations as to their practical worth: 'a fine sentiment no doubt but sentiment is not always at home in the world of commerce'. Admittedly, he might have changed his outlook in the 20-something years since he put forward this view of his, for, clearly, today's commerce is precisely all about getting closer to the user. With very good reason, too: sophisticated market research and demographic profiling are behind the success of many leading retailers and service providers all over the world. Actually, as Kujala

(2003) suggests on the basis of a careful analysis of the LIS literature, user involvement in information systems development has generally positive effects, especially on user satisfaction, and taking users as a primary information source is an effective means of requirements capture.

A systems-driven profession

The information profession is, by and large, systems driven; it shows an enormous interest in the processing and storing of information, to the detriment of the consumer. Indeed, the profession manifests a marked fixation with powerful, innovative information systems, sometimes irrespective of their direct suitability to users. A prime example of this mindset is libraries' recent attempts to halt the massive desertion of their patrons by succumbing to any digital fashion that comes their way: institutional repositories, portals, internet cafés, learning spaces, open access and social networks. What is more, once such facilities have been obtained it is on to the next powerful, innovative one, without any user evaluation of the former system or facility. The sheer pace of technological change provides the ideal opportunity and excuse. The qualities that are appreciated tend to be systems characteristics, such as speed of response, storage size, or number of network stations. If needs are considered at all, it is by and large in terms of how the system might meet these needs, rather than be built, developed or changed to meet them. No wonder, therefore, as Adams et al. (2005) note, that librarians are held to be possessive of resources rather than supporting and understanding users' needs. The words of the academic they quote do indeed seem to echo faithfully enough the popularly held sentiments on the topic: ' … the librarians are not user-centred, they're information resource centred … they want to protect their resources, not to gain access to them'.

Admittedly, in their deliberations and writings, the systems-driven of this world pay due allegiance to the idea of the user (generally mentioning the worn-out slogan 'user-friendly', which is, of course, a wholly systems phrase). It is almost as if by citing the term or having a conference on the topic, their guilt is assuaged. However, that seems to be the extent of it; hardly any libraries (or publishers for that matter) actually investigate users' information needs, follow their information behaviour and then relate their findings directly to outcomes and impacts. The following tale truly drives the point home: at a multimedia conference one of the authors attended a number of years ago, the delegates, from the top media companies in the country, were asked two questions: firstly, how many of them had online access, to which, with some alacrity, all put up their hands; secondly, how many of them conducted annual user needs assessments, to which just one admitted so doing. When confronted by the sheer disparity, most felt uncomfortable at first, but soon gathered their wits and asserted that this did not mean that they did not 'know' their clients – they did, of course! However, their main methodology for obtaining user data appeared to be osmosis. It truly looks as if information systems are seen as omnipotent, while users are too often perceived as the supplicants. This, when users are the ones who, after all, drive all the major changes in the digital information environment. How can we possibly see to it that we are delivering the right information services, unless we think about people's needs, rather than the allures of our systems?

Poor communication skills and insular and antagonistic attitudes

Information professionals tend to demonstrate a marked reluctance to keep in touch with their clients and, in result, they do not always know their clients as they patently should – though they would inevitably protest otherwise. Take, for example, Weintraub's (1980) gentle reproach of librarians, who, according to him, soldier on in brave isolation, as if they were a beleaguered community of martyrs, instead of dealing with the problems of the library by establishing a more effective interaction between them and the communities of which they are a part. However, a continuing dialogue between client and information professional is often a rarity – has always been a rarity – so that we cannot even blame it on the recent massive advent of disintermediation (loosely defined and understood as 'cutting out the middleman'). Why, then?

In defence of their customary ways, information professionals often cite shortage of time and work pressures. However, more frequently the real reason seems to be a characteristic insularity and four-wall mentality. Information professionals are typically inward-looking and tribal (something which seems to be particularly true of librarians): anything that happens outside their strictly defined discipline and/or job boundaries is not their prime concern, even though the user and the internet are dissolving these boundaries. In direct consequence, they are insufficiently concerned with information problems that occur outside the information unit – in the digital world, for instance. However, it is in the office, coffee bar and home that information needs are hatched and only occasionally, one would have thought, in the physical information space. This would necessitate that the information professionals go to their clients, which these days means both in the literal and the virtual sense of the word. Thus, it is important to interact with potential customers in their natural surroundings, say in the office or the laboratory, but it is no less crucial to follow closely the digital footprints of those who will never be encountered in the flesh. Luckily, we are in the enviable position that our predecessors could not even begin to dream about, of being able to monitor closely information seekers' many activities, as these take place anonymously in the virtual space.

Poor lines of communication can also be attributed to the low status of information professionals in the organisation, making it difficult for them to initiate contact and maintain ongoing dialogues. Generally seen as fulfilling a supporting role, information professionals are often overlooked and disregarded, and certainly not considered peers of the 'real doers' in the establishment. This perception of the information professional is especially prevalent in academe, as Biggs (1981) points out in her seminal work on the topic. Quoting a librarian, according to whom she and her ilk are treated as 'poor relations' and 'super clerks', Biggs traces this to faculty myths about librarians' alleged rigidity, meticulousness and lack of intellectual knowledge. More recently Adams et al. (2005, 183) also reported that librarians do not see themselves as being on equal footing to the academics with whom they work; as one interviewee of theirs puts it: 'There is also that whole professional thing as well that you have to be wary of that we're not seen as maybe their equal in knowledge or whatever and that maybe they feel that they're not going to learn anything gainful from us'. Regrettably, Biggs' (1981) conclusion is that the information professionals are the ones who, by their reluctance to confront their clientele, create a nearly insuperable barrier between them and their scholarly customers (although faculty members undoubtedly need to help things along by making an effort to listen and co-operate). Perhaps not very surprisingly, her diagnosis still seems to hold true today, not only in academe, either.

Further to this, it is not an exaggeration to say that a good number of information workers are antagonistic towards their users – such antagonism is bred of long and close proximity. It is an old cliché, but for battle-weary information professionals, people get in the way of the systems they are so busily building and defending. It is hardly surprising, then, that students complain of negative experiences with librarians, of encountering preoccupied, rude, inconsiderate and discourteous service, in result of which they apparently often think twice before resorting to professional help in resolving their information problems (Hernon and Pastine, 1977; Swope and Katzer, 1972). In fact, the phenomenon of library anxiety (Mellon, 1986) has been traced back, among other factors, to students' negative perceptions of library staff (Jiao and Onwuegbuzie, 1997; Onwuegbuzie et al., 2004), the result of previous off-putting experiences. In all probability not independently of this state of affairs, interpersonal skills, especially oral and written communication skills, have emerged as primary requirements for library positions, as content analysis of job advertisements appropriate for LIS graduates indicate (Kennan et al., 2006). Concurrently, theoreticians of the profession have been advocating the need to pay much more attention to communication and interpersonal competencies and skills in LIS education (see, for example, Gorman and Corbitt, 2002). Unfortunately, it is quite plain to all those who teach such courses that for many students acquiring communication skills-based oral competencies presents quite some challenge.

No single or easy method of collecting the data

Plainly, the method of analysis is only going to be as good as the data that are fed into it. Therefore, the data collection methods have to be effective and robust. There is, of course, a rich choice of data collection methods, to the point of too much choice, which, in itself, may put people off. To complicate matters further, there is also the vital need to use different methodological approaches (methods triangulation). The prevalent view in the literature may very well be that it is use or information-seeking behaviour data which point most directly to the needs experienced by people (see, for example, Cronin, 1981; Wilson, 1981). However, if we aim for effective information provision, we need to probe beneath the visible surface of people's actual behaviour, important as it is, into their needs, too (be they expressed or dormant, a point we will examine later).

Typically, since reality is subjective as well as culturally derived and historically situated (Crotty, 1998), phenomena need to be studied through the eyes of people in their lived situations (Hjorland, 2005), in an attempt 'to know what the actors [in a particular social world] know, see what they see, understand what they understand' (Schwartz and Jacobs, 1979, 7, quoted in: Wildemuth, 1993). This calls for qualitative research methods, which aim at studying people in situ, without constrictions of preconceived notions, so as to capture what their lives, experiences and interactions mean to them in their own terms and in their natural settings. However, not only are such methods very time consuming, but the practicalities of using them for obtaining data are such that the samples studied are by necessity relatively small and unrepresentative. Thus, crucial as the utilisation of qualitative techniques for determining people's needs is, it must be complemented by monitoring large (as large as possible) populations through the use of quantitative techniques. Only then can the veracity of the insights derived via qualitative methods be judged and put to a reality check, and the extent to which they are generalisable to a wider population established. By the same token, whilst quantitative techniques are invaluable for highlighting patterns of use and identifying broad sweeps of information-seeking behaviour, the data thus derived need to be further investigated for their validity and significance via quantitative methods. After all, quantitative methods tend to generate data of a more superficial nature: big numbers are there, but what it all means is not always clear. Therefore, it is truly vital that information need investigations combine quantitative and qualitative methods, for, as Hammersley (1981) and Greene and Caracelli (1997) suggest, the use of different methodological approaches (methods triangulation) serves to enhance the validity and reliability of the study by counterbalancing the flaws or the weaknesses of each method with the strengths of the others.

Expensive to collect the data

Another reason for neglecting information needs is that the data do not come cheap, at least not if you set out to attain an accurate and comprehensive picture, which, obviously, is the only way to do it. The problem is that providing the just noted necessary triangulation and reach necessitates the use of as wide a range of methods as possible, which comes at a (steep) price. The qualitative methods most suitable for running to earth information needs data (interview and observation) are typically very expensive indeed, although, luckily, the quantitative ones, offering the best insight into use, are often relatively cheaper.

In any case, as both qualitative and quantitative methods have to be used, information needs studies are a costly manoeuvre, especially as they have to be repeated regularly in these fast-changing times and, to make things even more complicated, the financial trade-off is not immediately obvious. Can the conducting of information needs investigations really justify taking money away from the Book Fund (the information professionals' original ultimate threat) or the website (the new ultimate threat)? Can it excuse removing staff from critical front-line routines, like shelving books, managing the short-loan collection or updating the website? With these comforting thoughts information professionals renounce the information needs survey. However, what is the point of efficiently overseeing a collection or website that amounts to no more than a dim and distant reflection of the needs of its users? It is bound to be so in a world that has probably seen more change in information needs and information behaviour in the last five years than in the previous 50! How can we be sure that the information unit or system is heading along the right track?

It seems, then, that the correct and only view must surely be that it is too costly *not* to collect needs data. The stance must be that, in these dynamic and fast-changing times, it is wholly *economic* to collect these data on a regular and ongoing basis. Not that it is going to be easy to convince people of the wisdom of this. On a recent short course, when one of the authors explained that needs data was best collected by interview and that the interview might take 45 minutes, a number of participants audibly choked. The implication was obvious: that is a lot of time (which it indeed is). Still, is it too long a time to ensure that people get the service and information they need and deserve? Would anybody choke if they were told it would take ten hours to design a website?

Lack of a commonly understood and agreed framework of analysis

There are few easily understood and practical frameworks available with which to explore people's needs. Many of the works looking into the topic have tended to be too personal, as well as too theoretical and academic. Rather than clarify the situation, more often than not they have muddied the waters; rather than encouraging people to conduct user needs surveys, in fact they have provided an excuse not to do so. Maurice Line (1969; 1974) did propose a suitable method many years ago, but it has not been widely adopted. This guide embraces and expands upon Line's original model in aiming to rectify the situation. Therefore, it offers up an analytical, off-the-shelf method that can operate in the hurly-burly of today's high-tech (digital) information centres and units. It is a method for the systematic collection of information needs data to facilitate the design, assessment and auditing of information systems, which, although highly practical, is firmly entrenched in sound theoretical outlook and principles. The main intention is to provide a practical, usable and reusable method of analysing and evaluating information needs, which can be employed by information managers, information system designers, publishers, records managers and digital information consumers alike.

There are, then, a host of factors that bring about the ongoing neglect of information needs. However, none excuse it. Indeed, this state of affairs has to be put right. There are good and pressing reasons why it simply cannot continue.

So why indeed undertake information needs assessments?

1 Increased competition and competitive tendering from within and without the profession force information services to get closer to their customers (or go to the wall).
2 The huge growth in end-use and migration to the virtual space, which so unnerves information professionals worried about their jobs, should compel them to monitor closely what their customers are thinking, doing and wanting.
3 The challenge facing today's information professionals, the provision of custom-made, personalised information infrastructures, tailored to the distinctive needs of individuals, can only be met through a nuanced understanding of information seekers' idiosyncratic needs.
4 The huge and rising costs of introducing IT-based innovative systems demand that these systems be evaluated in the light of people's actual information needs.
5 The increased rigour with which information units are being audited and questioned about how they spend money require that information services collect data on their clients and outcomes to justify their expenditure.

Competition and deregulation

We are ten years into an information consumer revolution occasioned by the arrival of the internet (and, increasingly, the mobile phone), which is changing society, education and commerce on a massive and global scale. Digital consumers worldwide, numbered in their billions, are rapidly transforming today's ubiquitous virtual information environment through a preference for search engine exploration, a dislike of paying for information and a short attention span. Moreover, they use their new-found freedom to relocate themselves and their activities in this altered and incessantly changing information landscape, taking on many of the tasks previously reserved for information professionals. Indeed, information professionals and their systems are no longer the first choice of supplier for many people looking for information. As a direct result, the traditional information flagships are heading towards the reefs, blown there by the hurricane-force winds that have been generated by the digital transition. Public libraries appear to be in real trouble, but academic libraries, too, clearly grow increasingly decoupled from their user base as information consumers continue to flee the physical space (Martell, 2008).

Complicating things even further, libraries, the traditional agents for the preservation and provision of knowledge, are facing probably the fiercest competition in the history of their existence. As part and parcel of the inter-communal strife among the core content providers – librarians, publishers, journalists and television broadcasters (Gunter, 2008) – librarians and publishers, especially in the scholarly communications field, are on the brink of coming to blows over the possession of the keys to information. Their territorial disputes and skirmishes, a direct consequence of the introduction of open access and institutional repositories, are bound to become even more ferocious with the inexorable growth of the popularity of e-books (Nicholas et al., 2007b). Thus, publishers and librarians already find themselves fighting for the spoils, with the threat of the loser being mortally wounded ever more looming over the horizons of both. At least for now, there seems a real possibility that librarians will be the ones to suffer defeat. Take, for example, the case of scholars, surely one of the most prominent information consumer communities: increasingly deserting the physical space for the virtual space, they move closer to the publisher and further from the library. As they become more and more anonymous and removed from the scene of scholarly information consumption, the librarians attempting to meet their needs grow correspondingly less and less informed about them (Nicholas et al., 2008b).

The conclusion to be derived from all this is truly inescapable: if information professionals do not get close to the consumer, others will and the information professionals will become an irrelevance (out of sight, out of mind). Whatever the reasons for the profession's neglect of information needs, it is surely the dearth of a robust and appropriate evidence base on information seekers that is responsible for the palpable danger of libraries becoming increasingly rudderless and estranged from their users and paymasters. It is clearly the reason why in this so-called information society, librarians, in particular, are increasingly marginalised, frequently under attack, in danger of losing their jobs and having their salaries depressed, with the organisations they so lovingly tend losing market share by the minute. The profession should look to successful businesses for guidance on how to survive the new climate. The advice of a past chairman of Kingfisher, the owner of B&Q, ScrewFix and other DIY brands, is certainly worth taking on board: 'We are concerned with meeting end-consumer needs. If you look at the success or failure of many organisations, the root of the problem often comes back to not anticipating how customer's needs have changed, and therefore not adapting to those changes' (Kay, 1994). Sound advice, indeed, and in the digital information world even sounder.

The end-user cometh and cometh again and again

Related to the above point about changes in the marketplace, there is also the huge number of connected end-users (digital consumers) now populating the information space. During the 1980s the profession constantly debated the outcome of end-use – some doubting whether it would ever happen and others forecasting the Apocalypse (how wrong could they be!). Since then, a veritable armoury of computers and modems have been built up in people's homes and offices, and, concurrently, the ultimate user-friendly tool – the internet – has become effortlessly accessible for all and sundry, so much so that, as Russell (2008) notes, access to the internet has become more the norm in a household than not. Indeed, the information landscape has been totally transformed:

millions and millions of people are connected directly to the information they need, courtesy of the ubiquitous search engine, on a scale that dwarfs any library, publishing or newspaper effort. The days of information seekers as supplicants are pretty much over. Who needs the traditional 'gatekeepers'? After all, people can now easily and expediently meet all aspects of their information needs on their own, and do so at any time of the day or night, too! The end-user is now king, truly the dominant player in today's information scene. No wonder disintermediation seems to be moving at such a rate.

The reaction of too many people in the profession to this upheaval taking place all around them is rather like that of a frightened rabbit in a car's headlights. They are paralysed by fear, possibly in denial. The appropriate reaction is surely to recognise that there is now much common ground, a common vocabulary, a willingness to discuss information problems; and the opportunity should be grabbed with both hands. The potential terrain for the information professional has increased enormously, although most of it lies outside the boundaries of the physical space. The key to mastering this terrain, of course, is information needs assessments. When you talk about end-users and digital consumers, you are really talking about information needs.

The challenge of custom-made, personalised information services

For many people the internet has resulted in the overnight transformation of an information-poor world into an information-rich one. We have moved from a situation in which information needs were rarely ever effectively met – certainly not without a tremendous expenditure of effort and cost, to one in which they are only too easily met, in theory anyway. To be sure, the internet fulfils information needs, triggers information needs and attracts people – information voyeurs and navigators, who have no needs at all. It has turned information seeking into a global (and fun) pastime. However, just broadcasting ever-greater amounts of information is not what it is about. There is a mistaken belief amongst the profession that the future is all about sharing information knowledge-management style, or storing and distributing information digital-library style; it is, in fact, about getting closer to what people need in the way of (instant) information and producing it in a processed, packaged form for individuals to consume at a particular point in time that they choose. Plainly, customisation, individualisation and segmentation in the information market are the next stage of the information revolution. Indeed, the Information Society will never become a reality until we can genuinely meet people's individual and special needs. There is still a long way to go.

However, although we talk glibly enough about the commodification of information, we seem to stop there: essentially, we – and the systems we provide – remain crude batch processors. At least for the time being, information products remain incredibly raw and general; even in the case of the web search, success depends largely on the lucky dip of single keywords or the input of a hieroglyph (URLs). This, when the future of information provision is surely personalised information flows; it would be an extremely brave (or foolish?) person who would argue against that. How else do you get personal information other than from information needs assessments? Undoubtedly, in the information-rich environment in which we find ourselves, with undreamed-of quantities of information just a couple of mouse clicks away, we need to be even clearer about consumers' information needs than ever before. What else is going to help steer a path through the information jungle? Certainly not any of the current search engines. What else is going to ensure the precision of searching and the filters for the push technology that is coming our way?

Cost of IT-based innovations

With vast amounts of money being spent on novel communication and retrieval systems (intranets, websites, blogs, RSS feeds), mistaken judgements have increasingly serious and perilous consequences. Also, the more rapid the pace of change, the greater the risk of investing considerable sums in passing fads or enhancements divorced from real needs. It is only through an understanding of what information people need, how they prefer to set about finding that information and whether they achieve positive outcomes from their information seeking, that professionals can ensure that scarce budgets are used for the provision of suitable information systems; professional judgement alone cannot be relied upon, certainly not in these fast-changing times. A case in point is libraries' recent experiments with Web 2.0 interactive facilities. In an attempt to ensnare today's allegedly new brand of information consumers, used to involving, dynamic and personalised content experiences that can compete with the likes of Facebook, many libraries now have profiles on social networking sites. However, as we will discuss in more detail later on, at least for now, libraries' presence on social networks, as well as the blogs proudly sported by many of them, attract very little positive use. Obviously, costly innovative endeavours need to be based on people's actual information needs, otherwise there is a real risk of wasting money on systems and services that fail to meet their intended purpose.

Accountability and auditing

Traditionally, the quest for knowledge and learning was seen as an end in itself and, in consequence, its major (if not sole) supporting agencies, libraries, were generously provided for from public funds to enable their fostering progress and education. However, with knowledge and information becoming commodities of major value, the state's financial resources have become reserved for producers and propagators of 'knowledge for use', rather than 'knowledge for its own sake' (Calas and Smircich, 2001; Delanty, 1998; Duderstadt, 1997), with a subsequent decline in the budgets of the latter. Furthermore, driven by the rhetoric of 'quality', 'efficiency' and 'value for money' (Harvie, 2000), whatever government funding remains is made more targeted by allocation mechanisms mimicking the market. Hence, public sector organisations are called upon to adopt 'new' management processes and systems for greater efficiency, even more marketisation and, especially, greater accountability.

Libraries, information centres and archives are thus part and parcel of today's value-driven environment, from which they are unlikely ever to escape. They are now on the same cost-conscious footing as any other business and, in result, they are subject to the same concerns, such as customer care, customer charters, cost benefit and the like. Whilst this is generally recognised as a *fait accompli* by the profession, few seem to realise that these concerns are nothing but a sham unless they are underpinned by the systematic collection of data on consumer needs and behaviour. How else is performance to be determined? Certainly not by the traditional measure of the number of documents on the shelves or new titles bought per year, or by the item that has superseded it: the number and power of computers on display. The yardstick unquestionably has to be changed, for it is only through customer satisfaction and outcome that success or effectiveness can be truly measured, and satisfaction and positive outcomes can only be obtained by meeting user need. It is customers who we should be proudly showing off, not computers, websites or shelves. Placing the customer care charter on show in the library, scattering a few complaints forms around and employing a number of staff to monitor a service is woefully inadequate, but it is too often the common response. No library that we know has a department devoted to the monitoring and evaluating of customer needs and usage of information, but they are taking on institutional repositories with some alacrity. These days, with value-for-money exercises having become the norm, there is really no other way to face up to the challenge they present, but through the careful collection and appraisal of information needs and use data.

All this seems to boil down to one point: the main reason for undertaking needs assessments must be that the information profession has neglected doing so in the past, a practice that has not got either the profession or the systems and services they provide very far; indeed, it continues to frustrate the progress of them both. Thus, unless information workers, from all walks of life, are reconnected with their user base, they are not doing the job they are meant to be doing: playing their part in supporting the information/knowledge society and economy. The message is loud and clear: the information community must stop thinking it knows best. The information consumer knows best. It is consumers who are calling the shots, so why keep them at arm's length? Bridging this gap necessitates, however, that we clarify to ourselves what information needs really are, which is the next question on our agenda.

2 What are information needs?

The concept of 'information need' is hardly unequivocal, although people talk about it as if it were, without ever bothering to define what they mean when they use the phrase. All the same, as Shenton and Dixon (2004) point out, citing a host of articles in ample proof of their assertion, there is a lack of a common understanding of the term 'information need'; indeed, the absence of universal agreement on the topic is a recurrent theme in library and information science (LIS) writing. True, there are very good reasons for refraining from the attempt to clarify the expression, for, when definitions are provided, they are often vague or highly complex in nature. Actually, they tend to cloud further some already muddy water and really serve very little practical use. Unfortunately, despite years of academic debate and much intellectual borrowing from other disciplines, like management and psychology, not too much has emerged that would aid information practitioners in their information needs deliberations.

Furthermore, people often talk about information needs when, in fact, they are referring to wants or use. Indeed, as Elayyan (1988), Green (1990) or Hewins (1990) contend, many studies that claim to be studies of information need are really studies of information use. However, while it is true enough that wants or use are both manifestations of need – and, as such, undoubtedly should be considered, they are neither identical to need, nor fully or accurately describe it. Thus, in order to attain a correct and comprehensive picture, we should be evaluating the need people have for information, the wants and demands they express for it and the use they make of it. Needs analysis may very well be fraught with difficulties and complexities, but still, we cannot always employ use indicators, such as website 'hits', as proxies. Therefore, as part and parcel of any definition, information needs have to be distinguished from some closely associated, but distinct information concepts, like want, demand and use, which are frequently (and sometimes deliberately) confused with information needs – to the general detriment of information provision and system design. We will attempt to do so in this section, which follows much of Maurice Line's original thinking, as set out in his 1974 article 'Draft Definitions: Information and Library Needs, Wants, Demands and Uses'.

Information needs: a working definition

For Line (1974), information needs were seen as the call for 'information [that] would further this job or this research, and would be recognised as doing so by the recipient'. Belkin and Vickery (1989) add that information needs arise when people recognise a gap in their state of knowledge, that is, when they experience 'an anomalous state of knowledge' and wish to resolve that anomaly. One can build upon these definitions by adding that it is the need for information that individuals *ought* to have to do their job effectively, solve a problem satisfactorily or pursue a hobby or interest happily. The operative word here is surely 'ought', the assumption being that for people to perform efficiently, effectively, safely and happily, they need to be well informed, that is, their information needs should be met. There is an implied value judgement in this – the meeting of need is beneficial or necessary to the person – and would be recognised as such.

Of course, people do not usually have information needs *per se*; rather, when they experience a problem or difficulty or are under some pressure, these cognitive and emotional needs of theirs may be met, or at least partially met, by obtaining and then applying some appropriate information. Indeed, information needs arise out of a desire to meet one or other of the three basic human needs: physiological needs (need for food, shelter, etc.); psychological needs (need for domination, security, etc.); and cognitive needs (need to plan, learn a skill, etc.). Thinking very much along the same lines, Norwood (cited in: Huitt, 2004) proposes that Maslow's (1954) well-known hierarchy of needs can be used to describe the kinds of information that individuals seek. Thus, individuals at the lowest level of the pyramid of needs, focused on their basic physiological needs, such as hunger, thirst, bodily comforts, etc., require *coping information*; individuals at the safety level, intent upon avoiding danger and ensuring their personal security, need *helping information*; individuals higher up on the pyramid of needs, at a stage where they are looking to belong, to affiliate with others, to be accepted, need *enlightening information* of the kind to be found in books on relationship development. Individuals on an even higher level of the hierarchy of needs, that of esteem, seeking to achieve, to be competent, to gain approval and recognition, need *empowering information*: information on how their ego can be developed. Finally, people who have reached the highest level of needs, that of a need for self-actualisation, for self-fulfillment and the realisation of their potential, seek sources (whether human or documentary) of *edifying information*.

All this, however, can in no way be taken to mean that information needs are any less important than the primary needs they serve; rather to the contrary, because success in meeting the one (the primary need) is dependent on meeting the other (the information need). True, the latter might be classified as secondary to the former, but in this increasingly information-dependent age, where information has obviously moved to centre stage, lack of information could certainly have serious, or even perilous consequences for the individual. Yet, despite the pivotal role accorded to information in all spheres of present-day social and economic life, people's information needs may go unmet, either because they are unaware of having a need for information, or because, for various reasons of their own, they do not set out to meet a recognised (but unexpressed) need.

Unrecognised and recognised (but unexpressed) information needs

People do not always know what their information needs are. They do not know they have an information gap, for they are not aware that there is information out there that could be of help to them. They do not know that new information has rendered obsolete what they know and, in result, has given rise to another information need. It is only when exposed to the relevant information that the need is recognised. This might be called *dormant need* or *unrecognised need*. Take this case as an example: a person goes down to the photocopying machine to copy a letter and in the queue overhears a conversation about a television programme, screened the previous night, about globe artichokes. The person in question is rather fond of this vegetable, so listens with keen interest. Apparently, globe artichokes contain a lot of chemicals because of the infrequent rain (in Israel, where they are grown), and because the washing process fails to penetrate their tightly closed petals. Now, the person did not come to the photocopier with an information need, but goes away having obtained a needed piece of information.

Conversely, users may be well aware of their information needs, that is, their needs are by no means dormant/unrecognised, but, nevertheless, they do nothing about meeting them, either because they cannot or will not. A case in point is the all too familiar phenomenon of people refraining from pursuing their information needs for lack of time. Such non-use of relevant information, as Wilson (1993a, 1995, 1996) points out, may not happen by accident or by mistake even in academe. Rather, it often reflects a routine and normal approach for coping with the prevalent situation, in which the concurrent pressures of the constant dearth of time, on the one hand, and the huge quantities of available information, on the other, combine to instigate a policy of deliberate disregard of one's information need. In fact, even at the best of times today's information seekers tend to be satisficers (a term resulting from the blend of the two words 'sufficing' and 'satisfying'). That is, they stop information seeking after finding material that is good enough (Savolainen, 2007), so that they can juggle the need for comprehensive information with the constraints placed upon them.

Clearly, in today's internet-based information world, in which information is being generated in ever-increasing volumes and people are connected to information sources of unparalleled power and reach, taking a conscious decision not to attempt to meet one's information needs, at least not fully, is commonplace and will increasingly become more so. At the same time, the huge popularity of the internet must be at least partly due to the fact that it has an unlimited potential both to uncover dormant information needs in the searcher and to solve recognised information problems expediently. However, turning to the internet, with or without a particular purpose in mind, frequently means relying on happy accident. This, in its turn, may come at some considerable cost: missing out on a vital piece of information. Thus, users cannot possibly count on this serendipitous method for obtaining all their information; it is too much of a lottery in these information-dependent times. The uncovering of dormant need, just the same as the efficient meeting of recognised need, has to be put on firmer and surer ground, but in this disintermediated age it is not clear who is going to do this: librarian, publisher or academic.

There is an opportunity for information professionals in all this: they are in many respects the best positioned to run to earth individuals' primary-needs-contingent information needs and to help them meet these needs effectively. They know what is available, on the one hand, and are able to control the information filters, on the other, so that exposure to information can be balanced with the problems that the availability of masses of information may bring about. This, of course, creates for them a positive and proactive role: where information needs are concerned, they are the experts. However, this is also where the big challenge lies for them: so far, information professionals have, at best, only really concerned themselves with satisfying the direct and specific articulation of information needs, but they need to go further if they are to win back a strategic place in the information chain. To attain the holistic understanding of their customers' information needs, wants, demands and uses, which alone can ensure that these needs are successfully met, they need to get very close to the information consumers and to remain steadfastly close. A clearer understanding of how information needs differ from information wants, demands and use, the issue we are about to tackle, may be a good place to start.

Information wants

Information wants are what an individual would like to have – *like* being the operative word here. Of course, in a perfect world information needs and information wants would be one and the same. However, we live in a far from perfect world, in which, for a variety of reasons, stemming from idiosyncratic factors of personality, time and resources, not all that is needed is wanted, and not all that is wanted is actually needed. Thus, for example, individuals may not attempt to meet their information needs fully, that is, may not strive to obtain all that they in fact need, for lack of time, skills or finances, or, alternatively, individuals may be tempted to obtain information that they do not in fact need (a prime example of this is the way people surf the web).

Nevertheless, people tend to equate wants with needs. Indeed, questionnaires, aiming to explore needs typically turn out to be want studies – with questions taking a 'would you like more information, more journals, enhanced facilities' line. Results can prove to be very misleading because users unreservedly tick all the want choices on offer, happy in the knowledge that they will probably never be required to exercise their options (but just in case!). The following story amply illustrates to what an extent 'real life' can differ from wish-lists. One of the authors, at the time a practising librarian in charge of reader services, was requested over and over again to see to it that her library's opening hours were extended until 10pm. A bit hesitant to expend the considerable sums the move required, especially in view of the limited number of patrons on the premises by 7pm or so, she decided to ask the potential beneficiaries whether they were interested in longer opening hours. The results left little room for doubt: people were overwhelmingly in favour of the option. However, when the plan was actually realised, the author and her colleagues were more or less the only ones around in the evenings.

In any case, where information wants are concerned, we are moving into an almost wholly subjective domain, where, as it has already been noted, personal characteristics, available time and affordable assets make themselves felt. It is, of course, taken for granted that a price has to be paid if information needs are to be met – time, effort and possibly money have to be expended. Still, individuals may not be motivated to chase information, perhaps because these days information so often comes to them unsolicited and at no cost, or because they may not have the time to look for it or the skills to locate it, or, maybe, just do not have access to the necessary information resources (through lack of finance, perhaps). Job satisfaction must be a big determinant of whether individuals go ahead and attempt to meet their information needs fully. If you like your job, you will want to do it well, improve it and keep yourself up to date. This will inevitably mean going out of your way to meet your information needs.

Be it as it may, one point is hardly arguable: society sends us confusing signals about whether we should want information. On the one hand, we are enjoined to sample the joys of the internet (surely, *the* information-enabling mechanism), and on the other hand, in today's atmosphere of relentlessly increasing demands for accountability in everything we do, we have less and less time to enjoy the fruits of this easily come-by information. Moreover, when we succumb to the temptation to pursue our information wants, we may end up burying ourselves with information, thus digging our own information graves. So, should we, or should we not follow up our information heart desires; that is, should we actually demand the information we want?

Information demands

An information demand is a request for an item of information believed to be wanted. This is where information seeking starts, where the potential consumer first encounters the information system, source (human or documentary) or intermediary. However, people may demand information they do not really need, perhaps because their initial perception of its value does not match with reality: someone tells them it is a good site, but on arrival it turns out to be a disappointment (lots of information seeking must lead to blind alleys, especially courtesy of search engines). By the same token, they certainly need or want information they do not demand, for instance, because they are not aware that it is there. Certainly the internet stokes up demand and leads inevitably to (very) large amounts of material that is demanded but not needed. Indeed, as the findings of the CIBER study into the use of scholarly journals (Nicholas et al., 2008b) clearly indicate, people download huge quantities of material, but not everything (possibly not much) that is downloaded is actually read or used. Much material is just squirreled away for another day, though that day may never come because of a shortage of time and the amount of squirreling that already has been undertaken.

Also, demand is at least partly dependent on expectation, which, in its turn, depends upon existing information provision. Indeed, as long as traditional libraries were the only game in town, customer expectations were notoriously low; after all, libraries only ever offered a limited window on information and could never respond within the tight time frames expected by most busy individuals. Also, as it has already been noted, there is a legacy of poor service in the profession. Add to this that many people are altogether unaware of what the information service can do for them, and the picture in its dismal entirety becomes all too clear. Seen in this light, the rush towards disintermediation (or doing it yourself) is less astonishing than it seems at first glance, especially as the advent of computers has raised user expectations enormously. Information seekers naively believe that these 'black boxes' can deliver anything and quickly, to boot. The web has raised people's expectations even more, to sky-high levels, in fact: plainly, it is seen as an inexhaustible source of (mostly) reliable information on anything and everything, which is effortlessly available 24/7. Indeed, web logs provide an awesome indicator of global demand for information, which, though, as we have already seen, is not necessarily synonymous with actual consumption or satisfaction.

Information use

Here we arrive at the more visible end of the information-seeking process – the information the individual actually uses or consumes. This is an area about which information professionals know most, but even here, not enough. So what exactly do we mean when we talk about information use?

First of all, use is both intended use and unintended use; that is, it may be the direct outcome of a satisfied demand, but, just as much, the result of browsing or serendipitous discovery, while not looking purposively for anything or when looking for something else. Not, it must be noted here, that browsing and accidental unearthing of information are invariably akin to unintended use, for browsing can be quite directed and structured. Some people browse because they have no choice; they cannot recognise and articulate their need until something they see reminds them of it. Indeed, humanities scholars are famously fond of browsing precisely because some newly encountered information may uncover for them a dormant need, bringing about the fortuitous discovery of connections between ideas and words (Saule, 1992). People also browse because they are forced to do so: the manner, whereby the information system – the web, for instance – displays the information, leaves little room for locating information any other way – and logs point to this being the dominant form of navigating the vast virtual space. At any rate, the difference between intended use and unintended use is an important one in terms of information system design. For this very reason, usage studies should really make an effort to distinguish between the two.

All in all, use is a word that comes with a lot of baggage, beyond the fact, which has already been pointed out, that it is certainly not the purported clean, hard, direct manifestation of need, which it is so readily assumed to be. To begin with, it is not all that easy to determine when the use being witnessed can be counted as 'real' consumption of information, for 'use' can and does refer to, at the very least, two clearly distinguishable levels of use. The first level of use simply involves determining whether something is worth using in the first place, for, obviously, use and satisfaction do not always go hand-in-hand. Thus, information seekers clearly need to establish at the outset whether a given item of information amongst a vast sea of data will satisfy or fail to satisfy need; but can we consider their actions, typically measured by transaction log analyses, as constituting 'use'? Probably better considered as power browsing. Still, this type of use might lead to other people being alerted to the potential worth of the information consumed, so perhaps it is use, after all! The second level of use is the actual consumption of information, subsequent to its having been found relevant, that is, the actual putting of some information to purpose-relevant use. This type of use, generally more effectively measured by citation studies, probably corresponds more directly to the popular concept of 'real' use. However, even use data of this kind can really tell us very little about many of the key needs characteristics: thus, for example, the need for information presented from a particular viewpoint, approach or angle certainly cannot be gleaned from usage data.

If the problem of what can be considered 'real' use and what cannot is not complicated enough, there is also the dilemma of how use is to be measured. After all, use has many recorded manifestations. What can be taken then to be an indicator or record of use? Citations and logs have already been mentioned, and there are also issue statistics, library loan studies, book sales records and the ubiquitous tick boxes in questionnaires, which seek to find out whether people used a particular information system daily, weekly, monthly, etc., during a given period of time (mysteriously, always assuming that information use is a rhythmic or periodic activity). Plainly, many of these use indicators are measuring different phenomena, each of which leaves plenty of room for various interpretations.

Consider, for example, what constitutes use on the web and what can be read into it. Putting aside for the time being the problems of actually determining use on the web (we will come to that presently), let us try to establish what 'hits' (pages viewed) really signify. For a start, with the loose and idiosyncratic method of searching on the web and the shotgun approach of most search engines to retrieval, the chances that you actually want to see the specific page you end up with have to be relatively low. However, you 'used' it and you are recorded on the logs as having done so, and action will be taken by others – advertisers, sponsors and web managers, on the basis of these data. Furthermore, how many times do you navigate through a site, going down numerous pathways, to get what you really want? Each page you go through on your way to the page you really need is another page 'used', but not actually needed.

Obviously then, use data are really very problematic, and need to be handled with great care, but are generally not. True, bean (use) counting does come stripped of the wish-list or fantasy factor that is so endemic of questionnaire surveys, which is an undoubted advantage. Also, data on use are generally to hand and plentiful, two very attractive features indeed where there is a chronic shortage of time and funding (and where is there not?). However, as we have just seen, use data have to be treated with caution. Also, perhaps even more importantly, use data are too crude indicators of need to serve as a comprehensive enough foundation for services aiming at the meeting of information needs: whilst use can be a manifestation of need, an information need is, in theory, greater than demand plus use. Moreover, as people can only use what is available, use is very heavily dependent upon provision and access, albeit this is less of a problem these digital days. Perhaps most disturbingly, where use studies are concerned, non-users – whose number can often amount to quite a significant percentage of the population, are not taken into the equation. Non-users may loom larger in certain fields and users may form a small, self-selecting group, but they may also prove to be a more financially attractive and/or influential group. We know, for instance, that senior managers have traditionally been the ones that have shied away from using information systems, as a senior partner of an accountancy firm, trying to explain why he never searched for information himself, told one of the authors who came to interview him: 'I know how to make coffee, but I don't'.

Evidently then, use data can only offer a partial view of need. Even when augmented by demand data, use data can only help an information system improve on what it is already doing, but since there is no guarantee that it was on the right lines to begin with, this is of limited value only; use data will not help build a system which will provide new services and solutions. Thus, use data may be very welcome for measuring the usage of what is provided, but it is no substitute for needs data in establishing whether what is provided is what is best. Plainly, the case for basing effective information services and systems on a holistic view of the need people have for information, the wants and demands they express for it, and the use they make of it is very strong. Before we leave the topic of information use, though, let us consider the term 'user' itself.

The digital consumer (yesteryear's user, reader, customer, client, patron ...)

User, along with its various synonyms in the professional literature – reader, costumer, client, patron – has traditionally been used to denote people who might avail themselves of an information service. The expression has never been too fortunate a choice of words (for one, it was employed to describe non-users, too), but, in any case, it is surely *passé* by now: user (and users) has lost much of its meaning. In many respects it is a tired, cheap, over-used and misused word, which provides the information profession with a debased currency. The word 'users' conjures up a picture of a featureless mass, a homogenous body – people who are accustomed to being fed (print-based) information in batch-processing mode, 1950s-style. It fails to reflect the close, complex and virtually incessant engagement that takes place between people and information in today's digital world, where knowledge, perceived as the key to success in all walks of life, is a major democratic right and leveller. Basically, then, 'user' is the wrong word, in the wrong place, at the wrong time.

What we really need is a more accurate term, much richer in meaning, which acknowledges the multi-dimensional relationship between an individual and the internet-redefined, vastly widened and 'viewing' information environment. 'Digital consumer', the term suggested by Nicholas and his colleagues in their recent book of the same title, could fit the bill, and 'digital consumer', rather than the more specific descriptor 'digital information consumer' it should be. This, because, as Nicholas et al. (2008a) contend, in today's information realities a digital consumer is, to all intents and purposes, the equivalent of an information consumer. True, people visit the multi-purpose, encyclopaedic virtual space that is the internet for many different objectives, much the same as they would go to a bricks-and-mortar superstore looking for goods, services, new experiences, titillation, excitement and amusement. However, as their pursuits on the internet invariably involve choosing or buying e-documents or information services, it is now almost impossible to say what is information and what is not; what is information seeking and what is not. Take the example of e-shopping: as Russell (2008) explains, first a person is a digital information consumer and then an e-buyer. Thus, people shopping at an e-store will be using the internal search engine to find what they want, navigating through the site, employing browsing menus and opening another window on a cross-comparison site, to make sure they are getting value for money. Only when the information-seeking component of the shopping process is successfully completed will they actually purchase the item they need. Thinking very much along the same lines, in a recent *New York Times* article on the growing reliance on the internet for health information Schwartz (2008) argues as follows: 'As patients go online to share information and discuss their care, they are becoming something more: consumers. [For instance,] Amy Tenderich, the creator of Diabetes Mine has turned her site into a community for diabetes patients and an information clearinghouse for treatments and gadgets ... '

'Digital consumer', not 'digital information consumer' it should be, then, but why this specific term? Well, to begin with, because 'digital consumer' is very much an internet-type word, which the word 'user' most certainly is not. The internet, with its own rich and picturesque language, is so very much a part of everybody's life today (at least in the so-called 'developed' countries), that there is a pressing need to get our professional jargon in-line with its vocabulary. We really cannot ignore the call for employing the 'right' language, for it is only by doing so that information professionals can address the much larger information audience that the internet commands.

Also, perhaps more importantly, the term 'digital consumer' is a truer representation of things as they really stand, namely, that it is the individual, rather than the system that now holds centre stage. Thus, while users of a bygone era used information systems, today's digital consumers explore the information space (cyberspace); while users were supplicants, standing outside the system, looking (beseechingly) in, digital consumers are part of the system. Indeed, the digital consumer has come to play a much more dynamic, complicated, creative and engaged role in the evolution of the information domain than the user of yore could ever have imagined. In fact, the digital consumer is now King, actually driving the changes in the virtual space with a wholly novel style of information seeking: frenetic, promiscuous, volatile and intent on the pursuit of quick wins. Exchanging the old term for the new one thus acknowledges this shift in power from information producer to information consumer.

Perhaps it is the adoption of this more accurate terminology that will help to convince librarians, publishers and media moguls alike – indeed, anyone who manages large, centralised, inflexible, batch-processing-style information factories – that their users/customers/patrons/readers have really flown the coop. Having become digital consumers, rather than passive users, they are no longer the captive audience of the past, wholly dependent on the information providers' goodwill; these days they are the ones who call the shots. After all, they have a huge digital choice and can quickly vote with their feet (mouse?). In fact, as Gunter (2008) points out, they will have even more choices in terms of sources of information about commodities and services. Thus, thinking about people as consumers is a key step towards delivering the right services to meet their needs. Information professionals had better take these relatively new developments to heart, challenging as they may be, or ignore them at their peril. If they opt for the latter, they run the risk of information seekers completely abandoning them and going their own way; there are plenty of convenient enough alternatives to the traditional information services. With disintermediation gaining momentum by the minute, the writing is there on the wall, for all to see ...

3 A framework for evaluating information needs

Having delineated in some detail the whys and wherefores of the imperative to undertake routine collection and analysis of information needs data, we now come to the thorny question of how to go about it. The secret to it all seems to place the slippery concept of information need in a comprehensive, clear-cut and understandable analytical framework, which is precisely the form of scrutiny offered here. Not that the parameters of such a framework too readily come to mind, for it is far more difficult to describe the characteristics of information needs than, say, those of housing needs. This is probably to do with the fact that information needs arise from other needs: as such, they are more likely to be accorded less individual thought and consideration, and, in result, their characteristics are not so easily remembered or disentangled. Still, despite the fact that information needs are perceived as less concrete and more diffuse, just as you can describe the key characteristics of housing need as being: building material, site location, type (apartment, semi-detached), number of rooms, architectural design/character, and age/period of the property, so too can the characteristics of information need be described.

Thus, it is possible to identify 11 major characteristics of information need: subject, function, nature, intellectual level, viewpoint, quantity, quality/authority, date/currency, speed of delivery, place of publication/origin, and processing and packaging. These characteristics combine to form a comprehensive evaluatory framework, for it takes the holistic consideration of the different attributes of an information need to provide a truly fitting answer to a problem encountered. Suffice to cite the example of the unsuitability to most UK-based high-school students of some information, which may be right on target subject-wise, but, say, highly scientific in its level, 20 years old and in Chinese, to demonstrate the point. It is important to mention at this juncture: although the portrayal of the various facets of need may take a lot of words, this does not mean that using the framework is a long and laborious task. It is the understanding that takes the time. Once the form of analysis is mastered, then the various sections outlined below shrink into a headings checklist.

The 11-pronged framework proposed here can, thus, ensure that information delivery is consumer-centred, targeted, personalised and relevant. Indeed, it can be profitably used at both a macro level – for effective strategic information management planning, and at a micro level – for the efficient carrying out of routine enquiry work and consumer online searching. More specifically, the framework can be put to use for the following purposes:

1   Laying the foundations for the design of personalised information services by benchmarking the needs of different information communities and making comparisons between them.
2   Monitoring and evaluating the effectiveness and appropriateness of existing information systems from a consumer perspective.
3   Detecting gaps in information service provision and remaining vigilant to changes in need necessitating modifications, adjustments and fine-tuning.
4   Aiding the assessment of the never-ending tide of new information products.
5   Ensuring that one-to-one information service encounters are set on a firm footing and conducted in a systematic and comprehensive manner.
7   Bringing the information consumer and the information professional closer together (something that is inherent to the information needs assessment process put forward here).
8   Providing an information literacy training tool for the enfranchised, but untrained, digital consumer.
9   Offering a self-help guide for the e-citizen who wants to maximise the benefits of the information cornucopia. Students of all subjects would particularly benefit.

Subject

Subject is probably the most obvious characteristic of information need, central to nearly all information need statements. Indeed, it is probably the one feature most readily coming to mind for describing an information need. Libraries arranging their document collections by subject and search engines providing access to the world's information resources by the means of keywords is a testament to the importance accorded to this aspect of information need. This is not to say, though, that describing information needs in subject terms alone will lead to wholly satisfactory outcomes. As has already been noted, only if all relevant attributes of the information need are considered, can a truly appropriate solution to the problem be found. Still, while subject is not the sole aspect of significance in the portrayal of an information need, it is plainly a very important one (hence Google's interest). Unfortunately, it is also one that often defies our attempts to get it right, for the successful matching of a person's subject requirements with the 'right' information is far easier said than done, and no wonder: subject requirements vary so with the idiosyncratic circumstances of each and every person, or even with those of the very same person at different times.

Inter- and intra-individual variations in subject requirements

In today's multidisciplinary and multitasking world most people undertake an ever-increasing variety of roles, each with its own subject requirements. On the job front alone an individual might function in a number of capacities. Thus a university lecturer might have teaching, counselling, consultancy, administrative, professional and union responsibilities, and, probably above all, research obligations. In consequence, people need to concern themselves with quite a few subjects: mastering some, learning a bit here and there about others; keeping in touch with some, occasionally (if at all) revisiting others. It is not necessarily the individual's lead role(s) either, where the most pressing need for information is. Indeed, it could be argued that the individual would already have ensured that arrangements were satisfactory in this department, for example by putting to good use one or other of the widely available current awareness/alerting/RSS services. It is elsewhere – outside the mainstream interest – where initiating 'jewel hunting expenditures' in a library or on the internet may be deemed necessary. Thus, for example, a focus group of academics attended by one of the authors, convened to discuss and reflect upon scholarly research behaviour, said they followed developments in their specific areas of interest mostly via subscriptions to alerting services, which sent them journal tables of contents (TOCs) on a regular basis; however, outside their immediate fields they considered Google searches the better option for the purpose.

What makes the whole matter rather tricky, though, is the fact that every role people undertake requires them to have detailed knowledge on some things and a broader understanding of many other things. Obviously, people have different information needs and different methods of meeting these needs in areas outside their fields of expertise, in which their knowledge is limited or even altogether non-existent, and in which they are certainly not as well versed in the literature, the methodologies and the jargon. Take again the example of the information needs of university lecturers. As Menzel (1964) points out, in their particular role of researcher alone, each scholar's area of attention comprises several fields or sub-fields arranged in concentric circles: the primary field of attention, at the centre, is to be kept up with in full detail; the secondary fields, at varying distances from the centre, are also to be kept up with, if not in the same detail; and fields towards the periphery merely warrant knowing about progress made. A similar differentiation holds true where university lecturers' other roles are concerned, too: in some areas they follow the advances made pertaining to their teaching in minute detail, while in others they dip into the material every now and then, just to gain a smattering of understanding of current professional issues. Thus, for instance, one of the prime teaching interests of Library School lecturers – on which they spend a lot of time and have done so for many years – is online searching. It follows that they would be grateful for everything newly written about, say, Dialog, a system they usually teach in depth. However, the same lecturers must also keep in touch with developments in the broader Library world, for they are training students to work in libraries. The need here, though, is for general, contextual data only: a general item on the financial problems faced by libraries would be acceptable, but perhaps only the one, not too detailed, item would be sufficient.

Furthermore, not only do different roles and endeavours call for material in diverse subjects and in a range of detail, but they may very well require information that also varies as to the extent to which it delves into a subject. It is very much a question of how deep the interest lies. True, these days people's 'concentric circles of interest' are getting smaller and smaller in span, as one academic explains: 'You know that you are unable to cover the whole field, and in consequence you concentrate on specific issues ... you deal with the trees, rather than with the whole forest'. However, at the same time, these circles of interest grow ever-more specific. In fact, the developments in this direction seem to form a self-perpetuating circle, for the need to cope with the huge quantities of information being constantly generated seems to dictate, as much as to originate in this ever-growing specialisation. Thus, a salient fact of contemporary life seems to be a focusing of interests and, as its direct derivative, a focusing of information needs. Another academic, also testifying to a focusing of his research interests and his information needs, elaborates: 'You have to specialise, otherwise you won't be able to cover all the knowledge in a given field, [and] because of the specialisation you need to inquire more deeply into your subject, you have to know more about it'.

However, just how specific a request is may greatly vary from person to person, or even from situation to situation for the very same person. An interest in, say, organic gardening might entail a need for some quite broad-spectrum information, if the person is a newcomer to the subject area – 'The Manual of Organic Gardening', for instance – or for some very specific, in-depth information, if it is for the use of an expert – such as 'The No-digging Approach to Potato Cultivation'. By the same token, a visitor to a health website may sometimes search the site for a specific purpose, looking for exhaustive information on a given subject, whilst at other times the same visitor turns to the site simply to browse the general health news. Of course, information seekers often have a very good idea of just how specific and detailed the material they are looking for must be, but does the intermediary or system know? If this is not untangled at the outset, either a flood of dense information is unleashed on the unwary, or the supply of information is choked off to the needy.

To complicate matters even further, people's interests and responsibilities change – nothing is set in concrete. Rather to the contrary, as a casual comment of a physicist, musing aloud on his information needs, seems to indicate: 'My area changes so much, that I constantly have to spread out to more and more domains, and in consequence I need to know increasingly more. It's not the way it used to be; in the past you accumulated the information you needed in the first few years of work in a field and from then on you only needed to keep track of further progress made. Now it's the other way round: with the passing of time I need to know more and more of things I have never needed to know before'. It seems, then, that routine and regular monitoring of the subject premises upon which the increasingly more widely available current awareness/alerting services are built must be carried out if they are to maintain their effectiveness. Virus-checking programmes today often update their scanning lists daily and information systems should take their lead from them. Updating needs profiles should be conducted at the very least once every six months to maintain their effectiveness. Once a quarter is better.

Having seen how differences in personal circumstances entail discretionary information needs and uses both on the inter-individual and the intra-individual level, we now come to the biggest challenge of all: the matching of a person's subject requirements with the 'right' information.

Locating pertinent information on a subject

The root of the difficulties encountered when attempting to find appropriate information on any given topic seems to lie in the problems associated with effective subject description. The conversion of the need for information into terms that adequately clothe its subject sounds easy, but it is not: people are unlikely to furnish all the terms the information system needs for it to produce the goods, or, even when prodded (by pop-up boxes, for instance), to provide the most productive terms. It all boils down to the problem of translating user-generated keywords into the retrieval language of the information system, which purportedly has been solved with the introduction of structured access to information. However, as the huge popularity of keyword-based information seeking irrefutably proves by now, bibliographic description and controlled subject access are not held to be as crucial to information work as librarians would have us believe. In fact, information seekers have long been 'voting with their feet' in manifesting quite some reluctance to locate the information they need on a given topic in the methodical, bibliographic-tools-based fashion wistfully recommended by information professionals. Thus, for example, Palmer and Neumann (2002) observe that academic researchers in the humanities are renowned for their propensity for serendipitous locating of information despite the plethora of secondary searching tools at their disposal, to which King and Tenopir (1999) add that science and social science researchers too have been found to prefer less systematic methods of information retrieval.

Perhaps not surprisingly: first of all, as Stoan (1984) points out, no subject heading or descriptor can adequately analyse a book or an article for the reader, as bibliographic access tools to the literature introduce another layer of human minds through which information must be filtered, evaluated, classified and labelled. Also, locating information through the use of the controlled vocabulary of a catalogue, an abstract or an index necessitates lighting on the 'right' subject terms, which for all practical purposes depends on the seeker's ability to second-guess correctly the indexer's choices. Happening on the 'correct' term is clearly difficult enough even in knowledge areas, most notably the sciences, where the information content of a publication is definable in concrete and universally accepted terms. It is obviously a far more formidable task in fields of a less predictable terminology, such as the humanities and social sciences, in which vocabulary is conventionally assumed to be fuzzy and hard to pin down. It is for this very reason that a university-based political scientist argues so hotly against unconditional reliance on alerting services in his efforts to keep up with new developments in his areas of interest:

> I'm constantly on the lookout lest I fail to spot relevant material, as I can never be sure that I can correctly predict an indexers' choice of terms! Just last week I almost missed an article of importance because it was under "prejudice" rather than "xenophobia"!.

There is, of course, a time-honoured (but increasingly less-used) solution to these problems of relevance and precision in defining the subject of an information need: professional assistance. Take, for example, the attempt to solve an information problem on a one-to-one basis. An information specialist will spend some time, ideally in the presence of the customer – not so easy in the virtual world – scanning thesauri and sample issues of secondary services, often coming up with quite satisfactory results: the broad-narrow and related-term networks will provide an excellent word map in which to place a topic, resulting in sufficient terms to effectively cover a subject. Yet, even enlisting the help of an intermediary does not guarantee problem-free information retrieval, for clients seem to find it very difficult indeed to pinpoint the subjects of their information needs.

One frequently encountered problem is that people, in their attempt to communicate to the information professional or system the subject of their concern, generalise the query. Mostly they do this in order to ease the way of the intermediary into what they consider a complicated and intractable problem that they have spent a long time considering, but to which the intermediary comes cold. Interestingly, people appear to do the same with remote information systems, too. However, there are other reasons for generalising requests: to provide browsing room to allow for the inadequacy of the keywords; to simplify things for the intermediary, who is not necessarily a subject expert; to minimise the risk of early rejection and to provide space for negotiation, in case the intermediary can only offer limited assistance; and to get a prompt reply by means of a short, perceived then as simple, question. Information workers, indeed telephone helpline operatives, all have their own pet examples of hopelessly general questions, such as the following gem: a request for books on fish in a public library. Now, in a public library there are books on catching fish, cooking fish, the biology of fish and fish as pets, to name just the most obvious possibilities. Take, too, this real-life query: 'I wonder if there is any information on new cars?' The actual requirement was for dealers' prices for the Honda Civic.

Closely related to general question-framing is vague question-framing – sometimes the two are indistinguishable. Confidentiality concerns can lead to people cloaking or camouflaging their interest from the intermediary or system (in case it is monitored), so that others are not alerted to their particular line of enquiry. This can happen in the information centres of newspapers, especially in those that serve journalists from a number of papers, as is the case at News International and the UK Mirror Group. More often, vague subject specification mirrors the users' own confusion and uncertainty as to what they want: it is difficult for them to verbalise their problem, although they will recognise what they want when they see it. After all, users are asking for information to fill a gap in their own knowledge: this must inevitably lead to some imprecision in the formulation of the query.

Not that all these are insurmountable problems; far from it. In point of fact, information professionals learn early in their careers to identify such obstacles to subject specification and deal with them effectively in the reference interview. Unfortunately, though, in these disintermediated days, where most searching is conducted remotely and anonymously, they have fewer and fewer opportunities to put their expertise to the test. Even before the digital information world became for many people a far superior alternative to the print-based traditional library, turning to the information professional was perceived as time consuming and labour-intensive compared to researching information independently. So much so, that even researchers, for whom attaining the right information at the right time is absolutely crucial, were found as long as some 35 years ago to shun professional librarians (Meadows, 1974), and this to such an extent that, apparently, they were 'prepared to consult almost anyone, except a librarian' (Line, 1973, 33). By now, this reluctance to use the services of an intermediary seems to have become an overpowering trend: in our age of ubiquitous desktop access to massive quantities of information on any and every subject, help yourself is very much the name of the game. After all, who needs information professionals performing their feats of conjecture to alight on the right subject descriptors when all it takes is typing in a keyword or two? Searching is easy, is it not?

Well, as it happens, it appears not. Thus, as Bates (1998) contends, in study after study, across a vast variety of environments, it has been found that for any target topic, people will use a wide range of different terms. Two examples help to illustrate the nature of the problem. A research academic, searching for material published on the topic of people doing work 'on the side', i.e. without the various government authorities knowing, uses the term 'moonlighting'. However, a comprehensive trawl of the literature would soon uncover more terms: second economy, underground economy, black economy, black market. All of these terms will have to be employed if the search is not to become a lottery, which much searching is. Similarly, a search for material on the elderly – a relatively simple concept one might have thought – is, in fact, even more problematical with the following possible alternatives: retired people, old age, the aged, senior citizens, pensioners, old people, old persons. It gets much more complicated than this when two or more concepts are involved.

Still, people seem to favour greatly what is in effect the epitome of the shallow thinking characterising 'trial and error' behaviours: the portrayal of information need through keywords alone. 'Google is doing a great job for us these days ... you only have to know how to search, how to choose the key-words', says a computer scientist, and his psycho-oncologist colleague joins him in extolling the wonders of the technique: 'I search for information by trying various word combinations which I think will get me to the information I need, all sorts of word combinations, until I find the ideal combination'. However, she seems to be unique at least in one respect: these days not even scholars construct searches with many terms in them. Typically one-third of users enter one word in their search statements, about the same proportion two words, and only the remaining third enter three words or more (Nicholas et al., 2008b). To be sure, today's information seeking is very different from that prevailing in the hard-copy environment of the late 20th century. Searching is no longer a serious activity in terms of thought, preparation and execution. No doubt, subject keywords are perceived as providing the easy and quick fix, although, of course, they fix a little as every user of a web search engine is only too aware.

Indeed, as the use of search engines is fast becoming the first-line option for tracking down pertinent information, there is a proportionate increase in the retrieval of irrelevant documents. It is easy to see how this comes about: today's information seekers, steering clear of 'superfluous' bibliographic access tools or professional support because 'it is so easy to conduct an information search on the web', forgo the benefits of accurate and comprehensive analysis of need, which alone can guarantee relevant and precise results. Also, the ease of use characterising search engines comes at a price: much of the material procured by this form of wide-angled (shotgun) searching will inevitably be irrelevant.

Apparently, then, the awareness that much of the material served up in spades by a search engine will probably be found irrelevant does not deter people from its use; they are quite happy to trade failure for convenience. This dovetails neatly with the waning of the hue and cry characterising the early days of the web concerning the problematic nature of locating information of relevance via search engines. Thus, for example, gone are the (not so long ago) days, noted in study after study (Kibirige and DePalo, 2000; Massey-Burzio, 1999; Voorbij, 1999; Wang and Cohen, 1998; Zhang, 1999), when academics consistently clamoured for librarians' professional intervention to remedy the problems seen as emanating from the lack of bibliographic description and controlled subject indexing of the information to be found on the web. Indeed, the CIBER studies into the use of various e-information platforms, most notably in the areas of health (Nicholas et al., 2007a), scholarly journals (Nicholas et al., 2008b) and scholarly books (Rowlands et al., 2007) find time and time again that whatever the specific audience, users tend to shun on-site menus, complicated interfaces and myriad search options, opting instead for search engines. Thus, the majority of users (the proportion normally varies between about two-fifths and three-quarters) find a relevant site through the use of Google or other search engines. Anecdotal evidence gleaned in the aforementioned focus group, discussing the information seeking of academics, indicates that even among researchers, with very specialist, sometimes esoteric fields of inquiry, the notion of discipline-specific databases seems to have bitten the dust in favour of convenient but incomplete generic services like Web of Science and Science Direct. The attitude appears to be that 'if the information isn't found there, it's not worth looking for'. This mirrors the behaviour of their undergraduates; it is just that they look for something a bit more 'select' than Google. No wonder then that, as Russell (2008) points out, there is a marked increase in search engine-based information retrieval: in 2007 approximately one-third of internet users utilised a search engine to find a site, even if they had visited the site before, whereas in 2003 this was just one-quarter! Furthermore, as the evidence amassed in CIBER's Virtual Scholar research programme (2001–08) indicates, this is just the beginning, for the younger the information seekers, the more likely they are to tackle an information need by keyword-based retrieval via the use of search engines (Nicholas et al., 2008b).

Not that this growing popularity of search engines, bringing about the habitual reduction of an information need to a few haphazardly chosen key-words, is all that surprising. Keyword searching may not be the most efficient information retrieval method, yielding, as it usually does, a considerable amount of 'noise', but it does provide the information seeker with a much wider and disparate view of what is on offer – more titles, older material, from more subjects. Also, it is certainly a far more convenient method of information retrieval than using an arbitrarily chosen descriptor or subject heading assigned by a third party. Finally, perhaps most importantly in today's hurried times, when 'fast, easy and trouble-free' is so often the overriding consideration in everything we set out to do, the use of a search engine serves the ultimate goal of the information consumer, the simplifying or short-circuiting of the information-seeking process. In addition, using a search engine is costless, except for the time spent – and it only takes a typical internet user 10 seconds to check out a page (Nielsen, 2000), and, courtesy of associated advertising, you might even find something to buy.

Thus, search engines offer the prospect of trouble-free, targeted and direct access to meet an information need, providing as they do massive choice in response to a query of a word or two. No wonder they are perceived as offering a relatively sophisticated search facility for people with limited knowledge about either information retrieval or the content sought. In this respect they might have become the digital equivalent of the 'returned book shelves', the place where the tried, if not necessarily proven items are to be found. The quest for effortless searching is so pervasive that young people even exhibit a strong preference for expressing themselves in natural lan-guage rather than analysing which keywords might be more effective (Williams et al., 2008).

The ramifications of this inexorably growing preference for unmediated and uncomplicated information activity may be quite far reaching. On the most basic level, as it unmistakably emerges from the substantial evidence base amassed by the CIBER research group over the years, search skills and levels of digital literacy are (largely unacknowledged) problems for a considerable number of people. There seems to be some disturbing data which indicate that much use appears to be passing and/or ineffectual, and could possibly constitute a 'dumbing down' in information-seeking behaviour. Thus, lots of hits are just searchers passing through; they put in the wrong word and got to the wrong place. Take the example of an investigation of the BBC website (Nicholas and Huntington, 2005), which found that a considerable number of users made input errors when entering their search queries, and often did not notice what they had done until the search results were displayed. When participants noticed spelling suggestions (i.e. 'were you looking for … ') they often welcomed them, although several users scrolled directly down to the results list. The recurrent indications of poor/limited searching do make one reflect on the effectiveness of information literacy strategy and programmes. It would indeed be ironic if the web that provided for the enfranchisement of the user in information terms was also guilty for the disenfranchisement of whole swathes of the population unable to take advantage of the information deluge.

Furthermore, this may be the first inkling of a major change underway in today's information consumption dictates. The fact that search engines, unlike browsing mechanisms like content, subject and alphabetic lists, do not require information seekers to have any prior knowledge of the formal literature, its structure and hierarchy might well mean that future users will bring with them less knowledge of the scholarly system, of which libraries are currently an important component. Seeing that most libraries were originally – and still are – designed so that their contents could be browsed first, this is quite a fundamental shift, which is not yet reflected in information provision.

Function (use to which the information is put)

People frequently need information for achieving the vast variety of their role-, task- or interest-dictated goals. The inevitable outcome of this state of affairs is that each individual puts information to work in diverse ways, contingent on the specific circumstances in which the need for information arises. Take, for example, the different functions information fulfils for individuals in their professional capacity alone. It begins with the organisation or professional community to which they belong: since the end products of each such organisation/community are distinctive, so are, as you might expect, their uses for information. In the case of journalists information is used to write stories; in the case of social workers it is often used to answer resource questions concerning their clients; and in the case of academics it will be used to root a new inquiry in its context, help compile a lecture or update a reading list. Further to that, within each profession (and organisation) the prime function to which information is put will vary according to the role and specialism of the individual. Thus, managers in social work departments would be using information to monitor the progress of the organisation, rather than to answer the resource questions of the client group. Nevertheless, there are some generalisations that can be made about the functions to which people put information. Essentially, people need information for six broad functions or purposes, and it is very important to distinguish between them, for they require very different information solutions. They are: (1) getting hold of answers to specific questions (fact-finding function); (2) keeping up to date (current awareness function); (3) investigating a new field in depth (research function); (4) obtaining a background understanding of an issue/topic (briefing function); (5) procuring ideas or stimuli (stimulus function); and (6) looking for interesting titbits of information just for the fun of it (recreational browsing function).

The fact-finding function

Very often indeed, people need information simply to obtain answers to specific questions. These questions are familiar to all reference librarians: they are of the 'who, why, what, where, when and how' kind. Such questions may be straightforward, like the address of an organisation or individual, a biographical portrait; or complex, like the number of aircraft near-misses that occurred in 1987. The huge popularity of such fact-finding tools as Wikipedia and the now electronically accessible 'The Statesman's Yearbook', and the enduring high regard in which the still print-only 'Whitaker's Almanack' is held, bear testament to the strength of the need amongst end-users.

Indeed, everybody has this fact-finding need and for most of us it is a recurrent, perhaps everyday need; many of the queries of e-shoppers, for instance, fall into this camp. Even practised and experienced researchers, who know their literature very well, frequently seem to encounter those gaps in their knowledge (Bernal, 1959) that send them in pursuit of a piece of necessary information: a bit of data, a method, the construction of a piece of apparatus, an equation … Luckily, the need is relatively precise and well-defined, generally met by facts, names, addresses, statistics and the like. Not a lot of information is involved in meeting this type of need and the interchange between user and information system/intermediary is consequently brief: therefore, such needs are by and large easily and cheaply met. They are also easily delegated.

There is a lot of evidence to suggest that nowadays fact-finding needs are met almost universally via the web; it seems to be everybody's handy encyclopaedia and telephone directory, and then, of course, there is Wikipedia. Hardly surprisingly, of course: this is simply part and parcel of the by now truly widespread tendency to regard the internet as the first-line source for meeting all information needs. Thus, for example, in the aforementioned comprehensive survey of the use and impact of key digital health platforms and services in the UK (Nicholas et al., 2007a) it has been repeatedly stated that the internet is now the first source consulted, with people saying that other sources were consulted only 'when I can't get what I need from the internet'. This was true even for one respondent working in a location where there was a medical library:

> I usually first try to find relevant info [sic] on the net, because it is easier than getting hold of hard copies of the same or similar info. If the net can't offer enough, then I will try to get the information from medical library at work.

Obviously, where easily solvable problems, necessitating only some fact finding are concerned, the convenient accessibility of the truly wide-range information on the web does indeed render it the prime option for resolving painlessly and quickly the occasional disruptions to workflow or thought processes caused by problems of this sort. Yet, interestingly, it is precisely this need for specific information which can at times still bring people to the physical library, despite its plainly diminishing importance in the eyes of many (Martell, 2008). Thus, for example, as it has been shown by Herman (2005), humanities scholars still regard the library as their primary option for fact-finding purposes, even though turning to a colleague or searching the internet could leave them comfortably seated at their desks. Apparently, as Brockman et al. (2001) point out, their investigations often raise questions pertaining to details which can be found only in lesser-known primary documents or secondary sources. These stand a better chance of being located in a traditional library, for, in many of the commercial full-text and indexing products available in the humanities the marginal and the esoteric are ignored in favour of the canonical and the influential.

The current awareness function

Moving on to another use to which information is put, we now come to people's need to keep up to date, to follow the new developments in their areas of interest. This is also a generally widely felt need, especially in today's knowledge- and information-based society, but in some fields and professions the concern is much more pressing. In fact, as Wilson (1993b) suggests in his essay on maintaining currency, for the large class of knowledge workers – i.e. knowledge producers (those active in research and development) and members of the professions – the requirement to keep up with one's field is an ethical requirement, sometimes even dictated by the law. However, social pressure strongly reinforces the demands of ethics and law: people do not want to appear to their peers to be behind the times, because that is likely to expose them to contempt. This is how a biologist puts it: 'I need to know what's going on so that I don't turn out to be the laughingstock of the field, proposing a 'new' project five other labs are already working on'. Further to that, Wilson (1993b) adds, there is a kind of 'logical' pressure involved, too: keeping up with professional advances made is, of course, plain common sense, as people's principal assets are likely to be their stock of specialised knowledge, which, for them, makes keeping up to date nothing less than a form of self-preservation. Literally so, apparently, as a neuro-biologist, mincing no words in getting across the message, explains:

> Keeping up is one of the measures you take in order to safeguard yourself ... otherwise you've no way of knowing what goes on in the world, and in science it's truly critical and essential that you do. If you want to survive, you've got to do it, if you don't know other people's work you're as good as dead.

Maintaining a hold on what is going on is a particularly essential part of professionalism in dynamic fields, characterised as they are by sudden, frequent and widespread change. This is plainly the case with all journalists, and enormous amounts of money are spent assembling complex information systems to enable them to keep track of events in real time, although they have been helped considerably in this by social networks, like Twitter and Facebook. In academia, too, it is the fast-moving areas that require constant vigilance over developments, although in the case of scholars, it is the research advances made that need to be followed, rather than events. Indeed, keeping up to date is considered a must in all scholarly fields, as an academic, an expert in philosophy, elucidates:

> Keeping current is very important. You can't conduct research ... if you are isolated from other people's work; that is, you can, but it will be much less efficient ... You can't discuss a problem without acknowledging that somebody wrote something on it recently, you can't write an article on a problem which somebody else has already solved ... Only if all researchers determinedly keep pace with the developments in their fields can scholarly progress be guaranteed, otherwise they'll re-invent the wheel over and over again.

Still, in matters of keeping up with the developments in one's field it has long been demonstrated that all researchers are definitely not created equal. Not that they differ as to the theoretical importance accorded to keeping abreast of new developments in their areas of interest; it is rather the definition of keeping up which differs from discipline to discipline and, in result, so does the pace of the activities aimed at attaining currency. Indeed, there can be little doubt that 'making every effort to keep current' does not mean the same for scientists, social scientists and humanists.

Scientists consider keeping current an ongoing task of great urgency and no wonder: as their fast-moving fields are characterised by rapid changes, unless they are invariably up to date, they are liable to put in jeopardy the successful outcome of their research efforts. Not realising that some research has already been done, they may repeat it and, as a computer scientist puts it 'you turn out to be an idiot ... because you have wasted your time, and because people will tell you: what, didn't you know?' Moreover, in addition to the waste of energy and resources and the loss of face involved, ignorance of new research developments may also slow down their progress to the point of thwarting a claim to priority of a discovery (Becher, 1989; Garvey et al., 1970; Garvey, 1979; Price, 1986).

In comparison, social scientists can afford to adopt a more relaxed attitude to the need to maintain currency, since, as Line (1973) contends, the penalty for refraining from doing so is not as severe as in the case of the science researchers; with the circumstances of the typically empirical research projects of the social sciences differing from place to place and from time to time, it is not too likely that any findings would be discarded altogether because somebody else 'got there first'.

As for the humanist researchers, they are altogether complacent about the whole issue of keeping current, far less concerned than their scientist and even their social scientist colleagues with making sure that that no new contribution in their subjects escapes their attention immediately upon publication. Thus, although they too are mindful of the need to keep pace with new developments, they are believed to contentedly adopt an 'if not sooner, then later (or even much later)' frame of mind to the whole issue (Fulton, 1991; Stone, 1982; Wiberley and Jones, 1989). Stone (1982) links this relative tranquillity attributed to the humanities researchers, with regard to following the progress made in their areas of interest, to the nature of scholarship in the humanities: since the humanist researcher's innovative contribution to knowledge can consist of different perspectives or different understandings of the same work and might not present any new 'facts', awareness that others have worked or are working in the same field is less important; there is small chance of actual duplication occurring and it may not matter much if it does, so long as each presents an original interpretation. Indeed, at first glance, this danger of reinventing the wheel does not seem very relevant where humanities research is concerned. After all, who dare claim that the ultimate word on, say, Hamlet has already been said? However, the following story, recounted by a professor of literature, clearly demonstrates that in the humanities, too, the danger is there:

> Having re-read Jane Eyre I realised that there was a recurring motif of opening and closing of doors and windows in it. Rather happy with my insight, I wrote a long article on the subject, only to discover that somebody else had come up with the idea long before I did and there was a very good article on the subject, far better, unfortunately, than mine. There was nothing to be done about it; I literally threw the article into the bin.

Evidently then, humanists, too, have very good reasons for following the scholarly advances made in their fields.

Not very surprisingly, then, seeing to it that current awareness needs were adequately met was a major concern of the information community up until recently, and with good reason. The huge amounts of information generated, often referred to as the information explosion (a phrase nobody uses any more), did make the systematic monitoring of advances achieved quite complicated, even with close support forthcoming from computerised information systems. Thus, despite the ready availability of Selective Dissemination of Information services – regular, pushed information services based upon user-supplied keywords that represent ongoing interests, now increasingly being replaced by RSS (Really Simple Syndication) feeds – maintaining currency does necessitate a great expenditure of time and effort on the part of the individual to be spent on vetting and digesting the data. Still, in the above-mentioned survey of the roll-out of digital consumer health services in the UK during the period 2000–05 (Nicholas et al., 2007a), one user type identified was people who rated medical news and research highly and wanted to keep up to date. In fact, almost one-quarter of the users were on the site simply to browse the general health news, rather than to search it for a specific purpose. By the same token, the ways of a psycho-oncologist, who five years ago still reported seeing to her needs for up-to-date information in a fairly regular manner 'because information becomes obsolete in a fraction of a second', were quite the norm. No longer, though.

Logs, as well as interview and focus group data tell us that people are not keeping up to date as they once did: with increasing time and resource pressures at most workplaces and in many households, current awareness is no longer a discrete or regular activity. Thus, for example, in the just-quoted survey of digital health services in the UK (Nicholas et al., 2007a) doctors testified that at least some of their professional updating was done in response to a specific need: on the comparatively rare occasions when they were faced with complaints that required information beyond their personal stock of knowledge, they turned to the internet to aid them in forming a diagnosis and advising the patient. That it should be so is perhaps not wholly unpredictable: after all, the need for keeping up is inevitably vaguer than the need for facts; therefore, it is an information activity that may more easily be put on the back burner, dropped or conveniently overlooked. Also, whereas fact-finding is usually associated with immediate and often urgent problem-solving – and hence has to be dealt with speedily – this is not the case with current awareness. There is often no direct pay-off; the effect is much more long term.

Indeed, even academic researchers, who, as it has just been noted, are very conscious of the need to keep up, do not, as a rule, routinely invest time and effort in proactive information seeking aimed at learning of new developments. True, as Herman (2005) points out, the range, variety and frequency of researchers' activities aimed at keeping current are determined by the level of awareness deemed necessary in their disciplinary milieu to the work being done by others. Thus, for example, in fast-moving areas, where the disciplinary culture dictated norm is the ongoing exchange of pre-print based information among researchers, users seem to appreciate greatly the benefits of obtaining early intelligence via e-print repositories, as an academic, specialising in high-energy physics, describes:

First thing in the morning, I check the new articles posted overnight. I'm addicted to this, I spend on average between half an hour to an hour each morning checking if there's something new and interesting, or something which may link up with what I've been working on ... Since everybody, from students to the most valued researchers, sends the results of their work first to this archive, and only later to some journal, this is all I need to keep up.

However, this is really quite the exception to the rule, for nowadays, contrary to widely held notions, academics seem to follow the progress made in their respective fields with what can be termed as 'serene interest', but no more than that. Thus, with the notable exception of perusing e-journal TOCs when these land on their desktops, they tend to update themselves when the need arises, tacitly relying on search engines to deliver 'current awareness on demand'. Indeed, libraries' attempts to interest their patrons in innovative alerting services, such as RSS feeds and the like, meet with very little success, if any (Nicholas et al., 2008b).

It seems, then, that these days keeping current is a tactical, problem-driven activity rather than the strategic, time-driven concern that it used to be. Presumably this is because keeping a finger on the pulse of the developments presents less difficulty in an electronic environment, in which the information tap is always in the on-position in any case.

The research function

Researching a new field in depth is a far less frequent and widespread concern. Most people encounter the need to review the existing knowledge on a topic only occasionally and irregularly, but, given the realities of contemporary life, it does not come as much of a surprise to find that this is on the increase. Indeed, the insatiable demand for a multi-skilled and mobile workforce in a world based on knowledge has turned us all into permanent students, if not amateur scholars. There can be little doubt that these days, when life-long study, as well as training and retraining have become customary and taken for granted by large segments of the population, assembling a solid information base in preparation for embarking on a new undertaking (and not necessarily in work-related circumstances, either) is fast becoming routine for many people. It is certainly no longer the prerogative of those in research and academe! Indeed, the survey of digital health platforms and services in the UK (Nicholas et al., 2007a) lent further support to the notion, held by various health information providers and researchers (London, 1999; Eysenbach and Diepgen, 1999, to name but two) that the internet is exploited at a deeper level than that which might be expected of lay users, with websites intended for medical practitioners accessed by non-professional consumers alongside healthcare workers. Thus, for example, one respondent commented: 'I prefer sites, which are written by Doctors for Doctors [sic]. I also like to see references to the research papers that back up articles'.

This increasingly more prevalent need for anchoring a topic in its information context often necessitates extensive coverage of the knowledge existing on it, a state of affairs which is not invariably problem-free. True, the computer-aided accumulation of data allows for the ongoing creation and easy management of a dynamic, growing knowledge base, which is so wide-ranging, that seekers of information have at their disposal an unprecedented array of information resources. Also, computer applications can be of immeasurable help in locating, accessing and retrieving relevant information. Still, the time required to absorb and put to good use the data resulting from a simple search for the information foundations of a given subject can reach such enormous proportions, that a seemingly insurmountable problem is entailed. Fortunately, though, the need to research a new field in depth does not equal a need to assemble all the existing information on a subject, not even as an ideal goal to which to aspire. This holds true even for academics, who have to base their investigations on steadfast information underpinnings just as much as anybody else, perhaps more, but, in addition, also need to identify the lacunae in it for further investigation. Indeed, among the academics interviewed by Herman (2005), while a few did testify to aiming for obtaining the maximum information coverage possible on the eve of a new research project, others were more in agreement with a neuro-biologist, who said that she only aimed at 'getting the general drift of things':

> I had quite a few arguments with colleagues [on the thoroughness with which the literature needs to be reviewed]. Each time I mentioned considering a new topic for investigation, I was told: 'Go read the literature first'. And I keep insisting that I'm not interested in the literature when I can see with my own two eyes what's going on ... I don't hold with performing a full review of the literature ... it should suffice that you know in general terms what has been done, and what hasn't, for you to go ahead.

It seems, then, that whilst it is all too easy to mix up a good search with a big search – and none come bigger than those associated with the research need, the two are by no means synonymous. The novice or naive user (and intermediary) may be particularly prone to pursuing such information needs much too exhaustively, but this really need not be so. Establishing at the outset of an information-seeking expedition the scope of comprehensiveness and thoroughness required can simplify matters considerably, whether it is end-users searching on their own or an intermediary searching on behalf of somebody else. Moreover, as Wilson (1995) suggests, evaluating the search results and then intentionally ignoring some of the potentially relevant information to be found on a subject, which is really a routine and normal strategy of research work, can be a very effective way to cope with the problem. Obviously, this tactic can only work if the decisions taken as to which items to use (and which to skip) are based on knowledgeable assessment of the quality, authority and value of the information found, rather than resorting to the popular practice of picking the first item(s) produced by Google, which, of course, only proves the vital importance of the much-discussed need for information literacy training.

One last point: it is important not to confuse a fact-requiring question for a research one, because the information outcomes are as different as they can be. The trouble is that the information need, which seems to occur most readily to people, is the need for finding all relevant information on a topic. As it has already been noted, even academics no longer consider it essential to locate 'everything' known on a subject under investigation, but, nevertheless, their instantaneous association of a need for information often seems to be with ostensibly gathering literally everything published on a given topic (Herman, 2005). The root of the problem seems to be the fact that so much Information Science research concerns academics. They really are a prominent group of information users, but they also commend themselves because they are a pliant and orderly population, who, to boot, are easily accessible for a university-based Information Science researcher. The consequence is a stereotype of information need, which, although no longer accurate even for academics, is carried over to the population as a whole. No wonder, then, that when graduates of Information Science programmes come to work in a practitioner environment, they tend to opt for information solutions more appropriate to academic information problems, both in the planning of information services and day-by-day work, much to the detriment of their adequately meeting their clients' information needs.

The briefing/background function

As previously mentioned, not everyone has the time or need to research a field in depth. However, many people need a briefing on topics with which they are broadly familiar, but perhaps insufficiently acquainted with the detail, and sketchily and fleetingly need to be. For most of them this need is probably met by the newspapers, which thus perform a key briefing function.

Generally, the broader the subject interest (which, inevitably, equals more information), and the less the time available, the greater the need for the background brief. Journalists, for one, caught between the need to say something authoritative about almost anything and with very little notice and time to do this, are great practitioners of the background search – cuttings traditionally fulfilled this need until the advent of digital newspaper archives. Another group of users frequently in need of briefing are politicians. They are expected to have a view on anything, so it is not surprising to discover that one of their preferred information forms is the background papers produced by The House of Commons Library. Indeed, this is a prime example of information professionals anticipating information needs, and an area where they can really bring their skills to bear.

Ironically, the web – the chief culprit for the information deluge we are all experiencing, is a great briefing source. Thus, for example, the overwhelming majority of the seekers of health information in the survey of digital health services in the UK (Nicholas et al., 2007a) said that the information found on the web had helped them in understanding more about an illness or injury, and more than a quarter of them reported that the information found was even sufficient, in their judgement, to meet their health query and substitute for a visit to the doctor. Coupled with the ability 'to search on a wide range of topics – much more than a local library, and to consult a range of sources and perspectives', it is hardly surprising that for many of them the internet fulfilled effectively enough the briefing function, providing as it did what one user described as 'information that just wasn't available before to normal [i.e. non-medical] people'. However, patients bringing in internet printouts or discussing information they had acquired through this medium is not without its drawbacks and dangers, as one health professional explained: 'we are inundated with half heard or understood fragments of information from the television or half read magazine articles'. In result, added his colleague, 'usually the doctor has to allay fears or iron out misconceptions'.

Perhaps somewhat unexpectedly, today's academic researchers have briefing needs, too, especially when they participate in a scholarly endeavour attempting to coalesce the kind of multifaceted, and often inter- or multidisciplinary expertise that one researcher working alone cannot always provide. Thus, they may on occasion look only for the basic level information needed to aid them in understanding the wider picture within which the specific point being investigated is embedded, as a psycho-pharmacologist explains:

> If I need some information in a subject ... I'm no expert on, I'll look for a source, which can provide me with the information on a sufficient level to answer my question. I won't delve ad infinitum into each subject, because I won't see the end of it.

However, they have their own strategies for fulfilling this kind of information need (Herman, 2005), although they, too, utilise the web for the purpose.

Apparently, more often than not a brief discussion with a colleague suffices to point the researcher in the right direction. Obviously, the best option is asking a renowned expert on the subject, which is indeed the course taken by the more senior people. An archaeologist, for example, a prominent authority in his field, has no qualms whatsoever as to the right way to proceed when he finds himself up against a need for some background information: 'I'll contact a friend of mine who is sure to know the answer, I'll just send him a quick e-mail, he'll get back to me in no time, and that's that'. His economist colleague, also of a standing in his field, takes much the same course of action, but he will insist on talking to the colleague who can provide the information: ' ... it'll cost the university for half an hour or an hour of a transatlantic phone call, but I'll have my answer on the spot'. However, life is not as simple for the novice academics, as a young philosopher explains:

> Sometimes, when you don't know the answer to a question, you're well aware that there are others who do. However, then it becomes a question of ... the people you are in contact with in your day to day activities: if you work in a central place, where the action is, you just ask your colleague down the hall, but if you're not ...

Clearly, the problem boils down to a researcher having the right professional contacts, for in this day and age, courtesy of the ubiquitous e-mail, technically everybody is 'down the hall' from everybody else.

Well, if having the answer straight from the horse's mouth, so to speak, is not feasible, there is always recorded knowledge, which is indeed an often-cited solution among academics. However, these days this is not invariably the preferred option, as a neuro-biologist explains:

> If in the midst of work I need some information, I leave everything and dash to the library to get it. Though nowadays it's best to search the internet, it saves going to the library, looking for the specific volume, which may not be on the shelf, and even if it is, you have to go to the photocopying service, where there is a queue ... Also, often a little e-mail, which you write in a second, can save you all that trouble, you just ask a colleague to send to you the information.

Still, when academics require a briefing on a topic, turning to the literature is a prime option, for they have to hand review articles and extensive literature surveys designed for such purposes. These handy summaries of the state of the art are obviously of considerable time-saving capabilities and, as such, are very popular indeed among researchers. True, as Herman (2005) found, the practice of making do with a synopsis of the achievements on a topic in lieu of assembling the original contributions comprising the information base of a new research project is held, at least notionally, in very low esteem indeed. Even in the sciences, where it should be definitely feasible to do so, for in the 'harder' knowledge domains one reads to discover the outcome of somebody else's research (as opposed to reading for retracing the discovery and analysis at the core of the research in the 'softer' areas), a summary of advances made is rarely taken to suffice for laying the information foundations of a new exploration. Still, the more pressured the researchers are, the greater is the likelihood that they will rely on literature reviews. Indeed, in these days of Research Assessment Exercises and comparable institutional evaluation measures, which exert ever-increasing pressure on academics to produce as much research output in as short a time as possible, literature reviews are becoming much more important for scholars; they are considered a particularly useful strategy for getting up to date and avoiding too much reading.

Having seen how information is put to work to fulfil the need for acquiring some basic knowledge on a given topic, we now proceed to another of its uses: procuring ideas or stimuli.

The stimulus function

The creative aspect of many a new undertaking feeds on information, which can often serve as a stimulating agent, the source whence initiatives for an original venture may hopefully ignite. This role of information as a fund of inspiration is nowhere as pronounced as in the case of academic researchers, intent as they are upon contributing new knowledge and understanding. To be sure, it is their relentless search for the next problem to pursue which so frequently accounts for their ongoing concern with access to information, and with very good reason, too. As Palmer and Neumann (2002) contend, scholars prime for future discoveries: by working at maintaining a high level of interaction with a wide variety of information, they develop a state of preparedness for new discoveries, a conclusion, which, of course, echoes Pasteur's well-known saying, 'chance favours the prepared mind'. This is how an archaeologist puts it:

> You read the literature, you know what you know, and all of a sudden you realise that something looks at odds with what's held to be true, something doesn't fit into the existing body of knowledge. So you think about it, and then think about it some more, and perhaps come up with an alternative solution, which provides a better explanation. The existing knowledge is the trigger, yes, indeed, always, there's no such thing as not relying on previous information. Even if the idea occurred to Newton because the apple hit him on the head, it was his previous knowledge, which enabled him to come up with it.

Hardly debatably then, information serves a particularly vital purpose in sparking off fresh ideas and spurring new projects or investigations; the only question is how exactly it happens. However, the processes that lead people to light on new insights and/or formulate problems of consequence seem to defy attempts to describe it (Schwartz, 1992; Bath University Library, 1971a). What we do know is that these processes, including the utilisation of information for the purpose, are obscure and intensely personal. Indeed, whilst information seekers generally know what they are looking for, it is not so when they are on the lookout for inspiration. Here they have only the vaguest idea of what they are trying to find – and sometimes no idea at all. In fact, they interact with information sources in the hope that this will result in their discovering just what it is that they need; so much so, that quite frequently it is by seeing something that they do not want that they are perversely alerted to something they do want. No wonder, then, that surfing the web is a prime example of the stimulating effect information is capable of affording. The full-text documents the web liberally offers, with their hyperlinks and idiosyncratic natural language indexing, can in fact uncover all kinds of dormant information needs by providing unusual and unexpected associations of ideas.

Consequent to this state of affairs, the information seeking associated with this particular need is unavoidably unfocused and unstructured, which often leads intermediaries who observe it to the mistaken belief that what they are witnessing is poor searching. Much of the rubbishing of end-users' searching skills found in the professional literature results from a poor understanding of the characteristic information behaviour that results from individuals trying to meet this kind of need. However, it is only through this kind of vague and wandering exposure to great amounts of information that users can discover what they want and uncover their dormant information needs. This is why, as we have already noted, humanities scholars, whose manner of conducting research is highly individualistic and subjective, are so fond of browsing. As Saule (1992) points out, their seemingly aimless examining of the catalogue, scanning titles of books in the stacks or skimming a document sometimes results in the fortuitous discovery of connections between ideas and words. Of course, what is meant to stimulate can also irritate – and it can all too easily happen that the individual is overloaded and/or led on a wild goose chase. Still, it seems to be a small price to pay for fulfilling an information need that can hardly be resolved in any other way.

Evidently, if people seeking novel insights and fresh ideas are to fulfil their rather vaguely defined need for information, they have to rely on serendipity. It is perhaps not very surprising to find, then, that people do not often deliberately set out to discover stimulating information; rather, they seem to be on the alert while they browse around on the web or on the library shelves. Still, scientists, with their ongoing awareness of what the truly significant issues at the frontier of the developments in their fields are, do report that from time to time they scour the literature with the express purpose of locating topics for new research (Herman, 2005).

So now we come to the last of the uses to which information is put: enjoyment, pure and simple.

The recreational browsing function

Information seeking is seldom seen as an end in itself; rather, it is viewed instrumentally, as a means towards achieving one's role-, task- or interest-associated goals. Still, unearthing interesting titbits of information just for the fun of it is a much-loved pastime: people while away many a happy hour rummaging among the displays in a bookshop, leafing through books, journals and magazines in a library and, perhaps most notably, surfing the web. Obviously, as Das et al. (2003) maintain, they regard such a non-goal-directed information-seeking activity as its own reward, a form of entertainment, relaxation and escapism.

There is, of course, nothing new about this leisurely use of information, but the ubiquitous and effortless availability of the web, with its enormous information reach and its ability to provide undreamed-of quantities of information from one's desktop, have made it more widespread than ever. Thus, for example,

Fallows (2006) notes that almost two-thirds of American users (78 million people) testify to having gone online to browse the internet for no particular reason, just for fun or to pass the time, a percentage that has held about steady since the Pew Internet & American Life Project, which is a daily tracking survey on Americans' use of the internet, began asking the question in 2000. Indeed, she says, surfing the web has become one of the most popular activities that American internet users will do: nearly one-third of them go online on a typical day just to hang out. In fact, compared to other online pursuits, browsing for fun now stands only behind sending or receiving e-mail (52% of American internet users do this on a typical day) and using a search engine (38% of American internet users do this on a typical day), and it is in a virtual tie for third with getting news online (31% of American internet users do this on a typical day). Not that the huge popularity of recreational information seeking on the web comes as a surprise for anybody living in our times (at least in the industrialised world); we all do it, all the time. We have all become information voyeurs, who set out to look for information when we have no needs at all. Of course we do: these online sessions of wandering around on the web just for the fun of it offer a smorgasbord of information, attractively spread out for the consumption of a tasty bite here and there, wherever the fancy takes us.

Interestingly, this manner of information seeking is by no means reserved for recreational purposes; rather to the contrary, as we are about to see in the course of our discussion here. However, first we need to see how people obtain the information they put to use for the variety of purposes we have just enumerated.

Coping with the call for information in an era of abundant choice

Having examined in some detail the different functions information fulfils for individuals, as well as the distinctive information solutions each requires, all that remains now is the question of 'how'. How do people go about meeting the considerable range of their role-, task-, interest- or entertainment-associated needs in today's plentiful, if not over-abundant information world? The answer emerges loud and clear from the vast evidence base that the CIBER research group have assembled over the past few years. It is a very, very different form of behaviour than the one that might be expected on the basis of reading the classic information-seeking texts of Ellis (Ellis et al., 1993; Ellis and Haugan, 1997) and Wilson (1999). This is partly because we have undergone a massive paradigm shift in information-seeking behaviour since they developed their ideas, and partly because it has only recently been possible to observe information-seeking behaviour on a huge scale and in minute detail. Indeed, the digital consumer revolution requires us to consign to the bin much of what we have been holding to be true about people's ways and means of meeting their information needs.

In result of being given digital choice, present-day information consumers manifest a widespread, pronounced, endemic form of digital information-seeking behaviour, best described as 'bouncing', although the terms 'flicking' or 'hopping' would equally do. This is a form of behaviour where users view only one or two web pages from the vast numbers available to them and a substantial proportion (usually the same ones) generally do not return to the same website very often, if at all. Thus, for example, all the CIBER studies showed that around 55%–65% of e-journal users typically viewed no more than three pages in a visit and then left; the studies also showed that around half of all users did not return or only returned after a prolonged gap. This suggests a promiscuous, checking-comparing, dipping sort of behaviour that is a result of being provided with huge digital choice, search engines constantly refreshing that choice and a shortage of time that results from so much to look at. In this respect the behaviour is best seen as being akin to television channel hopping using the remote control – you flick around alighting on things of interest and when the interest fails or wanes you flick to something else.

In addition, information seekers seldom penetrate a site to any depth; on average, most people spend only a few minutes on a visit to a website, insufficient time to do much reading or obtain much understanding. This, as the extensive literature review undertaken in preparation for the Google Generation project (Williams et al., 2008) clearly indicates, is very much in line with other research based on observations or surveys. Thus, for example, observational studies have shown that young people (boys especially) scan online pages very rapidly and click extensively on hyperlinks – rather than reading sequentially. Users make very little use of advanced search facilities, assuming that search engines 'understand' their queries. They tend to move quickly from page to page, spending little time reading or digesting information and they have difficulty making relevance judgements about the pages they retrieve. When all this is put together with the bouncing data it would appear that we are witnessing the emergence of a new form of 'reading', with users 'feeding for information' or 'power browsing' horizontally through sites, titles, contents pages and abstracts in their pursuit of quick wins.

Plainly, this novel style of information seeking, frenetic, promiscuous, volatile and viewing in nature, is eminently suited to browsing for recreational purposes. Indeed, it bears a close resemblance to the characteristic behaviour of an e-shopper confronted by the cornucopia of shopping opportunities offered by the web. The problem is that when the search is goal-directed, whether it is for getting hold of answers to specific questions, for keeping up to date, for investigating a new field in depth, for obtaining a background understanding of an issue/topic, or for procuring ideas or stimuli, it can be construed to point to inadequate information skills resulting in negative outcomes (not finding what you need/want). However, in today's new information realities people expect instant gratification at a click, looking for 'the answer' rather than for a particular format or source. At the same time, they seem to await entertainment even when they set out to meet their formal, work- or study-associated needs, looking for involving, dynamic and personalised content experiences that can compete with the likes of Facebook. No wonder they scan, flick and 'power browse' their way through digital content!

This state of affairs clearly poses an enormous challenge for librarians. Forced by circumstances to compete for the attention of information seekers, who seem to be turning their backs on the library as a physical space at an alarming rate (Martell, 2008), they are increasingly conscious of the need to find innovative ways to enhance interest without impeding the effective meeting of people's information needs. Hence, in an attempt to adapt to the change they perceive in information-seeking behaviour, many librarians have started to experiment with Web 2.0 interactive facilities. Paying homage to the astonishing success of Facebook, MySpace and YouTube with the young (and not so young), and cognizant that if you are not certain of your brand or presence, it might be possible to obtain this by association, libraries now have profiles on social networking sites. It is too early to tell whether this kind of initiative will eventually bear fruit, but for now library presence on social networks as well as the blogs proudly sported by many of them seem to account for a small proportion of use only; most people concentrate on mainstream, traditional bibliographic activities. Thus, for example, Williams et al. (2008) cite a 2007 OCLC survey, which asked both college students and members of the general public how likely they would be to participate in activities on a social networking or community site, if built by their library. The responses left little room for doubt: clearly, neither group was much interested, with the numbers of those who said they would be 'extremely likely' or 'very likely' to do so coming to about 6% or 7% in most cases.

By the same token, at the above-mentioned focus group of academic researchers, the idea that an e-journal database should adopt Web 2.0 facilities went down like a lead balloon. They could not see the need for this or how people had the time to indulge in what they clearly thought were side-show activities. 'There is enough to do without engaging in blogs, wikis, RSS and the like', was the general message coming from the group. It seems, then, that at least for the time being social software does not have much to contribute to the rebuilding of relationships with users in an increasingly disintermediated environment. Perhaps not surprisingly: as Nic Howell (cited in: Sherwin, 2008) points out, 'social networking is as much about who isn't on the site as who is'; thus, when libraries and museums start profiles on a social network, its 'cool' brand is devalued. Anyhow, it is not very clear that any such attempt can be the answer to libraries' current plight: in 2008 the number of (British) Facebook users fell for the first time, and MySpace and Bebo visits were down too (Sherwin, 2008).

In any case, concurrent to these valiant attempts to harness social networking to the reinstating of libraries, librarians also concentrate a lot of effort on what is considered home ground for them: information retrieval. Having picked up on the popularity (and problems) of search engine searching, they are taking Google and the Google generation head-on by developing their own engines to stop user flight. The latest initiative and, maybe, the last hurrah, is federated searching, also known as meta-searching, broadcast searching, or cross-searching. The various federated search tools allow users to search simultaneously multiple library databases, catalogues, multimedia sources and other collections via one common Google-like interface, and to get the collected results in a succinct and unified format devoid of duplication (Cox, 2006). In doing this librarians aim to create the kind of simple and straightforward (not to say 'dumbed down') search environment that today's information seekers want, but with a difference: their search tools feature the components missing from the big search engines and Google Scholar: authority and quality. The early signs are quite promising.

Nature

This information need characteristic seems to defy any attempt at straight-forward definition, although a clear enough idea of what is involved emerges from a look at the various types of information in existence. Thus, on one level it is possible to differentiate between conceptual or theoretical, historical, descriptive, statistical or methodological information. On another level, there is the distinction between primary information (that is, uninterpreted evidence) and secondary information (books and articles reporting the results of research). Plainly, information of different types is available on any subject, in consequence of which, the nature of the information being sought is a crucial factor in ensuring that the answer found is truly relevant to the question asked. After all, when people specifically need one type of information, say, some statistics to prove a theoretical or conceptual point, their finding any other type of information on the subject most emphatically will not do. Yet, the type of information does not play the pivotal role in information seeking that it might conceivably do.

In fact, it seems that information seekers do not pay much attention to the nature aspect of the material they need; not even academic researchers, for whom the judicious use of information is truly vital. Thus, for example, in a questionnaire survey, canvassing the entire population of researchers at an Israeli university, more than a third of the participants rated the notion of setting out to look for a specific type of information as altogether irrelevant to them (Herman, 2005). Apparently, the kind of information required only comes to the fore when it is a truly prominent feature of the information need. Thus, for example, an academic researcher, musing aloud on the subject, remarks that she really should look specifically for methodological informa-tion, as she does not always know the new statistical techniques in vogue. Her colleague goes even farther than that, remarking that his ways are quite typical of biomedical and physics researchers: he actually sets out to look for parti-cular types of information, for example, if he wants to learn how a certain procedure is done or what the best equipment is to be used for a specific pur-pose. When he does need such information, searching the internet is his favourite solution to the problem, 'as it has sources, which are practically handbooks, telling you do this and this, the procedure goes like this'. However, on the whole the nature of information sought is not a matter with which people custo-marily concern themselves; indeed, it is not very often consciously formulated in the context of information seeking.

In view of the scant attention given to this aspect of information need, it is not very surprising to find that designers of information systems have traditionally neglected it. Systems seldom provide for retrieval along these lines, although most, offering a wide degree of access through their subject or word indices, do enable access to specific types of items, such as statistical accounts.

In any case, whilst there are different kinds of information on any subject, not all of them are equally suited to the needs of different individuals. As a matter of fact, some of these information types will prove to be highly unpalatable to some people, as a computer scientist interviewed by one of the authors insists: 'Stories are not for me; I leave them to my humanities colleagues'. Arguing much along the same lines, another interviewee, an economist, draws a clear demarcating line between information that he terms 'opinions', as opposed to what he calls 'facts':

> In the areas we deal with in economics we don't concern ourselves with opinions ... When it's a matter of opinion, you collect the facts ... , and then form an opinion ... , [but then] somebody else can have a different opinion about the same facts ... However, in economics it's not what I think, it's what's actually going on ... if I say that you need 5 percent to reach your goal, and somebody else says 4 percent will suffice, reality will soon put one of us right ... so it's not a matter of opinion; the concept that will be accepted is the one which reflects reality more accurately, and reality is usually not disputable, it's easily verified ... if I tell you the price of tomatoes, and you don't agree, the two of us go to the market ... and see what tomatoes cost.

Plainly, the nature aspect of some information depends in no small measure on its intended readership/audience. Thus, for instance, social science practitioners will hardly ever require their information produced in a theoretical manner or from a historical point of view – though their academic counterparts most probably would.

Indeed, it is scholarly research, which, intent as it is on querying every aspect of life on earth, perforce involves the use of the whole range of information types in existence: theoretical, conceptual, empirical, historical, descriptive, factual, statistical and methodological. Needless to say, though, that the nature of the information required in scholarly work is subject-contingent, that is, it varies first and foremost with the subject matter of the research underway, inclusive of the disciplinary-conventions dictated approach taken to it. Hence, if theoretical, conceptual, factual or methodological information is probably indispensable in any academic endeavour, regardless of its topic and the knowledge domain in which it is embedded, other types of information are, on the whole, reserved for specific disciplines. Thus, for example, historical information, so central for much of humanities research, will rarely, if ever be needed in science enquiries. By the same token, statistical information, the bread and butter of most social sciences research, is more often than not quite uncalled for in humanities scholarship.

Actually, even when researchers of different subject areas need the same kind of information, the extent of its utilisation may vary from one discipline to another, as Garvey et al. (1974) found in their extensive studies of over 2,000 sciences and social sciences researchers. Apparently, when physical scientists set out to look for methodological information, it is more frequently needed to formulate technical solutions and to design equipment or apparatus, whereas for social scientists the greater need is for information to select a design or strategy for data collection and to choose a data-analysis technique.

Further to that, since the activities associated with the successive steps of the 'typical' research process involve different kinds of mental processing, different kinds of information are required at the various stages. Thus, in the initial stages, the perception of the research problem involves heavy use of theoretical and conceptual information; at the stage of reviewing the existing knowledge on the subject being queried historical and/or descriptive information is needed; the formulation of procedures appropriate to the inquiry necessitate methodological information; in the intermediate stages that follow, when information is required to solve problems as they come up, specific information is usually the answer, along the lines of statistics or details of techniques and methods; and in the final stages, when researchers seek to fully interpret their data and integrate their findings into the existing body of knowledge, the need for information is focused yet again on theoretical and conceptual, as well as descriptive and/or historical information (Egan and Henkle, 1956; Garvey et al., 1974; Menzel, 1964). Very much in agreement with the conclusions arrived at in these studies into the matter, an academic researcher, describing the way he usually works, links the different stages of the research process with different types of information:

> At the initial stage of a research project, when I'm at the conceptualisation stage, I go to the literature in order to see what questions to ask, so I read theoretical works. [Then], when I'm at the stage of research where I'm looking for tools, I read works on applications of concepts and tools, that is to say works which investigate empirical parameters I am not familiar with or works which investigate issues in a new way, one I haven't tried yet. And when I analyse [my] data, I need theoretical information, which helps me to interpret my data, because in my field theory and data interact. I try to understand the data in light of what I've read, and I try to answer the question, what do I know now that I didn't know before, that hasn't been already covered in the literature. That is to say, at this stage I turn to the literature in an attempt to find out how to interpret the answers.

It seems, then, that even academics, who undoubtedly have very wide-ranging information needs indeed, present a rather nuanced picture of the requirements for the different types of information in existence. For other populations it must be 10 times so, with many people needing mostly descriptive and historical material. Theoretical information, for instance, seems to have a very limited circulation. It is descriptive, methodological and statistical data that are much more the province of the practitioners in all fields. The need for methodological information, however, cuts across the academic/practitioner divide: it is required by practitioners such as teachers, engineers and social workers, as well as by research scientists of all kinds.

Finally, if we interpret the 'nature' aspect of an information need widely to include 'how to do' information, then hobbyists of all kinds are certainly among the most ardent seekers of specific kinds of information. In fact, as a Pew Internet & American Life Project survey proves, looking for information about hobbies is among the most popular online activities in America, on par with shopping, surfing the web for fun and getting news. Fully 83% of online Americans say they have used the internet to seek information about their hobbies and 29% do so on a typical day (Griffith and Fox, 2007). Incidentally, the need for such 'how to do' information is not reserved for hobbyists alone, as a neuro-biologist, sounding very appreciative indeed of the capabilities of today's information services to steer her to this particular type of information, reports: 'I wanted to investigate some animal behaviour using a labyrinth, but I had no idea what the labyrinth should look like or anything [else about it]. So, I searched in a database, found an article which described the kind of labyrinth I wanted to use ... and asked our technician to build for me a replica of the labyrinth described'.

Having explored the nature aspect of an information need from one angle, we now come to another way of grouping the different types of material to be found: primary information versus secondary information. Stoan (1984) makes the following useful distinction between the two types of information: the term 'primary information' refers to essentially uninterpreted data, which may be gathered in the field, in a laboratory, in a library or in an archive, whereas the term 'secondary information' is used to denote the books, articles and papers in which the results of research are reported. Obviously, each discipline has its own kind of primary data and its own techniques for gathering and testing that data, as Wiberley and Jones (1989; 1994) point out: humanists use as their primary evidence existing sources created by the subjects of their research; in comparison, scientists and social scientists initiate and participate in the creation of their sources, the former in their laboratories and the latter in the field. Therefore, while in the sciences and the social sciences no primary evidence exists until the researchers begin to work, as the primary evidence is the product of the scientific quest, in the humanities the primary evidence is there first, for the researchers to reconstruct, describe and interpret. Moreover, as the subjects of humanistic research create the primary evidence of the humanities, these sources are the products of a specific place and time and shaped by the distinctive personalities of their creators, with primarily qualitative and aesthetic dimensions. No wonder, then, that humanists, unlike their scientist or social scientist counterparts, are wary of accepting even true-to-life replicas as substitutes for the original source they are about to analyse.

The fundamental nature of primary information may thus vary from field to field, but its vital importance for expanding human knowledge is indubitable; indeed, it is the genuine core of any research undertaken. Happily, in the course of the past few years, access to primary sources of information, especially current information, has been greatly enhanced through the ubiquitous availability of internet-based resources, as an academic explains:

> We download the latest 'Human Development Report' in a jiffy, whereas in the past we had to wait two months for it to arrive ... today you can download everything so easily, reports of the World Bank, of the Palestinian Central Bureau of Statistics, the Israeli Central Bureau of Statistics ... you can check the price of oil every few days, the exchange rates, the reports of the banks in the Middle East, everything, all the time.

The vast improvement in the ability to obtain primary material is nowhere more conspicuous than in the case of information deemed unmarketable by commercial presses. Indeed, the elusive character of the primary sources of information dubbed 'grey' or 'fugitive' (non-commercial literature, which is produced by government, academies, business and industries) has been radically changing. As Cronin and McKim (1996, 165) sum it up: ' ... grey literature is no longer the step-child of primary publishing. The web invites and envelops semi-published, unpublished and vanity items, blissfully unmindful of provenance or pedigree – grey becomes black and white on the World Wide Web'.

As we have just noted, somewhat in passing, much of the primary evidence so readily accessible on the internet is of the kind that is particularly useful for seekers of current or recent information on human behaviour (both on the group and the individual level), and the social and environmental factors affecting it, such as data sets, original archival material, and legislative, governmental and demographic information. However, there is also a wide availability on the internet of science primary information, such as raw data and technical reports. Perhaps somewhat more surprisingly, there is also an abundance of humanities primary information to be found on the internet, from the facsimiles of manuscripts and artefacts, through films and music recordings, to archival material. True, as Stone (1982) clarifies, it is really vital that people, especially scholars, who criticise or study the history of paintings, sculptures or buildings, see the genuine article, for information absorbed from an original artefact cannot be gained in any other way; however, even in the humanities the need for access to original research reports is more questionable. Apparently, then, the oft-heard argument that humanists would use electronic alternatives to the primary material they need, perhaps not invariably, but to a greater extent, if only their need for old, if not antique material could be met, that is, if more primary sources of theirs were digitised (Brockman et al., 2001), seems to present only part of the picture.

All the same, where access to primary material is concerned, there are very good reasons for singing the praises of the internet. Of course, it is the realm of 'current history', truly the forte of the web, which is probably the best proof of the vastly improved access to primary material in today's world. Still, the by now routine practice of allowing public access to research data 'milked dry' in a given project is also quite some improvement over past practices. The resulting databases of primary information surely would have been impossible to come by in the days before the electronic era! There can be little doubt then that the likelihood of locating primary information has risen quite dramatically thanks to the internet, to the great benefit first and foremost of academics, but not only them. People pursuing topics of interest or study can be quite pleased, too, at the ease with which they can now come by original letters, photographs, audio recordings, moving pictures or video recordings.

Intellectual level

This characteristic refers to the minimum extent of knowledge and sometimes the level of intelligence an individual might need in order to understand the information available. However, it is not simply a question of matching the intellectual powers of individuals with documents of appropriate academic level, because intellectually advanced individuals might require elementary knowledge in a related or marginal field. Thus, a research scientist coming to grips with spreadsheets for the first time could be on the same information footing as a school secretary. In fact, matching people's information needs with the suitable level of information dictated by their requirements and abilities has more to do with the intelligibility of information (or, all too often, its dearth ...). Thus, information is made complex not just by how much knowledge and education it assumes, but also by how abstract or compressed it is. Writing styles and skills do count here too; after all, some broadsheet newspapers deal with some very complex ideas, but their articles are made comprehensible by excellent presentation of the data. Indeed, journalists play an important role in making the contents of academic reports and research accessible to a much wider public. Thus, for example, the medical correspondents of broadsheet newspapers, like *The Guardian* and *The Independent*, regularly repackage articles from *The Lancet* or *British Journal of Medicine* for an essentially lay audience.

Unfortunately and, perhaps, somewhat paradoxically in our age of omnipresent information, locating a piece of information fitting to the knowledge and intelligence level of the person requiring it seems to have become more problematic than ever. Obviously, with so much information everywhere, rounding up something on any given topic rarely, if ever, poses a problem; however, finding an answer matched to an individual's needs, with all the intricate combination of subjective and objective factors that enter into it, is something else again. This is nowhere more apparent than in the case of meeting an information need on an appropriate level: clearly, for a child who wants information on the amount of food his newly acquired dog will consume daily, to be presented with a scholarly article in a learned journal on the topic is hardly the right solution for his need, and a zoologist would likewise find little joy in a children's book on pets. Each to his own, of course, which until recently was a widely accepted and easily adhered to information behaviour norm. The academic went to his research library and the child to the neighbourhood public library or the school library, content in the knowledge that their information needs were sure to be met on an appropriate level. No longer, though. With the easy accessibility of myriad items on the web, the effortlessly discernible dividing lines of yore between popular/scientific, elementary/advanced, detailed/superficial information are apparently not as visible as before. More amazingly, distinguishing among them is not deemed very necessary at all, regrettable as it may be.

In point of fact, regrettable it is: getting the pitch right can be of utmost importance, as there is a huge spread of values between the advanced user and the elementary user, and between advanced information and elementary information. This seems to be true even where relatively homogenous populations are concerned. Thus, for example, academic researchers may all want scholarly level information, but, as Menzel (1964) notes, scholarly communication channels are overwhelmingly tailored for the specialist in a given field. Opining that seekers of information from a disciplinary area that is not their main concern could benefit greatly from a different sort of selection, editing, grouping and packaging of information than that which is most suitable for insiders, he suggests the establishment of special channels of communication that would be dedicated to 'information from field A for researchers in field B'. Thinking much along the same lines, Kircz (1998) proposes the breaking up of the classical scientific or scholarly article into modules. This, in order to cater to the different levels of information needed during the various stages of a research project, in the course of which an academic alternates roles between an uninformed reader, who is out to learn something entirely new, in a field that is either unknown to him or her, or of which he/she has only a rudimentary knowledge; a partially informed reader, who is not conversant with the specific research as such, but is interested in the general aspects that might be of use for his or her own investigations; or an informed reader, who is well-versed in the literature of the field.

Despite their obvious merits, neither Menzel's nor Kircz's proposed solutions to the problem of different levels of information required have ever been realised, although probably not for a lack of a very real need for them. After all, information systems are cognisant enough of the requirement for suitably written material, which is why they index documents according to their intellectual level. Thus, for instance, ERIC, an educational database, allocates academic/research, practitioner and consumer codes to documents to assist with their digestion. However, the construction of a truly finely-tuned modularised system was hardly feasible before the widespread utilisation of information technology, whereas today, when the technical know-how could easily allow for such an undertaking, nobody seems to be clamouring for it. Given the scant attention paid these days to information-seeking strategies – as it has already been noted, searching for information is no longer considered a task requiring serious investment in terms of thought, preparation and execution – this comes as no surprise.

Furthermore, nowadays the sharply delineated demarcation between the need for popular as opposed to scientific, elementary as opposed to advanced, detailed as opposed to superficial information is truly crumbling down. In direct consequence of the vital role played by knowledge and information in contemporary life, which has turned us all into life-long learners, practitioners and even amateurs will read academic/research literature. Indeed, findings of the Virtual Scholar research programme (2001–08) clearly indicate that users from outside academe are heavy consumers of the Open Access scholarly material on the internet (Nicholas et al., 2008b). By the same token, as it has already been noted, lay persons use extensively the health sites on the internet primarily intended for healthcare professionals and researchers. No wonder, then, that many academic health websites, mindful of the obvious demand for their services, now often provide pages targeted at the general public as well. Developers of the academic cancer website, Kimmel Cancer Centre (at www.kcc.tju.edu), for example, having found that their database of currently open clinical trials, designed for physicians, was frequently accessed by non-professionals, began to include lay descriptions in their trial listings (London, 1999).

Interestingly, there is a move in the opposite direction as well: perhaps not very often, but at least every now and then internet-based popular databases are utilised for research purposes, too. Apparently, when academics need information in areas outside their chosen spheres of expertise for gaining some essential understanding of an issue at hand, they can and do compromise on the level of the material required, making do with consulting an information resource of a more elementary level (Herman, 2005). Thus, for example, a psycho-oncologist, who looks on occasion only for the basic-level information needed to aid her in understanding the wider picture within which the specific point she is investigating is embedded, says: 'for the fundamental medical information necessary for my investigations at times I turn to those popular health sites on the web'. However, her psycho-pharmacologist colleague, who joins her in testifying to sporadic use of non-scientific material or material not published via scientific channels for research purposes, clarifies: ' … of course I know enough to sift out the wheat from the chaff'.

Having said all that, much as today's information seekers tend to ignore any considerations pertaining to the level aspect of their information requirements, their competencies to understand and handle information, be it in electronic or hardcopy form, do vary quite considerably. This, obviously, can be quite problematic for information providers: their potential customers, coming as they do from different educational backgrounds and possessing diverse levels of computer literacy, reading skills and reading comprehension capabilities, may find the information presented to them unacceptable level-wise. Either too complicated, deep and detailed, and as such uninteresting and unappealing, or else too simplistic and superficial, and therefore not only just as uninteresting and unappealing, but also patronising and lacking in authority. Seeking to address this problem of people's varied abilities to comprehend information, Williams et al. (2003) came up with the idea of organising information into 'vertical' layers of pages. These would offer information on each topic at different depths or levels of detail, in addition to the 'lateral' arrangement of material organised by topic. Clearly, the designers of any such system would have to be cognisant of digital visibility issues and consider how the information could be displayed in the fewest hierarchical levels, perhaps with the informational levels 'side-by-side' on the menu option, e.g. 'treatment of kidney disease: basic information; more detailed information; advanced information' – where each option was an active link.

One further point of considerable relevance to the intellectual aspect of information needs: the much debated possibility that in the new digital environment information-seeking behaviour is increasingly being 'dumbed down'. Indeed, the CIBER studies exploring the information work of various communities, most notably those associated with news (Nicholas et al., 2000), health (Nicholas et al., 2007a), voluntary and charitable work (Nicholas et al., 2004a) and scholarly publishing (Nicholas et al., 2008b) point to characteristic patterns of information behaviour, which, taken together, could possibly amount to such 'dumbing down'. Indeed, there is some disturbing evidence that much of today's information use, shaped by massive digital choice, unbelievable (24/7) access to, if not bombardment from a vast array of channels, disintermediation, and hugely powerful and influential search engines, constitutes passing and/or ineffectual activity. Everyone exhibits bouncing/flicking behaviour, which sees them searching horizontally, rather than vertically. Power browsing and viewing are the norm for all; reading appears to be undertaken only occasionally online, probably undertaken offline and possibly not done at all. Promiscuity is endemic as a direct result of a combination of massive choice and the constant refreshing of choice by search engines. Much digital activity involves navigating and not using. The quality and reliability of some information is judged by its popularity; the wisdom of the crowd is the key measure of worth. All this arouses a real fear of a world full of 'information malnutrition', where people consume vast amounts of the information equivalent of fast food: easily obtainable, flattering to the undiscerning palate, but of little actual value at its best, harmful at its worst.

Viewpoint

The particular viewpoint, approach or angle from which (overtly or covertly) some information is written up, is obviously very important for its potential consumers. Indeed, this is one needs characteristic that really gets information seekers worked up. More often than not people require information sympathetic to the views that they hold, to the point that information on the same topic, but tackled from a different point of view or slant would be unpalatable to them. This is probably most commonly seen in newspaper readership, where people like to subscribe to those newspapers that present news and views from the same political and social standpoint as their own. Still, as we will see further on, information perceived as representing a different viewpoint from one's own, or even as biased and/or one-sided can nevertheless have its welcome uses.

In any case, this aspect of an information need is very much subject field-contingent: the nearer the subject of a piece of information is to the hard end on Storer's (1967) 'hard' to 'soft' continuum of knowledge domains, the less applicable becomes the notion of its being reported from a specific viewpoint. After all, Newton's laws are Newton's laws, regardless of how they are put forward; they are hardly open to different understandings or interpretations, are they? However, the 'softer' disciplinary fields, the social sciences and the humanities plainly allow, if not outright call for different approaches to writing up information, so that topics are frequently treated from a certain angle or with a particular perspective. So much so, that social sciences information, for one, is almost by definition 'information presented from a specific perspective', as an academic, an expert on social welfare, explains: 'I proceed from the more or less always given notion that information is subjective; it is based on the subjective theoretical approach and presented through the subjective perspective of its originator. I never even expect anything else'. Indeed, this disparity among the different disciplinary areas is so widely accepted that it is considered among the most fundamental axioms of information work. No wonder the aforementioned psycho-oncologist has no doubts whatsoever when she ponders the topic:

> I always want facts and data, and although it's not mathematics, it's not open to different interpretations, either. It's in history that they mess about with interpreting the data this way or that way; in my field, if the statistics say that 80% of the patients prefer a certain surgical procedure, neither you nor I can say that it's not the majority of women who feel this way … it's not debatable, is it?

Indeed so, which is why in those areas where the subject matter is open to different interpretations, any piece of information encountered may vary by one or more of several determinants of viewpoint: school of thought, political orientation, positive or negative lines of attack and, in interdisciplinary fields, discipline orientation.

School of thought

Schools of thought, those informal bodies of people united by a general similarity of principles, opinions, points of behaviour and practices, are most evident in the social sciences, although clearly the humanities have their own schools, too. These schools are large, widely known and have handy labels to describe them, such as feminism, Marxism, monetarism, neo-classicism/modernism and structuralism, to mention just the first ones coming to mind. In addition, there are countless mini-schools or 'departments', which inhabit nearly all disciplines. In the field of Information Science, for instance, we have the systems-driven and user-driven schools of thought. It is at this rather more specific level that it is possible to discern schools of thought even in science. In fact, Thomas Kuhn (1963), the renowned American philosopher and historian of science suggests that progress in science is based on the existence of precisely such schools of thought, for it is through the breakdown of old paradigms (i.e. theories or ways of looking at the world) and the emergence of new ones, which 'attract an enduring group of adherents away from competing modes of scientific activity', that world views change. Thinking much along the same lines, Max Planck (1968) even contends that ' ... a new scientific truth does not triumph by convincing its opponents and making them see the light, but rather because its opponents eventually die, and a new generation grows up that is familiar with it'. In addition, in scientific fields, too, ethical considerations bring about the fragmentation of information so characteristic of social science disciplines. Thus, for example, the ongoing intellectual battles over abortion, animal-testing, genetically modified food and organic farming techniques are every bit as heated and polarised as they are in the social sciences.

It is hardly surprising, then, to find that in many academic disciplines values may be highly charged and the incidence of major ideological disagreements quite prevalent. However, since the scientific ethos stipulates for scholars to be impartial and unbiased in their communications even as the existence of different schools of thought entails the possibility that a topic would be treated from a particular approach or with a particular perspective, they must routinely evaluate the material they handle for any tell-tale signs of a specific angle of reporting. This, as Ellis (1989) and Ellis et al. (1993) point out, can greatly aid researchers in establishing the worth of some material for their investigations, for information appearing in sources which take a similar perspective to their own is more likely to be pertinent to their needs. However, as Meho and Tibbo (2003) add, in this process, which Ellis (1989) calls differentiating, researchers also aim to detect biased information, the product of scholarship which has a hidden (or not so hidden) agenda. Obviously, identifying such slanted information for what it is forms an important part of research work, striving as it does to present a disinterested and open-minded picture.

Still, if the lack of objectivity is openly acknowledged, or at least once it is detected, there seem to be important benefits to be derived from information that is not presented objectively, or, in point of fact, because it is not presented objectively, as a historian suggests:

> I may definitely set out to look for an article, which has been written from a specific point of view, because in many instances you can deal with a topic only if you are well aware of the points of contention involved. If you're not familiar with the controversy concerning the subject, if you don't know who's against whom, and what each contender has to say for himself, you can make mistakes, you can misunderstand the situation.

His philosopher colleague apparently is of much the same opinion:

> As long as you realise that some information has been written from a particular point of view, there's no problem whatsoever with using it. Quite the opposite, actually: this way you learn that there is such a viewpoint, that it's possible to think ... and to answer the question ... differently; it can be of tremendous help even, because otherwise such an approach may not have occurred to you.

Indeed, the one-sided or non-objective nature of some information can render it all the more useful, but, probably just as often, also altogether unusable. A telling example of how this might happen came up in the aforementioned survey of the use and impact of key digital health platforms and services in the UK (Nicholas et al., 2007a). One health information seeker, a staunch supporter of homeopathic medicine, professed to a general mistrust of the information to be found on the NHS website because its philosophy of health and treatment was at odds with hers:

> I guess I never just trust what the NHS says. I always research their diagnosis as well as their proposed remedy before using it because Western medicine in general is myopic in its approach to the matter of health. Basically I feel there is too much of the notion that current medical practices can 'heal' you and too little on the concept of responsibility for one's own state of health; mentally, physically and spiritually. I guess you could say that I fall into the category of people who really do subscribe to the notion of a holistic approach to life. What the NHS offers is just one part of the whole.

The problem is that recognising the school of thought a piece of information represents can be quite tricky, seeing that authors – founding fathers and key disciples aside – do not normally identify which, if any, school they are writing from. True, for academics, familiar as they are with a field, discerning the school of thought guiding the writing up of some information is a manifestly undemanding task (Herman, 2005), and no wonder. After all, they develop such an intimate knowledge of the literature of their areas of interest, that they are easily able to match the features of the source they are examining with those long known to represent various schools of thought, viewpoints, approaches and perspectives. Thus, they can effortlessly recognise the point of departure of the information under consideration by the sources cited and the terminology used. Also, apparently they look for certain 'codes', which, for them, clearly signify the author's ideological affiliation. As a senior historian, well-versed in the ways of the research enterprise, elucidates:

> There are these little symbols ... for example, in an article [written by somebody] from the post-modernist school of thought, the opening lines

send you to a footnote citing Foucault or Derrida; now, this is a code, a sign, which says 'I'm a post-modernist, I accept the main tenets of post-modernism', even though he is actually writing on, say, the relations between Britain and Kuwait in the 17th century. There's no connection whatsoever? True, but this is how he pays allegiance, how he tells you 'classify me correctly'.

Obviously, not everybody is familiar enough with a given field to be able to identify in this manner the tacit evidence pointing to the school of thought; thus, expert help can come in very handy here. However, given the afore-mentioned trend towards a widespread marginalisation of intermediaries in information seeking, it is not too often that the viewpoint aspect of an infor-mation need is deemed important enough to dispatch people in search of a librarian. True, some information systems do help by providing viewpoint indexing – the British National Bibliography did so for a time with its PRECIS system – but, as we have already noted, the use of search engines, rather than information systems, is the first-line option for unearthing pertinent informa-tion. Still, today's practised information users seem to have their ways of dealing with the problem, if and when they are aware of it at all. Thus, they may simply search for an author representing the 'right' school of thought, possibly supplementing their findings with the names of the authors who subsequently cited the original publication (on the assumption that there is a good chance that they all follow the same intellectual traditions). After all, tracking down a list of subsequent citations of some information no longer poses too much of a problem: no need to resort to complicated bibliographic tools, or, for that matter, to the help of information specialists; suffice that you are aware of the existence of Google Scholar, which routinely offers citation data. Also, many people are experienced enough information users to realise that the organisation the author works for is the best guide. Thus, when it comes to organic farming, we know clearly where the Soil Association and the National Union of Farmers stand.

Political orientation

If there is one area more susceptible to subjective reporting of information than others it must be that of politics, as a university lecturer, an expert in mass communications, notes: 'I always teach my students to try and find out who the author of some information is; if he is, say, a politician, think of his party; if he is a journalist, you have to be cognisant of the political points of view represented in his newspaper'. Indeed, information can be, and often is written up from a political point of view: there are right-wing, left-wing, conservative, socialist stances – to name the most obvious. Of course, school of thought and political orientation may coincide. It would be difficult, for instance, to characterise the pro- and anti-European standpoint that drives much of today's politics in the UK. While people feel more comfortable with, and more disposed towards reading information sympathetic to their own political allegiances, it would be wrong to assume that they would not be interested in information emanating from a different political persuasion. Thus, politicians will often scan the opposition parties' newspapers, hoping that they can use something there as ammunition to throw at the opposition in debate or interview. A quote from *The Guardian* (a left-of-centre newspaper) used by a Conservative politician in the debating chamber can prove most effective.

As with school of thought, the political perspective of information is not always immediately recognisable, except when it comes from a mainstream political party, of course. Nevertheless, here again, if you are privy to the terminology typically used by holders of a specific political stance, discerning the point of view, approach, or angle from which some information is presented becomes much easier. Thus, for example, where the heavily politics-laced issues of the contemporary Middle East are concerned, if the term used is 'the Zionist state' instead of 'Israel', it is clearly written from a particular point of view, effortlessly recognised by all those in the know. However, what if you are not among the chosen few who are wise to such subtle representations of political orientation? How is your need to be met then?

Unfortunately, little help can be expected from the available information systems, but there are shortcuts, because so many organisations are associated with a political point of view. We are not just talking about political parties, either; think tanks, research centres/organisations, associations, unions, voluntary/ pressure groups, governments, newspapers and even university departments can be associated with a political point of view. A document on the environment by the Automobile Association is likely to differ fundamentally in tone from one issued by Friends of the Earth, for instance. Therefore, compiling lists of suitably-minded organisations can help a lot in the meeting the need for information shaped by political considerations.

Somewhat surprisingly, information professionals, especially those in the public service, sometimes fight shy of providing information presented from a political point of view, believing that this might compromise them in some way. However, there can be nothing wrong with providing information corresponding to the political stand being avowed. Indeed, at the House of Commons, where the Library has to walk a political tightrope, librarians frequently prompt the inquirer as to for what political end the data is required. That way the information can be used to its best advantage. If they, of all people, have no qualms about this, why should anyone else?

Positive/negative approaches

Sometimes there is a need for information to be presented in a positive or negative form – as the existence of 'spin doctors', those political press agents or publicists employed to promote a favourable interpretation of events to journalists, confirms. The demand for information presenting the facts in a favourable/non-favourable light is greatest amongst those in politics, the media and business. Thus, for example, both the Labour and Conservative parties in the UK have what they call 'dirt' databases on individual MPs, in which they keep unsavoury stories, injudicious quotes, incidences of poor behaviour, voting inconsistencies – all data to be leaked or exposed at a suitably telling time, such as a media interview with an opposing politician. The need for this type of data is best shown in an enquiry one of the authors conducted for a national newspaper. A prominent politician was suing the newspaper over being quoted as having said something, which made him look bad, although, according to him, he had not. For the newspaper the best defence was to get the 'dirt' on this politician in order to show that in the past he had said things, only to deny them later, proving that his memory/word could not be relied upon.

Apparently, then, it is not all that rare to find that there is a definite need for information that presents the issues being considered in a positive/negative light. No doubt, if more information systems catered for this approach, the demand would be even greater. Yet, there are not many people who would or could easily field this important and valid information need, and even information professionals consider such requests just as controversial and challenging as the above-noted need for information put forward from a specific political point of view. Information science students are particularly aghast when told that this is a legitimate characteristic of information need. Certainly 'dirt' in this context is unlikely to feature as a database keyword. Indeed, needs of this kind are best met through oral and informal channels of communication, but to have its greatest impact, the information obtained has to be recorded. Still, the problem is not unsolvable. Thus, for instance, there are publications that are only ever going to show some politician or personality in a bad light: *Private Eye* and some biographies, for instance. Also, a politically motivated organisation that is opposed to the views held by the person under consideration can be a great source of negative information.

Today the web is the best peddler of 'documented dirt' information, as The Drudge Report political site, for one, amply proves. In fact the web, especially the blogs, seems to meet much of the strong demand for the controversial, gossip and plain dirt. For many people, but especially journalists, the fact that the internet contains information of uncertain, but interesting quality is a plus. In particular, features journalists and those charged with producing articles of unusual 'human interest' or of a generally lighter nature tend, as might be expected, to be most interested. So much so, that they may even use information of dubious authenticity.

Subject orientation

In interdisciplinary fields, where authors and information providers possess a number of different subject backgrounds, there is the need to consider the subject orientation of an information requirement. Criminology provides a good illustration of this. University criminology departments are staffed by academics who approach the subject from a wide range of disciplines. Thus, for instance, the criminology department of Middlesex University studies criminology from the perspective of sociology, whereas the academics at the University of Manchester study criminology from a psychological perspective and those of the University of Cambridge from the standpoint of law. Any assessment of the information needs of criminologists must take this into account.

It seems, then, that diverse interpretations of facts and data are possible, if not expected in certain knowledge areas, although even there users may at times actually want information that is wholly objective. Given this state of affairs, detecting whether a particular piece of information on hand is written from a certain point of view, approach, or angle becomes an important component of information work. Indeed, as the above quoted philosopher suggests, every piece of information should be treated as potentially representing a specific point of view:

> You have to take into account that people often write with hidden layers of meaning … it's important to be aware of the possibility … [and] to recognise the concealed elements in the text. In fact, part of the understanding of a text is identifying whatever the author assumes to be self-evident and therefore leaves unsaid, or whatever he chooses to conceal.

No wonder the vast literature on information literacy unanimously acknowledges the need to keep a wary eye on authors' possibly slanted presentation. Concurrently, as we have seen, people may at times look for and happily use information representing specific viewpoints. However, perhaps somewhat surprisingly, nothing much seems to be happening in result of these parallel trends in information work; information seekers certainly do not clamour for a solution, either because the problem is not all that pressing, or because they do not even realise that they have a problem (of course, it is hardly a rare occurrence that information needs go unrecognised, or at least unvoiced).

Quantity

Life in our present-day postmodernist society, at least in theory, requires us to be better informed than ever before, emphasising as it does plurality of values and diversity, tolerance of ambiguity, acceptance (indeed celebration) of innovation and change, on the one hand, and challenging of convention and authority on the other (Buschman and Brosio, 2006). Now that we no longer rely on tradition or past experience (for the circumstances of yesterday have surely changed by today), or on the decrees of some authority figure (for who knows what is suitable or good for us as well as we ourselves do), how else can we weigh up the possibilities, the pros and cons of proceeding one way or the other? Plainly, nowadays we are only able to cope in all walks of life by getting hold of information to serve as the basis for competent decision making.

Not that attaining the necessary information poses any problem in today's information-saturated world; rather to the contrary. We may no longer live in fear of drowning in a vast sea of information, a point we will examine in more detail shortly, but we do have (literally) at our fingertips a dynamic, constantly growing and changing knowledge base, which is so wide-ranging, that it is truly all-encompassing. However, while all people require information to do a job or solve a problem, the size of their information needs (though, as we will see presently, not necessarily that of their information appetites) varies greatly, not only between individuals and groups, but also according to the nature of the need. Motivation, diligence and the amount of time available to take in information are all influential factors in determining the amount of information actually consumed, although the very presence of huge quantities of data in every form encourages excessive demand. Indeed, by now we have all moved from a situation where the main information problem was getting hold of information, to a situation where the chief difficulty is digesting (or avoiding) the information that all too easily flows our way. So the quantity aspect of an information need is unusual in that it can also be an information constraint.

It is not that information seekers never, or even rarely, want all the information on which they can lay their hands. Someone starting a new job, for example, might feel that the more information to be had on the organisation he/she is about to join, the better. An investigative journalist embarking on a new story might think similarly. Thus, the request to 'give me everything you've got on ... ' is far from uncommon in journalist–information worker exchanges. Indeed, quite a few of the journalists interviewed by one of the authors actually said 'you can't have too much information', although admittedly this was a few years ago, and the web might have changed that. The prime example, though, of people with truly voracious information appetites are academic researchers, and no wonder. As it has already been pointed out, they have to make sure that they see almost every new publication in their respective fields in order to keep up with the developments at the research front of their specialisations. Moreover, for each new research endeavour they undertake, they need to amass, as comprehensively and exhaustively as possible, the knowledge accumulated on their subject, first to identify the gaps necessitating further investigation and then to anchor the topic to be investigated in its information context. However, given today's unprecedented availability of vast quantities of information, 'everything on the topic' may be too tall an order even for academics. Have not we all heard ad nauseam about the problem of information overload, at least as a threat, if not a reality, to quote Wilson (1996)? However, is it a threat, or a reality, or perhaps neither?

The past few decades saw an ever-increasing concern with the possibility that the growth of knowledge had surpassed the growth of the knowledge of how to manage it (Gaines, 1995), to the point of its having assumed the stature of a widely accepted truism. Any mention of the subject seems to have served to unleash a flood of woeful prophecies concerning the difficulties to be encountered in a world plagued with excess quantities of information. Not any more, though. Plainly, the gloomy forecasts as to the huge availability of data resulting in 'information overload', or its more dramatically put counterpart 'information explosion' simply never came true (in fact, both terms may very well be on their way to becoming misnomers). Today's information consumers, far from being beleaguered by problems of information overload, consider the current state of almost unlimited access to information unproblematic, if not eminently satisfactory. Indeed, it looks as if somewhere along the way many of them have fallen in love with the information affluence characterising our times, actually revelling in the abundance of information unabatedly accumulating all around them: 'There is a fantastic amount of information available ... you can access wires, you access libraries, you access information all around the world ... in an office ... or at home ... it is quite fantastic'.

Even academic researchers, with all their patent awareness that an attempt to read everything that may be relevant to their scholarly interests is perforce doomed to failure, seem to be at least resigned to this state of affairs, regarding it as one element of the academic assault course, and a small price to pay for the unbelievable level of access obtained (Nicholas et al., 2008b). However, many go even further than that, considering the large quantities of information flooding them not merely an acceptable trade-off for the ease with which they obtain it, but a veritable blessing (Herman, 2005). Thus, for example, an academic communications expert explains: ' ... there truly is an inordinate amount of information all over the place, though I'm glad that it is so ... ', and his colleague, a professor of social welfare, apparently feels the same. True, he does point out the evident hopelessness of knowing everything, of reading every piece of possibly relevant information, which, according to him, entails an insatiable thirst for new material, along with some stress and guilt, but still he insists: 'I would never go back to the time there was less information around, I'm overjoyed with this explosion of information'. He is not alone, either, in happily taking avail of the wealth of information at his disposal, as the CIBER findings on the information behaviour of the digital information consumer amply prove. Take, for example, the levels of activity associated with scholarly sites. The volume of their use is very impressive indeed and seems to be rising inexorably. We are witnessing not only constantly escalating use on the part of the core audience of these sites, although that too, thanks to their ability to access the site anytime and anywhere via broadband, wireless, the Blackberry, mobile phone and the like, but also a surge of huge masses of non-subscribers, coming in via search engines and making enthusiastic use of the scholarly net (Nicholas et al., 2008b).

However, it is a mistake to assume that more (and faster) information increases knowledge: rather like food consumption, after a while it does you more harm than good. Similarly, it would be wrong to believe that there is always something essentially important about getting (more) information. Take, for instance, this quote from an academic researcher:

> It's important that I keep current, but ... it is my thinking, which is the core. All the rest [i.e. the information generated by others] just testifies to my having made my investigations, that I know what's going on, but it's

marginal to the heart of the matter, which is your own opinion and your reasons for forming that specific opinion ... Additional reading will not matter much for your thesis; in fact ... it'll be redundant, it'll obstruct your train of thought, it'll impede your ability to say to yourself: 'O.K., what do you make of this, where are you going from here'.

All this is very much in line with what a respondent in the Information Requirements of Social Scientists (INFROSS) research project (Bath University Library, 1971b) had to say on the subject more than 30 years earlier: 'The importance of information can be overrated. More information does not always result in increased knowledge and probably seldom produces increased wisdom'.

Unfortunately, it is precisely at this juncture that information professionals so often get their customers' requirements wrong. Too many judge their own information prowess by the amount of information that they can provide in response to an enquiry, considering a long list or bibliography the physical proof that they can do the job. The following incident amply illustrates information professionals' mindset where the quantity aspect of information need is concerned: a class of information science students were set an online exercise to discover what the winter of 1989 was like. After about 20 minutes a very unhappy student put up a hand for help. The problem? Well, they had only found one newspaper article on the subject. The fact that the article gave all the details mattered not; something was driving them on to find more of the same!

Actually, people do not always have the time, inclination and, perhaps most importantly, real need to wade through large volumes of information. The dearth of time necessary to make effective use of the information resources available can be especially problematic in this context, as people may find it difficult to come to terms with their inability to deal with the piles of documents accumulating on their desks or the long lists of unread e-mail messages awaiting their attention, to the point where they feel actually overwhelmed by the situation (Bawden et al., 1999). There again, people today are, by necessity, fairly efficient managers of time and they have certainly mastered the art of coping with the profusion of information characterising our world: indeed, they tend to be satisficers (a term, which, as it has already been noted, results from the blend of the two words 'sufficing' and 'satisfying'). That is, they stop information seeking after finding material that is good enough (Savolainen, 2007), so that they can juggle the need for comprehensive information with the constraints placed upon them. Thus, if need be, they are quite content to have sufficient, but small quantities of information, preferring limited information that meets deadlines rather than complete information that does not, which is why senior managers, for example, often insist that all written communication fit on one-side of an A4 sheet. Indeed, people ignore what they perceive as unnecessary or irrelevant; they sample and select, choosing the best/most suitable/most interesting; or they even information gamble, taking a chance on what comes to hand (say, the first item among thousands of search engine-generated items).

These tactics are by now such a customary element of contemporary information behaviour that even academics opt for them (well, one hopes for the first two only) in order to deal with the profusion of scholarly and scientific publications at their disposal. Thus, as Wilson (1993a, 1995, 1996) contends in a series of studies on communication efficiency in research, contrary to conventional understanding, non-use of relevant information in a research enterprise may not happen by accident or by mistake, but rather reflect a routine and normal approach to coping with the huge quantities of information in each and every field. Indeed, he suggests, rather than overdosing on information, researchers consistently and deliberately ignore material of which they are aware, even though it may be pertinent to their enquiries, as part of their individual research strategies. True, they do so only after more or less careful perusal and prioritisation of incoming information, much along the lines of the 'differentiating' component of Ellis's (1989) model of researchers' information-seeking patterns, through utilising the differences between sources as filters on the nature and quality of the material examined. Herman (2005) ties the obvious prevalence of this information management strategy, which, in effect, amounts to no more than the age-old policy of selective reading, to the lowering of academic standards associated with the present-day profusion of scholarly publications (the 'publish or perish syndrome'). This, she maintains, has brought about a change in attitude to information in academe: perceived to be declining in quality, information is no longer treated with deference bordering on reverence; rather, it is customarily appraised for its merits, just like any other commodity, and of the more easily available and plentiful variety too. This is why the key to contemporary researchers' effective information consumption is selective reading. This is why their strategy for coping with the time pressures typical of today's scholarly endeavour, on the one hand, and the vast quantities of information incessantly flowing to them, on the other, is screening, evaluating and filtering, not just to distinguish relevant from irrelevant, but to separate dispensable from indispensable relevant material.

To be sure, by now the real predicament for most people is not that they do not have effective enough ways and means of dealing with the inundation of information; they certainly do. It is rather that they cannot resist the temptations of the information affluence surrounding them. In fact, the behaviour of today's information seekers may very well exhibit the characteristics of 'The Sweet Shop Syndrome' (Ball, 2004): just like children, who, suddenly given the freedom of a sweet shop, will gorge initially far beyond the true limits of their actual needs, they too may get overly excited when they encounter the (as yet still) novelty of easy access to a seemingly unlimited array of information. This, coupled with the behaviour characteristic of the e-shoppers that they are, which is fashioned by the dictates of what could only be described as a sales mentality, results in a tendency to accumulate far more material than they actually read or use.

In the way that shoppers are easily swayed in their choice by 'offers', so too are present day information seekers. This point could not have been made clearer than by the findings of a CIBER study of Emerald (www.emeraldinsight. com), a scholarly journal database, the policy of which is to offer for free the articles from two journals once a week. It transpired that for these two journals – whatever they were – use jumped immediately by a factor of 10, only to drop down again to pre-offer levels once the promotion was over. Clearly, users hastened to download the articles while they were free, rightly surmising that this state was a temporary one. An analysis of download times before and after the free week suggested that a squirreling (or access expectation) behaviour was being witnessed: download times during the free week were much shorter, an indication that people were simply storing for a later day, rather than 'reading' at the time (Nicholas et al., 2008b). Indeed, the same behavioural trait was displayed by off-campus e-book users, noted in another CIBER project, Superbook (Nicholas et al., 2007b). Much material is just squirreled away for another day and that day never comes because of a shortage of time and the amount of squirreling that has already been undertaken. However, the increase in use for the two journals, on offer free for a week, was so remarkable, that it must have had something to do with their enhanced digital visibility at the time as well, with the very fact that they were part of a promotion.

It seems, then, that in our information-rich and information-driven world the quantity aspect of an information need has certainly come to the fore. However, flying in the face of popularly held notions, it is no longer the threat of information overload which is a cause for worry. Having masterminded the intricacies of coping with the ever-growing abundance of information at their disposal, today's information seekers see no problem whatsoever with the vast quantities of information available on almost any topic imaginable. However, whilst people perceive the situation all in all as a happy state of information affluence, they also find it hard to curb their information appetites, demonstrating a propensity to bite off far more information chunks than necessary, or even consumable.

Quality/authority

Assessments of the value of information are not easily made, especially in the digital environment, with the ever-more conveniently accessible internet bringing to the desktop of the contemporary information consumer a truly alluring array of material on every conceivable subject. Knowing that the information needed may be only a mouse click away seems to pose an almost irresistible enticement to opt for the instant information gratification so easily provided by the web, especially these days, when speed is so often the paramount consideration in whatever we set out to do. Inevitably, then, quality and authority concerns loom particularly large in our era of ever-present information of unprecedented volume: the extremely vocal, ongoing debate about the questionable reliability and worth of information to be found on the web is a testament to this. Hardly surprisingly, of course, for the more information there is around, the more tempting it is for people to power browse, to scan huge lists rapidly, grabbing an item here and an item there, without giving much thought to the relative merits of each. Often it is simply a question of fancying this rather than that, but even when the choice is more considered, it is likely to be made on the basis of where an item ranks on Google. The higher the item is on a Google-generated list, the more it is invested with quality, but of course quality is hardly the prime determinant in Google's ranking. This when, given today's information affluence, the key to effective information management can only be well thought-out selection: locating first the relevant and then, from among the relevant, the indispensable in terms of value.

Selection thus being the choice strategy for coping with the vast quantities of information surrounding us, obviously far better that it is conducted along logical grounds than arbitrary ones. Surely quality and reliability are better criteria for knowledgeable information selection than congeniality: after all, people do not really want to base a decision or a course of action on unstable foundations or be sent on wild goose chases, do they? Indeed, the quality of information, its veracity, trustworthiness and accuracy, are held to be, at least in theory, critical considerations, and for some fields and occupations particularly so.

Health is obviously a case in point, for poor information provision on ailments could have serious, even fatal consequences; but journalism, science, finance and business also come to mind. Take, for example, the following quotation from a leading crime correspondent:

> There is a problem with inaccurate information and particularly in my field that could be very dangerous because we run into problems of libel and we run into problems of contempt. Reporting crime if you get bogus information or inaccurate information about people's convictions or about crimes – then you are in trouble and I am wary of the internet for that reason.

Indeed, journalists are extremely concerned with authority and accuracy. Much of the unsolicited material that comes to them looks suspiciously like propaganda, public relations or advertising: it is difficult to distinguish fact from hype. In consequence, a good deal of cross-checking is done. At *The Economist*, for instance, where none of the articles are signed – and, in result, the reputation of the whole magazine is at stake, unchecked facts and unverified sources are simply not used. An advertisement for the journal once stated: '*The Economist* believes in collective responsibility. It commits its own reputation to every sentence it writes, good or bad'. To be sure, *Economist* journalists take the authority invested in them extremely seriously, as the following story amply proves: at one editorial board the following week's edition was being considered and the conversation got around to an article about Mozambique. The question was: should the article appear the week before the forthcoming elections or during election week? One journalist argued that the article should appear the week before, because, that way, the powers that be in Mozambique would read it and that would stop them making the same mistake as they did the time before!

Academics are another group with stringent requirements for excellence and dependability of information. They are very much aware of the importance of paying attention to the quality/authority aspect of their information work, and no wonder: they simply have too much at stake to neglect doing so, given that the inevitable prerequisite of every new scholarly progress made is its firm anchoring in previous knowledge and peer review. It is hardly surprising, then, that they are rather wary of information that is not endorsed by the formal scholarly communication system:

> ... for the purposes of my research work ... I use a good journal, something written by somebody from a good university. I can't base my hypothesis on findings posted on the web, which haven't been published in a journal, it's just not reliable, that's why, even if the idea is terrific, I'll still take it for something unreliable.

By necessity, then, academic researchers are considerably more skilled and competent at the task of evaluating the information on hand than most people – and it does take quite some expertise.

For one, determining the quality of information is rather more difficult these days than it used to be: the digital environment is a complicated one in which to make quality and reliability judgements. It is a relatively new (for some) and fast-changing environment, with new sites appearing all the time. Also, there are so many parties associated with the production of a digital information service – experts, governmental, scholarly or commercial content providers, broadcasters and publishers (and Joe-public in the likes of blogs), to name just the major ones. It is clearly a situation in which authority is 'up for grabs' and worth is by no means assured.

Further to that, in today's information realities the task of sifting out the wheat from the chaff in the information of potential relevance often falls to the user; the value and trustworthiness of information is no longer a priori established for its potential consumers. The traditional library-driven user of the not so distant past relied on the library for (limited) choice, and for a stamp of quality or authority. Seeing that ascertainment of quality was part and parcel of the authoritative professional preparation of information for its central storage and provision in a library, the not wholly unfounded assumption was that if it was in the library, it was good. In any case, the choice was largely made for the consumer because the intermediary conducted the search. Today most people search for themselves, often from non-library or -evaluated information environments. To stay afloat in the ever-expanding, mostly digital information environment they need to evaluate, and evaluate well. Presented with massive and increasing choice via internet-based, often unvetted channels, they are forced to make the evaluations once made by librarians; in this context the phrase 'we are all librarians now' is an especially apt one. With so much choice and new products coming on stream, they have to make many, many evaluations, and quickly. No mean feat, that, as for a user to select information on quality grounds involves multiple layers of interpretation derived from their experiences, perceptions and private knowledge related to the particular information need at hand (Park, 1993).

Seeing that the perceived quality and reliability of a document thus rests on a mix of highly personal knowledge, past experience and accumulation of information, the best way to assess its value is simply reading it 'cover-to-cover' to see what it says. However, the convenient availability of huge amounts of information on any and every conceivable topic under the sun renders the attempt to do so unrealistic; so much so that nowadays even academics are far less inclined to take their quality decisions on the basis of a straightforward perusal of the information presented to them. Instead, people look beyond the inherent appropriateness of documents in information need situations, making judgements about the *source* rather than the *content* of the information. In point of fact, they resort to long-standing aids or 'props' for picking out as efficiently as possible the worthwhile items from among the huge amounts of information at their disposal.

Thus, knowledgeable users aim to single out from the abundance of obtainable information the items of appropriate authority and quality, employing one or more indicators of value, often using all available indicators in combination. Indeed, establishing the authority and/or determining the quality of information is for many people a two-tiered process of first selection made on the basis of both information giver/sender and source (authorship and channel of publication/dissemination), followed by a more in-depth scrutiny of the items, which have been found to merit further consideration. Hence, the value and trustworthiness of some information is often assessed by first noting who recommended it, who its author is (with what organisation the author is affiliated, the author's academic background, etc.), and the journal in which it is published or the site on which it is posted. It is only if by this stage the information looks worthwhile that a more in-depth examination of its contents is deemed to be in order.

Starting out the evaluation process of some information with its giver/ sender makes eminent sense in our era, when more and more information comes to us, rather than vice versa. With social networking on the web having become almost normative, friends and colleagues seem to be behind much of the new information that flows to us. Indeed, Schwartz (2008) cites Ted Eytan, medical director for delivery systems operations improvement at the Permanente Federation, who says that 'patients aren't learning from websites – they're learning from each other'. Given this state of affairs, the following quotation, which captures the popularly held sentiments concerning the information giver/sender, sounds more pertinent than ever: 'One of the filters on what stuff you read is who sends it to you; the weight given to the information will depend on the source providing that information and more weight will be given to information provided by a source if that source has a high position in an organisation'. Indeed, the aforementioned study into the use and impact of key digital health platforms and services in the UK (Nicholas et al., 2007a) found a relationship between how users heard about health websites and the sites' rating. Those users who were recommended the site were least likely to say that site trustworthiness was poor or okay. Users who arrived at the site via an advertisement or a search engine were most likely to rate trustworthiness as either poor or okay.

Beyond the perceived authority and trustworthiness of the information giver/sender, it is the source of the information that is often the basis for determining its quality; therefore, a very good appreciation of the information producers in the subject field is quite important. This is how one academic put it, pondering the rationale behind it all: 'If I know the author, I know exactly what to expect: I know his areas of interest, and more importantly, I know the worth of the information he'll give me'.

Indeed, another important factor in determining the reliability or quality of some information is the reputation of its author and that of the institution with which he/she is affiliated, as these are perceived by the reader, with the latter, as Liu (2004) notes, considered even more significant than the former. This presents no problem for those in the know, for, as Becher (1989) points out, one of the striking features of academic life is that nearly everything is graded in more or less subtle ways, institutions, departments and, possibly above all, the scholars in a given field. Thus, to quote an economist, well-versed in the ways of academe, academics:

> Walk around with invisible ranks ... they all look the same, not even wearing suits or ties, or perceptible ranks ... and yet, whoever has to know, knows without any doubt who's leading and who's led, who makes the decisions and who follows.

It is not very surprising, then, that academics can form a well-founded first impression as to how good and solid a given piece of work is almost at a glance: if the information being considered originates with somebody who holds a senior rank in a 'first line' university with a 'good' department in the relevant area of specialisation, whose name is known in professional circles, it passes muster. So much so, that, as Park (1993) notes, a prominent scholar in the field tends to become an independent quality/authority parameter, regardless of the subject matter of the publication being considered (along the lines of 'anything he writes is bound to be good'). In fact, as Kling and McKim (1999) assert, a non peer-reviewed posting on a website by a high-status and well-respected scholar may well be trusted and valued more than a peer-reviewed journal article by someone not as well-known in the community.

Yet, with all the importance accorded to the author's status in the evaluation process, basing 'a vote of confidence' solely on the author's standing is obviously inadvisable, as an experienced academic researcher explains:

Clearly I treat differently the work of somebody, whose contribution to the field is indisputable, than that of a fledgling, who still sports a few bits of the eggshell on his head ... Of course I do, and so does everybody else ... Still, it is always possible that in some of his articles the author just reiterates previous sayings, and if so, prominent or not, these articles go straightaway to the pile of 'not worth reading'.

Moreover, basing quality/authority judgements on the reputation of the author is pertinent to no more than a small segment of information consumers; it would be hardly reasonable to expect that outside academe information seekers always or even often be aware of the scholarly weight of the authors, the actual producers of some document on hand. Still, things are very different indeed when it comes to the standing and dependability of the organisations with which these producers are affiliated.

People are well aware that certain organisations, because of their economic or political power, command particular authority or respect and, as a consequence, their publications or websites are in effect brand names, which carry a lot of clout. Thus, for example, BBC Radio 4's Today programme is widely recognised throughout the media and political worlds as being agenda setting – largely because of its flagship status and because important and authoritative people are drawn to its studios. Perhaps as a consequence of people's concerns over the quality of the information on the web ('I think that most people realise that there isn't any particularly effective restrictions in place as yet on the internet, therefore, anybody can set up a website containing false, misleading, incorrect or offensive content'), the websites of government, the European Union and some academic establishments, for instance, are particularly popular. Indeed, they are frequently used by journalists. A case in point is the science editor at *The Guardian*, who regularly consults sites such as The NASA Pathfinder mission, The American Association for the Advancement of Science, or The Global Seismology Unit, in pursuit of quality information. However, if not so long ago people unquestioningly accepted that information from such governmental bodies would be accurate and reliable (whether conveyed via the internet, hard copy publication or any other means) and were prepared to use it straight off, this no longer holds invariably true.

The findings of the above-mentioned health survey (Nicholas et al., 2007a), which, having canvassed hundreds of thousands of users on a national scale, can be taken to be very indicative indeed of generally held views, serve as ample proof of this point. Apparently, people may be by and large supportive of the British National Health Service (NHS), declaring that they trust the NHS 'to a large extent' or 'on the whole', but nevertheless, they also look elsewhere for information. They largely do this checking on the basis of long experience of searching the web, a lot of practice in making constant comparisons and through a process of trial and error. Plainly, people apparently take full advantage of the above-noted capability provided by the web to 'suck it and see'. Here is how one survey respondent put it:

> I trust the info [sic] provided by the NHS. However, like treating any other ... sources, I usually check up a few other professional websites for the same info, so I get a more complete picture of the subject, instead of relying completely on ... one source.

This seems to suggest that not even so-called 'authoritative' publications and sites are believed to be always correct. Rightly so, it seems: as the literature testifies, even 'official' information published by the NHS and other government bodies can be of dubious quality. Coulter et al. (1999), for example, point to a multitude of problems: much of the information at the time of their research was inaccurate and out of date, technical terms were not explained, and few materials provided 'adequate' information about treatment risks and side-effects. Huntington et al. (2004) also found that the NHS Direct site was in fact poor at sourcing its information, possibly, or so they surmise, as the NHS considers itself an authority in its own right and hence does not see the need to quote its information sources. The site was also found wanting in terms of date-stamping its information.

Further to users' awareness of the possibility that even organisations formally qualified to furnish authoritative information do not always live up to expectations, there is also the problem of government bodies being suspected of having an official 'axe to grind'. This, obviously, may greatly impact on the perceived quality and credibility of the information these establishments offer. In the words of one participant in the just-cited health survey, the NHS is considered:

> Trustworthy in the sense that the information present will be accurate on the whole but biased in the sense that there is an economic consideration with healthcare provision and the NHS is representing the Department of Health (DoH) policies and may not promote treatments that are not available widely on the NHS or new research.

Another instance where users can and do put brand indicators to good use in accrediting the information found is when their source is a peer-reviewed scholarly publication. Each discipline has its fairly well-defined, if unwritten hierarchies of scholarly journals and publishing houses, with some publication venues considered of a higher quality than others. This pecking order of scholarly information dissemination channels is so well-known, so much part of the disciplinary culture of any given field that active researchers can rank publishing venues on impact or quality grounds, and the level of agreement amongst them would be exceedingly high. They usually acquire this intimate familiarity with the relative standing of the different 'brands' of information dissemination routes in their respective fields as an essential part of their socialisation to their chosen profession, but also the hard way, through the process of submitting manuscripts (first-line publications are in such high author demand, that they can afford to be very choosy indeed). Accordingly, although more often than not they know exactly what the quality of their research is and send the manuscript to a journal that reflects that quality, if they cannot get into the journal of appropriate ranking chosen, they go to the next one down the ladder. Quality thus tiers down and, in result, the archiving of scientific ideas and findings is in fact on a continuum, with varying degrees of value, reliability and peer validation, from the most prestigious and rigorously reviewed at the top, to what is virtually a vanity press at the bottom (Harnad, 1990; 1999). Indeed, it is by no accident that a relatively small number of the titles available account for a relatively high proportion of use, a long-known characteristic of information-seeking behaviour, which has been proven to hold true in the electronic environment, too (Nicholas and Huntington, 2006).

This state of affairs is well-known to potential information consumers, certainly within academe, but often without it, too: 'If I read an article in *Nature* or *The Journal of the British Medical Association* then it is not an unreasonable assumption that the guy knows what he's talking about and that his colleagues believe he knows what he is talking about'. Furthermore, if in the past only the leading information dissemination 'brands' were known to the general public (*Nature* and *Science* may always have been household words, but not many other examples readily come to mind), it is hardly the case these days. The ethos of the knowledge society, with its emphasis on knowledge and information as the key to success has brought about a huge demand for scholarly information (Nicholas et al., 2003a). We are all amateur scholars now, and thanks to the greater access afforded by Open Access and institutional or disciplinary repositories, we have a library of immense power at our beck and call. Indeed, as Nicholas et al. (2008b) found in their Virtual Scholar research programme (2001–08), the so called disenfranchised users of Open Access material (that is, users from outside academe) are large in number and are fuelling a lot of the growth in scholarly information consumption. With many of the general public thus having joined the army of virtual scholars, they, too, are quite familiar with the literature in their areas of interest, inclusive of the aforementioned 'pecking order' of the scholarly information dissemination channels. In result, they are almost as adept at judging some information by its brand, that is, by the reputation of its venue of dissemination, as their academic counterparts.

Let there be no mistake, however; scholars we all may be by now, but amateurs, not professionals: translators of research into actionable outcomes – practitioners, research users, policy-makers and opinion-formers. Most people are, then, readers of scholarly information rather than its producers. Thus, amateur scholars may recognise brand names of publication outlets as readily as professional researchers, but they have little need or use for the time-honoured tool widely utilised in academe for identifying qualitative and authoritative information: citation analysis data. Actually, citations are very important, offering insights into which journals are, on average, the most highly cited (ISI impact factor), which journals researchers turn to first (immediacy index), and the long-term value that academics ascribe to particular titles (cited half-life). However, all these are indicators of value from an author perspective, providing as they do reliable information about the preferred publication outlets in a given field. For the vast constituencies of readers who do not write papers, citation data cannot be of much help. After all, the fact that an article has been highly cited does not necessarily testify to its reliability or commendable quality – the very opposite may well be true, with the citations reflecting refutations of its content! Indeed, Rowlands and Nicholas (2007) propose that we systematically measure, at the individual article level, journal use ('votes by readers') as well as journal citation ('votes by authors'), among other purposes in order to aid all scholarly information consumers, and not just the authors among them, in acquiring a good understanding of the usefulness of some research.

In any case, at least for academics, who need trustworthy and high-quality information for most of their work-related purposes, it seems to be a foregone conclusion that they will give much more weight in their choices to the brand names in scholarly publications, the ones considered to be as near as possible to the top end of Harnad's continuum. After all, many people set great store by a brand precisely because it is perceived as providing special benefits and added values. Indeed, as it has already been mentioned, the esteem in which a journal and/or a publishing house are held is often well-known and frequently used as an indication of the quality and authority of information, as one academic, summing it all up, says:

> The author, and in fact the whole journal, serve as parameters for deter-mining the quality and authority of a publication. As it happens, some very, very interesting things appear in negligible journals, written by authors you don't know, but when you have such an avalanche of material, that's the way you work.

However, contrary to popularly held notions, this building on brand names in quality and authority assessments of scholarly material cannot be taken as a sure-fire defence against alighting on information that is not really up to par. In fact, these days a degree of wariness seems to be called for in our dealing with scholarly information, the consequence of the ever-more perva-sive doctrine of 'publish or perish' in academe, which, according to the editor of a history journal amounts to 'far too much publishing and not enough perishing' (quoted in Garner et al., 2001, 253).

Originally coined by Logan Wilson in 1940, the term 'publish or perish' has become the universally accepted shorthand for the onus on academics to pub-lish copiously, as Schauder (1994, 82), summarising Wilson's thesis, describes:

> ... because publication is one of the main measures of academic produc-tiveness, there is pressure on authors to fractionise their research projects into as many separate articles as possible to 'add yardage to the author's

bibliography' ... [Since the] publishing of articles ... [is] a principal means by which academics can achieve visibility, and therefore, advancement ... , [these] situational imperatives dictate a 'publish or perish' credo within the ranks.

Unfortunately, the 'publish or perish' system, focusing as it does on the quest for quantity of publication, may lead to inconsequential publications: 'salami publications', wherein material adequate for a single paper is sliced into several 'least publishable units', or 'meat extenders', i.e. papers re-issued with no new data or papers that are in fact two previously published papers merged into a new one. The result of this perceived need in academe to skew research toward what is 'acceptable' rather than toward what may be important is, at least at times, a decline in the quality of the information, as Ziman (1970) puts it:

> Not only is there too much scientific work being published; there is much too much of it ... the need to get recognition by publication forces each of us to shout a little longer and louder so as to be noticed at all in the gathering, swelling crowd of voices ... The result has been a proliferation of semi-literate, semi-scientific, half-baked and trivial material which threatens to swamp the system.

It seems, then, that these days even governmental/official or scholarly establishments can no longer be unhesitatingly considered purveyors of innately valuable and authoritative information. Rather predictably, commercial organisations are held even more suspect in this regard. So much so, that in the UK survey of health platforms and services most respondents, 63%, said that being too commercial would be a reason not to visit a site (Huntington et al., 2004). Indeed, over half of the people polled said that they had not returned to a site because it was too commercial (Nicholas et al., 2007a). In the same vein, when a site carried 'obtrusive' or too many advertisements, people were much more likely to rate its trustworthiness as poor or only okay. No wonder, then, that clicking on a banner advert was found to be the least popular way of finding health information.

True, some commercial establishments do carry a lot of respect in result of the quality of their work and excellent track record. A particularly telling example of this came up in CIBER's above-mentioned health survey (Nicholas et al., 2007a). People who used the touch-sensitive screen health information kiosk at a Safeway (supermarket) Pharmacy were asked about the authority of the information provided by the kiosk and the trust they exhibited in it. In reply, users tended to say that they had 'every trust in the information', but also to assume that it was a Safeway service (it was, in fact, an NHS-provided one). When told that this was not the case, many were disappointed, and the younger the users, the more disappointed they were. This, because Safeway was seen as a very successful business, whereas the NHS was always being criticised in the press for not coming up to scratch. Moreover, even when it was or became clear that Safeway was just the host organisation, its reputation carried over to serve as a guarantee for the provision of quality information only on its premises: 'Well, they wouldn't let any cowboy stick a kiosk here, would they?'

By the same token, newspapers, with their wide and large readership – including lots of decision-makers, have great impact. Indeed, articles in newspapers like the *Financial Times* and the *Wall Street Journal* can actually move financial markets and bring down economies (in one of its advertising campaigns the *Financial Times* played upon the crucial role it has in meeting the information needs of the business world: 'no FT, no comment' was the advertising slogan). Undoubtedly, for-profit ventures of this stature are invested with special authority by many people, but they are the exceptions to the rule, certainly not the rule.

All this seems to lead to the conclusion that by now the time-honoured reliance on the source of some information in the initial assessment of its authority and quality certainly has undergone fundamental changes. Not that it has become any the less important; rather the contrary. Given the surfeit of choice characterising the mostly online information environment of today, singling out the items of intrinsic merit on the basis of a preliminary judgement of their extrinsic characteristics is an inescapable imperative. Indeed, the evidence that the CIBER research group has amassed in several projects points to the fact that on average most people spend only a few minutes on a visit to a website, insufficient time to do much reading, but perfectly adequate enough to note some indicators of its worth as a source. However, if this preliminary assessment of the information on hand is as crucial a component of information seeking as ever, if not more crucial, the way people go about it is much changed in today's web-based world. People simply shop around for information and on the basis of comparisons take decisions for themselves on what they perceive to be 'good' information. Present-day digital consumers are what can be termed 'promiscuous users'.

Promiscuity results from consumers' uncertainty in the face of massive access and choice, coupled with short attention spans and a tendency to leave their memories in cyberspace. In information-seeking terms it manifests itself in two ways. Firstly, people visit a (large) number of websites to find what they want. Secondly, and this is related, they do not often return to sites they have once visited. This form of information behaviour may sound like a dumbed-down form of information searching and retrieval: people are seemingly unable to make up their minds and, in any case, succeed in obtaining just a thin veneer of information. However, it is simply a different way of tackling an information need. One is minded of the father watching his young daughter using the remote control to flick from one television channel to another. A slightly irritated father asks his daughter why she cannot make up her mind and she answers that she is not attempting to do so; she is actually watching all the channels! She, like today's information consumer, is gathering information horizontally, not vertically. The single, high-quality and authoritative source, which is always consulted and deeply mined, seems to be a thing of the past.

Indeed, a recurrent finding in the various CIBER projects evaluating the information-seeking behaviour of a number of information communities, most notably those associated with news (Nicholas et al., 2000), health (Nicholas et al., 2007a), voluntary and charitable work (Nicholas et al., 2004a) and scholarly publishing (Nicholas et al., 2008b), is that appraisal of the quality and trustworthiness of information is largely undertaken by making comparisons, which seems to be a key element of digital literacy. People will look at several internet sites (and, therefore, consult several organisations) for information. This appears to be true even when people 'trust' one site, or when they go to 'brand name' sites. Perhaps not surprisingly: as Simon (2001) observes, brand recognition has taken on a new dimension on the web, with the surfeit of choice online producing 'a concomitant change in consumer attitudes', moving them from what he describes as 'receptive space' to 'sceptical space'. Users can afford to be sceptical about the attributes of an individual site, as these attributes can be maximised by visiting a number of sites. Indeed, in the aforementioned health services survey (Nicholas et al., 2007a), a relationship was found between a respondent's rating of the content and the number of health sites visited. As the number of health websites visited increased, so the user's appraisal of content depth, breadth and trust declined. The ease of information access has made internet users into information connoisseurs.

Hardly surprisingly, then, loyalty might be a thing of the past, too, although we have loyalty to Google, Facebook, BBC and ebay in bucketloads. Coming back to a site constitutes conscious and directed use, which clearly suggests that it is a tried and trusted source of information. This 'site stickiness' (as the industry calls it) makes return visits indicative of the perceived quality and authority of the site. Indeed, a service with a high percentage of returnees can be regarded as having a brand following, the goal of all service providers. However, loyalty or repeat behaviour generally is not a trait of the digital information consumer. Thus, for example, a study of the SurgeryDoor website (Nicholas et al., 2007a) found that over a relatively long period of 12 months, two-thirds of visitors never returned and the remaining 33% visited the site only two-to-five times. By the same token, in the 'Google Generation' project (CIBER, 2008), the data on the return visits to ScienceDirect, a scholarly journal database, show that over a five-month period 40% of users just visited once, 24% visited two-to-five times, 15% visited six-to-fifteen times and 21% visited over fifteen times.

It seems, then, that in today's information setting people have become consumer 'checkers' or 'evaluators'. They may happily avail themselves of innovative information services, with some of them actually describing their routine usage of websites and internet-based repositories as being 'hooked', but often they are also very cognisant indeed of the perils entailed by indiscriminate use of information distributed this way:

> ... these electronic archives are definitely no substitute to a regular journal. For example, if you log in today and find a pertinent article, tomorrow

you may discover that it is no longer there, in all probability because the author has decided to retract it for corrections ... an item posted there has not been refereed, so you've got to be very careful, you can't trust the information too much.

Indeed, the information seeking of the present-day consumer has more in common with the behaviour of shoppers than with that of traditional library users. This is because there is now a huge, rich market for information, and obtaining information is part of the shopping experience. As a shopper it is our duty to be a smart shopper, who plays the market. Nobody wants to spend time and money on obtaining information of inadequate quality and authority, and with good reason, too, as Nicholas et al. (2007a) found in their evaluation of digital health platforms and services in the UK. A person's trust in a site was a significant factor on health outcome, with those users demonstrating the greatest trust being more likely to claim a positive health outcome. Thus, those rating the site's trustworthiness as either good or excellent were more likely to say that they had been helped a lot and were less likely to say that the site was of no help.

There is a possible role here for the information professional in providing quality assessments, especially in the construction of information-filtering mechanisms that take account of quality and authority criteria. Plainly, web search engines and their relevance-ranking methods are not always sufficient. However, neither are the commonly cited quality criteria for online content, as a 2008 study into breast cancer information online clearly indicates: apparently, no quality criteria or website characteristic, singly or in combination, reliably identified inaccurate information (Bernstam et al., 2008). Librarians seem to be facing up to the challenge by developing their own search engines. These are meant to offer the trusted and effective searching environment that is missing from the big search engines and Google Scholar.

Date/currency

Everyone works with a mix of new and old information: even stockbrokers, preoccupied as they are with the telephone and real-time services, need to place data into a context. Thus, two closely related questions have to be asked regarding this information needs characteristic: firstly, how up-to-date does the information need to be; and secondly, how far back in time the information is required to go.

Information seekers are always likely to require the most up-to-date material, even if they do search for data back in time, too; by definition – the new captures the most interest. This seems to hold all the more true in today's information society, in which people consider keeping informed of new developments in their diverse areas of interest and attention an essential part of their customary pursuits. Thus, currency may be only one aspect of the date-range requirement, but these days the pressing need to always have the very latest information puts it very much in the spotlight. However, 'current' may have quite different meanings for different people and even for the same person in different circumstances, from 'this very moment' to 'nowadays', although the web has raised everybody's expectations. Thus, as Wilson (1993b) points out, one may claim to be current without claiming to have information about what is happening in 'real time' – i.e. right now. A market maker in a leading stockbroking firm would probably consider the last few minutes' information to be current, but for the historian the definition of current might well extend to a year or more.

Be an individual's precise definition of 'current' what it may, conventional wisdom holds that an information source is at its peak of use just after release, becoming less and less frequently used with time. This truism might not have gone uncontested – for instance, Rothenberg (1993), reviewing the body of literature testing the notion, argued that studies had failed to show the expected measurable decline in use. Still, whether there are demonstrably fewer readings of older materials or not, they are rated more important than new articles, more time is spent reading them, and a higher proportion of them are consulted to prepare a formal publication, such as an article or a book (King and Tenopir, 1999; Tenopir and King, 2000). Indeed, early retrieval systems traditionally proceeded from the notion that the most current information was the most important for users. This is the reason why they ordered their output in reverse chronological order. In fact, the provision of current information was long held to be the hallmark of a good information system – and for many people it was the performance indicator by which they measured its efficiency. Clearly, users are, and have always been interested in the new, but, as Odlyzko (2000) prophesied almost a decade ago, and as the data gleaned in CIBER's Virtual Scholar research programme (2001–08) prove beyond doubt, it would be a mistake to go on believing that this is the picture in its entirety. Apparently, once the visibility of older material increased, thanks to the massive improvements in access to back files, on the one hand, and the ubiquitous use of search engines that prioritise relevance over age, on the other, a much wider usage of older materials followed (Nicholas et al., 2008b).

Indeed so, but what do we mean when we say 'older material'? Undeniably, if people's perceptions as to their currency requirements vary greatly, so do their notions of how far back in time information may still be relevant to their needs. Hardly surprisingly, though, for obsolescence, the decline in the use of published material over its lifetime, is the result of change in general, and in the individual circumstances of the information seeker, in particular. Indeed, new discoveries, new equipment, new technologies, new legislation, as well as political and economic factors can render valueless – even dangerous – what we know and do. For instance, consider the value today of a book published on central heating systems for the home in the 1990s – books that can still be found in some public libraries. The relative prices of fuels have changed; much of the equipment featured would be obsolete; and new energy-saving features would not be mentioned. No wonder that it is the shelf-life of technical information that seems to be the shortest, on par with that of news. However, information decays in all fields, as the following account of an archaeologist amply illustrates:

> Without a doubt, in archaeology information does become obsolete. A book published, say, in 1932 is worthless by now ... you can't use the information in it, because it is no longer correct ... the dates given are wrong, the facts are incorrect ... I have in my private collection some older books, but not one line therein is still valid.

Given that the decay of information is so much contingent on change, it comes as very little of a surprise to find that obsolescence is clearly a discipline-specific phenomenon. After all, as it has already been noted, the various areas along Storer's (1967) continuum of 'hard' to 'soft' domains are characterised by a very different pace of change and development. Thus, the knowledge domains towards the 'hard' end of the continuum are fast-moving fields, characterised by rapid and linear changes. Since, as Meadows (1974) puts it, scientific knowledge grows in the orderly fashion of a skyscraper being built, with each new floor depending on the previously constructed floor for support, steps forward can be made only when the current problem at the frontier of research is resolved. This state of affairs obviously dictates a dynamic tempo of information creation, bringing about frequent change and a correspondingly high rate of obsolescence. Take, for example, the above-quoted psycho-oncologist's description of her field:

> ... the world of medicine is one of the most rapidly changing, one of the most dynamic ... whatever held true five years ago is more or less rubbish by now ... just like my PhD dissertation, which is all but ready for the bin by now, since the huge progress in the prevention of the side effects of chemotherapy for cancer has rendered all I had to say on the subject of patients' coping with the treatments just a few years back very much outdated.

In comparison, the humanities do not normally evolve in a linear fashion; one discovery is not necessarily the result of a prior one and will not necessarily lead to a later one. As such, to use again Meadows' (1974) picturesque simile, growth in the humanities might more reasonably be compared with the construction of a rambling country house. Therefore, new developments in the knowledge domains towards the 'soft' end of the continuum occur at a much more leisurely pace, in consequence of which information decay occurs much more slowly. Still, if in the past obsolescence in humanities research was an almost unheard of phenomenon, with new research usually supplementing rather than superseding previous knowledge, nowadays there seem to be instances of information becoming obsolete. This is what a historian has to say on the subject:

... in the humanities too, in history, philosophy, theology, there is so much research going on that now, and it was not so in the past, material does become obsolete ... A significant part of this innovative research truly sheds new light on the issues being considered, provides us with further understandings and different approaches ... some humanities research done ten, fifteen years ago has simply become obsolete and it never used to be the case! So you can't say today 'I don't get to the recent work in my field', it won't hold water, because in most every area there are some new, very central, very important works, which have changed in one way or another the concept, the outlook, the understanding, the whole information infrastructure.

As a rule, the very nature of information use in the different knowledge domains (particularly for research work purposes) dictates these differences in the levels of reliance on past information. As it has been previously noted, at the 'hard' end of the continuum information consumers must have the results of previous research pertaining to their own work, though not the specific writings reporting it, for where the findings of previous generations of scientists are still relevant, they are part of the building blocks of science and, therefore, readily available in textbooks, treatises, handbooks, etc. In stark contrast, in disciplines at the opposite, 'soft' end of the continuum, seekers of information cannot incorporate prior knowledge in their own undertakings unless they get hold of the specific documents that convey it, for the unique insights of the author form a vital part of the breakthrough reported (Bates, 1996; Stoan, 1984, 1991). No wonder, then, that there are distinct, discipline-specific patterns of the time-depth needed in information work.

Obsolescence of primary ('raw') material occurs (if it occurs at all) more slowly towards the 'softer' end of the continuum of knowledge domains: thus, for example, nobody could ever substitute an article summarising, say, Plato's thinking for the original works of Plato, and not only because the reviewer may have misunderstood the great philosopher or made a mistake in interpreting his work, but also because new insights can only arise from the original text. In fact, such primary information can actually gain value with age. Something written by Churchill during the Second World War would be valued for its age – it would be a source document; by its very nature it cannot be superseded. However, secondary works, which interpret the primary material, may very well age and become obsolete as new scholarly advances are made in the 'soft' disciplines too, although, again, the process is likely to take much more time. To be sure, citation studies show that the shelf-life of information in the 'softer' areas is a great deal longer than in the 'harder' domains (see, for example, Line and Sandison, 1974).

Even in the sciences not all information ages rapidly: the theory and fundamentals of many subjects are fairly constant and, in result, long-established (but revised) textbooks and manuals are still well-thumbed. Moreover, in every field there are key publications, which, having shaped the course of research, left an indelible imprint on its development: ' ... these are the most important works on the subject, the corner-stones of a knowledge area', says a biologist, 'which everybody seems to remember and cite, no matter when they were written. Therefore, I cannot say that I only need current material; sometimes I may go back as much as fifty or sixty years for the basics'. In the same vein, medicine often needs long-term retrospective information in considering the development of a disease. Also, apparently, there are instances when going back to the original publication is important, if not essential, in the sciences too, as a mathematician explains: 'I've often found that if I encounter some difficulties in understanding something, then the original article, the one which first reported the breakthrough on the issue I'm trying to understand ... clarifies things for me. Since the original article explains what the author really wants to do and how he goes about it, it gives you a different perspective. In the books subsequently written on the subject you find all sorts of things he never thought about when he wrote his article, and the improvements made on his initial notion, but you are better able to understand the original idea, the message nobody had come up with till then, when it is being described for the first time'.

However, as people often intuitively know what the obsolescence factor is in their field, they customarily set out to look primarily for materials from a given age spectrum (from the almost unlimited time-depth in the humanities to less than five years in many areas of the sciences and social sciences). In direct consequence, they frequently use date of origin as a means of selection – sometimes, as a substitute for quality. Date can indeed serve as a useful cut-off point for a search that produces a lot of documents. Information professionals have long understood this, which is why the aforementioned reverse chronological display is such a well-established practice. Still, it is important to remember that the shelf life of the information is not the only factor that determines the date range required – the amount of time that a person has available to read and digest information also comes into it.

Of course, information units and systems themselves have a need to weed, discard and archive information, because of the cost and space involved in storing information. This is often done using date criteria. However, where information professionals often have got it wrong is in holding on to information long after it has become deceased (the collector syndrome), and in failing to understand the complex relationship between occupation/job role and currency requirements. Thus, for example, just because journalists deal with news as it is breaking, it does not mean that they do not need archival information. In point of fact they do – to put the breaking news into some kind of perspective.

For information to retain its currency it must be distributed quickly – something that is taken up more fully in the next section. Some information channels are more conducive to the rapid transmission of information than others: hence the tremendous popularity of e-mail and the mobile telephone. Traditional information systems have never been geared to providing access to really current information – typically, abstracting services still serve up information that is three-to-six months old, although they no longer claim they are providing a current awareness function. Indeed not, for online technology and the internet enable the provision of services that are much closer to what people regard as acceptably current information. Thus, for instance, in the Western world same-day access to the full text digital edition of the major newspapers is quite the norm by now, and in many cases the digital edition is available before the hard copy.

Still, as the participants of the above-mentioned focus group of researchers reported, innovative alerting services, such as RSS feeds and the like, meet with very little success, if any. For example, on the eve of the 2008 elections in the USA, when online news consumption tripled (fully one-third of Americans reported getting most of their election news online, up from the 10% who did so four years earlier), still only 4% of American internet users subscribed to receive campaign or political information through an RSS feed. Even among voters who used the internet in one way or another for political purposes, who did take somewhat greater advantage of the ability to customise their news and get the latest updates on the campaign, only 5% set up a politics-related RSS feed (Pew Center for the People & the Press, 2008; Smith, 2009). Generally, people much prefer to rely on search engines to deliver 'current awareness on demand'. Mistakenly, as it happens, for the internet may be doing much to raise the currency performance, but too often it flatters to deceive. Sites are sometimes not even as up-to-date as their hard-copy equivalents, and when they are, their 'date stamp' is frequently either not very prominent or missing altogether.

Yet, currency is popularly held to be a prominent attribute of internet-based information. True, in the aforementioned survey of digital health platforms and services in the UK (Nicholas et al., 2007a) few people cited currency as an advantage of the internet over other sources, but that because their assumption must have been that digital information, almost by definition, was up to date; a dangerous assumption, of course. Nevertheless, people did say that the 'fact' that it was up-to-date information was instrumental for them in replacing other sources. Thus, for example, according to a company director 'books are too out of date relating to medical matters'. Similarly, another respondent felt that 'you will always be able to access the most up to date information on the internet, whereas a library may not have it available'. Information professionals have long taken it upon themselves to alert their customers to the importance of evaluating websites not only on the basis of content, but also on the basis of other key elements of digital literacy: authority, access, design, currency and interactivity, to name only the most important. Indeed, this is what Friedewald (2000) must have had in mind when he urged medical practitioners to cultivate professional websites of their own, because doing so could help them steer their patients towards current and authoritative information on the internet.

Speed of delivery

Speed of delivery is all about getting information to people quickly – as quickly as the need for it. Obviously, information should not go 'off' in transit or transmission. This is ever-more true these days, when time is such a rare commodity. However, the centrality of this aspect of information need goes beyond the unprecedented time constraints characterising life in the 21st century. Clearly, we also seem to have set ourselves new standards for the speed with which information is counted on to reach us. Hardly surprisingly, of course, for the easy availability and effortless accessibility of the host of resources, channels and facilities truly enable the transferring of information from one end of the world to the other in a matter of seconds. Indeed, the host of internet-based information services, with their live broadcast qualities, on the one hand, and the omnipresent electronic information communication tools, the e-mail, the fax and, more recently, even the mobile phone, on the other hand, add up to a seemingly boundless capacity to satisfy every information appetite on the spot. Inevitably, then, where speed of delivery is concerned, people's expectations are by now sky-high. Total access, as quickly as possible, appear to be the present-day information seeker's key information needs requirements. Nobody wants to wait; nobody wants to queue – even if they could. We are all impatient and have zero tolerance for delay, as the CIBER studies (Nicholas et al., 2003b; Nicholas et al., 2004b; Nicholas et al., 2005; Jamali et al., 2005; Nicholas et al., 2006a) have shown time after time. Needs must be fulfilled immediately and information needs are no exception. A computer scientist, for example, admittedly of the ilk constantly preoccupied with 'getting there' faster than his colleagues, thinks nothing of setting the standards of speedy information delivery quite high when he says: 'who has the patience to sit and wait for an hour until a piece of information arrives?' Real-time information, once the exclusive and treasured domain of the journalist/stockbroker, is open to all and is now what everyone wants, it is the benchmark.

Indeed so: with IT-enabled increased speed of information delivery, a more instant response is demanded of everyone; knee-jerk reactions become the norm. Take the case of the stockbroker. Some 25 years ago human messengers would bring price information from the Stock Exchange twice a day and maybe this information would arrive 20 minutes late. On arrival of the prices a frenetic period of activity would begin. This would subside after a while and then the stockbrokers would prepare themselves (perhaps by reading) for the next price announcements that came much later in the day. Now, though, thanks to real-time online systems, they watch the prices change on the screen in front of them, seconds after they have been posted. This goes on all day long, there is no relief or quiet time; they watch the screens all the time. Stockbrokers are not the only ones who work under such time pressure; rather the contrary. Today's working environments are characterised by the urgency and immediacy with which tasks have to be done, which is of course the reason why rapid information delivery is so highly prized – almost above everything else. In newspapers, for instance, if information cannot be obtained within half an hour or so, it simply will not be used. By the same token, a physicist readily admits that he will give up on a worthwhile idea if he is too short of time to do the information work involved:

> I may very well have an idea which necessitates that I go to the library. Now if I don't have the time or if it's too much trouble, it's not that I'll write the article without information, but I may decide that I won't try to solve the problem at all.

Thus, even academic researchers look forward to as swift a solution as possible to their information needs, and it is not merely because they want to avail themselves of what there is for the taking. Actually, obtaining information quickly is a very real need of theirs, as a historian explains:

> When you are in the midst of this process of investigation and analysis, and you get to a certain link which seems to be missing, you go to your information reservoir … if you find your answer there, then you can continue with your work, but if it's not there, and you can only get what you need later on, you're stuck at the point you've reached until you do … So the velocity of the information flow is indeed immensely important for people engaged in intensive research work.

Another academic, an expert on social welfare, goes even further than that. Contending that working under pressure is inherent to research work, he believes that in consequence the speedy meeting of information needs is an enduring prerequisite in academe:

> Even when you already have a reputation in your field, you still feel that you're under pressure to publish quickly, and therefore, you also feel under pressure to obtain information quickly … First of all, I think that in academe you're socialised to work under pressure, so when you no longer need to do so, you're already 'infected', so you keep working in the same manner. When you work on something, you always want it either validated or refuted so that you can get going, and this is not contingent on your academic rank, it's just how our work is. Also, when you're in the midst of developing something, you don't want to defer gratification for lack of information.

If researchers' perceived need for speedy access to information is the direct consequence of their feeling compelled (for extrinsic or intrinsic reasons) to produce and announce the results of their work quickly, it is particularly so in the highly competitive disciplinary culture of the sciences. Indeed, their circumstances are not conducive to tranquillity in any aspect of work, inclusive of its information-gathering component: 'When somebody comes up with an idea', says the above-quoted physicist,

It may very well happen that simultaneously five others in the world come up with the same idea. You want the idea to be chalked up to you, but if somebody precedes you, you can't very well say that you've done it too. If you look at it from this angle, there is a definite need in my field to obtain information quickly.

So much so, in fact, that according to Herman (2005), researchers' ability to find the time necessary to handle a certain quantity of information may occasionally even impact on their choices of topics for investigation. Firstly, the rigorous dictates of the 'publish or perish' mentality in academe, coupled with the externally imposed norms of gauging faculty productivity, enforce these days a brisk pace in every scholarly field. In addition, though, in the sciences and the social sciences the greater potential for profitable research findings, and the aforementioned much greater danger of those revenue-generating discoveries being 'scooped' by somebody else prescribe a more intensive – occasionally frenetic – rate of activity. In result, scientists and social scientists, especially the young among them, who still have to prove their abilities, are more inclined to weigh among the pros and cons of a planned project the amount of information needed, as it can have an impact on the time investment required.

No wonder, then, that many of the visitors to scholarly sites seem to be in a great hurry: they 'power browse', skimming titles, contents pages and abstracts, view only a few pages and do not stop long enough to do any real reading (Nicholas et al., 2008b). Seekers of scholarly information are not alone in manifesting this manner of behaviour, either. Indeed, the current interpretation of how quickly is 'quickly' has clearly become much more stringent in the universally felt pressured atmosphere we all inhabit now. In these times of electronic access to information, 'quickly' seems to be no less than 'immediately'; not 'in a few minutes', not 'soon', but now! Plainly, it is not that we all have to have our information needs met in real time, or with a high degree of urgency, but that even people who do not need information that quickly are impressed by rapid response – after all, it is another performance measure. It is synonymous with efficiency and efficiency at all times and in all respects is one of the hallmarks of life in our time-starved realities. Computer experts' conduct is perhaps the quintessence of this attitude, as one of them explains:

> I strive for efficiency; anything slow is inefficient and as such, irritating. My wife likes to recount how in the cafeteria, where there is a choice of two soups, one chock-full of vegetables and noodles, but more expensive, and the other watery and unappetising, but cheap, computer people unfailingly opt for the low-priced alternative, because it is the more cost-efficient choice. What about the pleasure factor? Well, for computer experts that doesn't enter into it … That's how we are, that's the way things are in our field; we try for maximum efficiency. We relentlessly struggle to improve our solutions … constantly seek to find ever-more efficient ways to solve the very same problem … so anything inefficient gets on our nerves, really offends our sensibilities.

Unfortunately, traditional information services generally respond relatively slowly, though perhaps not as slowly as they used to (a prompt information service, according to librarians of the old school, was putting a book on the shelf within three months or so of the request made for its acquisition). Still, it was not so long ago that The British Library Document Supply Centre's inter-library loan performance of five-to-seven days from query to receipt of document was being trumpeted as a success story. Given the standards we are used to by now as to the speed with which information can be delivered to our doorsteps, it becomes more understandable why information seekers grow-ingly desert the physical library (Martell, 2008). Thus, even academics, whose work is ostensibly done at a relatively leisurely pace, increasingly consider taking even a short journey to the library building the least preferable option for fulfilling their information needs, if an option at all, for:

> If I don't have the information on-line, I have to go to the elevator, wait a long time, go down to the library, only to discover when I finally get there that somebody has just checked out the item without which I'm unable to continue working. It can mean a waste of three, four, five days of work.

Indeed, none of the participants in the aforementioned focus group of prac-tised and experienced academic researchers used libraries in any regular or strategic sense. 'Libraries are empty nowadays', said one of them. Another volunteered that he had not been in the place for three years and he said this with no sense of guilt. Many researchers, especially scientific ones, really seem to have fled the library (Nicholas et al., 2008b).

Yet, the regrettable fact remains that many information units still trundle along in a rather unhurried fashion, ignoring the huge changes that have occurred around them, which makes them look almost prehistoric by com-parison. Thus Amazon's ability to get a book to a user within a day has shone the spotlight on the performance of most libraries in getting books to their customers. No wonder, then, as Nicholas and his colleagues argue (Nicholas et al., 2008b), that the consumer is moving closer to the publisher or dis-tributor and away from the library as a provider of information. True, full-text online services, electronic document delivery, the fax and, above all, the internet have all come to the aid of the information centre to make for – in theory, anyway – a much more responsive service. However, as Moss (2008) contends, making a strong case for bringing the library back to its rightful place at the forefront of the information chain, the technology-driven access and service focus of the present-day library is hardly the way to go ahead, in any case. Rather, he suggests, it is the time-honoured curatorial actions of the library which should be emphasised, the selection/appraisal/privileging of content for user communities. Quoting Levy (2001, 197), he thus calls for reinstating the library as a warehouse of organised and ordered knowledge, a move that, alone, can ensure that it fulfils its true role as a space for reflection and contemplation:

> For some of us, books and libraries symbolize some of the very qualities and modes of being that are threatened in our fast-paced instrumented lives. Books speak of time and depth and attention. They speak of a slower rhythm of life ... Libraries are places not just where books can be found, but where people can temporarily remove themselves from the speed and busyness of life, where they can read and write and reflect.

It is speed, speed and more speed that appear to be what most people want, whether they wish to get from place to place or have their information needs met. It is in cognisance of this fact that web designers and computer manufacturers continue to see the reduction of response times as their main goal. There can be little doubt about it – everybody wants quick wins, pure and simple. So much so, that, as Russell (2008) points out, speed is often preferred to accuracy (or authority), which is why, according to Lippincott (2005), students usually prefer the global searching of Google over the more sophisticated, but more time-consuming, searching system provided by the library, where they must make separate searches of the online catalogue and every database of potential interest. In a similar vein, as the findings of a benchmarking survey of e-book usage and perceptions in more than 120 UK universities indicated, when searching (rather than browsing) was used as the means for locating e-book content, the most popular search, by a considerable margin, was the quick search (Nicholas et al., 2008c). Indeed, as Russell (2008) goes on to say, website usability is not just about making sure that everything on the site works and relatively easy to navigate and use; it looks at speed of use, as well. Thus, when it was still common for sites to exhibit advanced technological facilities that had the effect of slowing down page loading, visitors were more likely to try their luck elsewhere. By the same token, those sites that offered a range of search methods were preferred, for then users could find and select the fastest method to suit them. Therefore, he concludes, where internet users are concerned, registration or application needs to be as simple and quick as possible, and any feature that speeds up the process is an advantage.

Finally, one last word about speed of delivery and its affect on currency. The faster people can get information, the more current it is, and that drives up their currency expectations further, with people wanting ever-more current data. Thus, for example, news has a shorter and shorter shelf life. Should, say, an abstracting service provide abstracts of news items months later, as sometimes is the case (*British Education Index* for instance), then its value as a publicist of news information is severely circumscribed. Because of this it is not wholly implausible to imagine a time when news will migrate totally from hard-copy newspapers to newspaper websites, possibly reducing newspapers to features magazines.

Place of publication/origin

The term 'Global Village', by now a rather worn-out cliché, nevertheless captures particularly well the essence of the contemporary information scene:

information production, communication and use certainly seem to have moved into a worldwide, borderless arena, unimpeded by technical barriers. Still, the place or country from which some information hails may not be invariably inconsequential to its potential consumers, and not because of any racist, discriminatory or derogatory attitude on their part. In ample proof of this point suffice to remember that unless information seekers can understand the language in which some material is written, it is of no use to them, especially since the automatic translation services available on various websites are still far from providing adequate conversions from one language to another. It is in recognition of this that search engines routinely offer the opportunity to restrict a search by language. The place or country of origin of some information can thus be very significant; just how significant, is contingent largely on three factors: (1) subject; (2) whether the user is a practitioner or academic; and (3) language proficiency.

Subject

The profiles of internationalisation differ between fields: the subject matter of some is truly international, whilst that of others is less so. In direct consequence, the importance accorded to the geographical origins of information is decidedly discipline-specific. The social sciences transcend national boundaries much less well than either the sciences or the humanities.

The sciences cross national frontiers readily by virtue of their universality ('an atom in New York is an atom in Moscow', says Brittain, 1984, 11), as well as their highly codified language. Therefore, academics studying say, cancer, or salmonella poisoning, are likely to be interested in research emanating from anywhere in the world. The humanities, too, 'travel well', concerned as they are with unique topics that have universal relevance, such as an event, a person or a work of art, literature, or music (Tibbo, 1994).

Not so, though, the social sciences, which, as Line (1973, 29–30) asserts, are characterised by an inherent instability, the result of their concern with human beings, and particularly their interactions with one another, whether this interaction be social, political, or economic. Thus, he maintains,

> … however carefully a particular study or experiment is carried out, and however valid the data that may come from it, a similar study of a different population – in a different town or country, or at a different time – will almost certainly give different results.

In addition, the lack of universally accepted methodologies and definitions, and the existence of uniquely national social institutions (like the UK's NHS, for instance) further contribute to the locality-specific nature of social science information. All this adds up to an overall tendency among seekers of scholarly information in the different fields of social science to be much more parochial in their information needs and information behaviour.

Not that this is always the case: some subjects in the social sciences – economics and psychology, for instance, do have broad international horizons. Still, in subjects like law and social welfare, communication is country-bound, although the European Union is increasingly drawing even law out of its traditional insularity. In the case of social welfare the concerns are even more local – at the regional rather than national level. Also, in the cases of some social science and humanities subjects – history, political science and geography come most immediately to mind – countries are frequently the subjects of study and, in result, place of origin is of special importance to them. Thus, for example, if you wished to study, say, the politics of Cyprus, then you would be well advised to examine the publications emanating from that island.

However, even in fields characterised by world-spanning scholarly communication, users will place a higher priority on the literature of some countries than others. Citation studies have long borne testimony to the fact that international scholarly communication is not a two-way or reciprocal process; rather, as Arunachalam and Singh (1992) point out, the actual distribution of scholarly and scientific research among different nations is rather skewed. Indeed, a small number of countries produce much of the mainstream research, whilst a very large number of countries contribute very little to the generation of knowledge. Naturally enough, the literature of the countries renowned because of the quality and size of their research, most notably the USA, the UK, Switzerland, Sweden, Canada, the Netherlands, Denmark, Australia, Finland and France, is universally held in high esteem, whilst the publications of the developing countries, because of the poverty of theirs, is generally ignored. Thus, for example, a professor of literature professes to a pronounced partiality to information originating in the Western world (and sounds rather apologetic about it, too):

> In my field, there's quite a lot of information coming from India, and somehow I have this somewhat derogatory attitude toward it; I keep expecting that it won't be all that significant. I don't know how justified I am for thinking so; I can't say I've read the piece and found it superficial, but my expectation is not the same it would have been were the author from the UK or the States or Holland. In fact, in India they have great English, we don't come near their level, and yet I have the feeling that whatever they write in India can't be serious. Part of it is the quality of the book: you see how cheap it is, both the paper and the print, and on the spot your expectations drop. It's not right, there's no justification to it, but that's how it is. You see something from Princeton or Oxford, and immediately think it is God knows what, although that's not always the case, not at all, but …

In defence, scholars point out that if someone from a Third World country had something really worthwhile to say, he/she would say it in a Western journal, on account of the recognition and prestige to be gained in so doing. True enough: in scientific journals, no matter what the geographic origin of the publisher, the authorship is likely to be international. Thus, it is mostly through international conferences that academics (qualitatively) sample the non-Western literature, especially since, as a mathematician points out, 'if a journal is published in, say, a third-world country, there's a good chance that you've never heard of it and it will not be in the library either'.

True, as Russell (2001) observes, the shift to electronic scholarship could, at least in principle, bring about a change in this state of affairs, seeing that these days, researchers in developing countries can interact with their colleagues in any part of the world unhindered by geographical constraints. Also, Open Access is clearly hugely beneficial to people in poorer countries, where users cannot afford access to expensive journals (Nicholas et al., 2007e). However, even if information poverty is no longer the barrier that it used to be, academics from the periphery may still find it difficult to assume a more central position in international scholarship, for it is still questionable to what extent today's information consumers are prepared to take note of possibly valuable work done and published outside the Western world.

The problem does not seem to be a dearth of aptitude, knowledge or skills on the level of the individual researcher. After all, international research collaboration is especially prevalent between scholars hailing from small or developing countries and their colleagues in the wider academic world (Thorsteinsdottir, 2000). The phenomenon of 'brain drain', the significantly increased mobility of academics in the global knowledge society from low to high knowledge intensity places also speaks against such a possibility (Meyer et al., 2001). Yet, as Arunachalam (1999) contends, developing country scientists are not easily accepted into mainstream science: they can rarely get their research published in well-known journals and, even when they do, their work may not be quoted in subsequent work as often as papers published in the same journal by scientists from the advanced countries. Thus, the genuine inequities in opportunities, from less-developed infrastructures for electronically mediated research, through a shortage of research funds, to inadequate statutory and organisational environments both at the government and institutional level probably do not tell the whole story. Rather, as Russell (2001) suggests, there are also social and cultural barriers that prevent academics from the developing world taking their rightful place in the international community of scholars, due to a measure of subjectivity in scientific evaluations. Thus, until neither the objective conditions for the conduct of the scientific work, nor the subjective perceptions of its quality measure up to Western standards, the scholarship of the developing countries is bound to be approached warily.

Having seen the impact of the country of origin on information production and consumption, we need to probe deeper than that in order to see a more finely-grained picture. Thus, taking the place of publication aspect of information to its logical extreme, to the immediate work environment, it is important to note that it is in-house information, that is, formal and informal information produced within the organisation, which is the more valued. Hardly surprisingly, of course: inside information is immediately relevant and directly touches upon the individual. Indeed, internal information flows are perceived as most critical and, in result, fellow workers seem to be the most frequently utilised information sources for work purposes (Baldwin and Rice, 1997; Huotari and Wilson, 2001).

Practitioner/academic divide

Academics, because they tend to be more interested in ideas, theories and comparative approaches, adopt a more international approach to information gathering than practitioners or, for that matter, amateurs; although, as it has already been noted, with scholarly information having become available at everybody's desktop, a much wider range of people have been drawn to its products. Nevertheless, information seeking across national boundaries is particularly typical of the scholarly enterprise (Nicholas et al., 2008b), and one which has been gaining considerable momentum throughout the 20th century and into the 21st. This, obviously, happened as part and parcel of general globalisation trends, although policy initiatives on national and supranational levels also contributed their share (Smeby and Trondal, 2005). In addition, the increasingly widespread availability of information and communication technologies not only enabled and underpinned the developments in this direction, but further accelerated them, too.

Practitioners and consumers of general-interest material also feed off a more international diet of information, though not necessarily intentionally or even knowingly. Thus, people may still obtain much of their foreign information second-hand from the national news services, but the ever-increasing popularity of the internet and the growth of satellite television have certainly brought the world to almost everybody's doorstep. Here again, the web has had a major impact. The impact is not a straightforward one, though. By making it much easier to get hold of information from any country on earth it is promoting the use of 'foreign' material. However, because the vast majority of information on the web is from the USA (although this is being challenged now by the economic growth of China), use is even more concentrated.

In any case, the world is indeed getting smaller (hence the term 'the Global Village'). Even Americans, long held to be quite self-sufficient in their use of information, take considerably more interest in the literatures of other countries. This is best illustrated by reference to two CIBER studies (Nicholas et al., 2008b): one, of the British Library's learning site for young scholars, the other, of Intute, a Joint Information Systems Committee (JISC)-sponsored scholarly gateway site. In both cases the UK audience was a minority one and US scholars were the majority user group, as was the case with *The Times* five years earlier (Nicholas et al., 2000). This might be explained by the perceived high quality of UK education, which, gratifying as it may be, plainly has big implications for decision-makers. After all, what will the tax payers say, in this specific case in the UK, if they learn that government money is going to help the Americans become better and more informed searchers?

It seems, then, that on the national level the advent of the Global Village may not be wholly devoid of problems. Another instance of this is the ever-more heavy slant of today's globalisation-induced realities towards the so-called Anglo-Saxon culture. Suffice to cite, in ample proof of this, Google's initiative 'to organise the world's information and make it universally accessible', which, to all intents and purposes, is tantamount to a universal library of mostly Anglo-Saxon origins: a digital file of 15 million English-language books available on the web. No wonder the president of the French National Library has launched a counterattack, aimed at redressing the situation, which, he believes, will result in an unbalanced treatment of the literature of other countries (Jeanneney, 2007). Such a development, in its turn, will, as Gerald Grunberg, Senior Consultant to the Project Bibliotheca Alexandrina argues, run counter to the need for assembling and conserving the collective memory of a community or of a country, a need which has clearly become especially important now that globalisation has become an all-pervasive fact of life (cited in: Moss, 2008).

Language proficiency

Another problem associated with the geographic origins of information is what seems to be the most obvious of them all: the language barrier, which may thwart the attempt to read the literature of another country. Linguistic ability thus clearly enters into the question of whether information from foreign countries is consumed, although it seems that even when people can read literature written in another language, they are not highly motivated to do so. Mindful of this, the European Union publishes all its significant papers in all the languages of the Community. In any case, with the universal trends of globalisation and internationalisation, English has truly become the Esperanto of our times (only far more thriving than the original has ever been). Indeed, the dominance of the English language in contemporary international communication is indubitable, as Jorna (2002, 158) asserts:

> English is the geographically most widespread language of the world ...
> [It] is the official language of relatively affluent and influential countries in
> North America, the British Isles and Australia, and has special status as a
> second language in over 70 countries ... Across the world there are about
> 350 million native speakers and 250 to 350 million people who speak
> English as a second language ... [although] if the most basic level of English
> is included, one might count up to 1.5 billion English speakers ... Also, three
> of the most important international organisations communicate primarily in
> English: the United Nations, the World Bank, and the European Community.

If rallying behind English as a *de facto* lingua franca of international discourse is the way to overcome language barriers, then the web has certainly been instrumental in helping things along. Firstly, it is encouraging people of all languages to disseminate information in English to obtain the largest audience. Indeed, well over 80% of websites are in English. Secondly, as has already been noted, a number of search engines provide a translating facility.

In point of fact, the use of English as the one, commonly agreed-upon language of dialogue between people from all over the world looks as if it is fast becoming quite the norm. Academe is a prime example of a milieu where this has actually happened. Indeed, by now proficiency in English is absolutely vital for academics; so much so, that the above-quoted Israeli-based computer scientist considers not having English a disability and his mathematician colleague actually likens it to not being able to breathe! With good reason, too, as another colleague of theirs explains:

> The whole of the Western world these days is centred on the U.S. and U.K ... When somebody publishes in his native tongue, in local journals ... it is inevitably less of a contribution, just like in our case with Hebrew ... What you really want is to present your work to the international scientific community, to measure up to the standards set by the scientific community, which today begins with publishing in English ... If an author did not publish his work in English it's probably not because he hadn't wanted to, but because his work was rejected.

Yet, interestingly, at least in the 'softer' knowledge domains, academics consider not having other languages detrimental to their work; perhaps not always seriously damaging, but certainly disadvantageous (Herman, 2005). First of all, as we have already seen, at least the social sciences are more insular in their scholarly activities, in result of which considerable quantities of information are published domestically and in the local language, too. Indeed, in an interview with an academic researcher, whose multidisciplinary interests frequently send him in pursuit of information in various fields of the social sciences, he greatly lamented the problem incurred by his linguistic limitations:

> I only know two languages, Hebrew and English, and it's an obstacle in my research, a real obstacle ... I'm very interested in Germany ... their constitutional organisation, both from the legal and the political point of view is probably the best achievable ... [However,] I don't read German, and they hardly ever translate themselves ... two, three, four, five publications in my field have been translated, and they are the most important ones, but you can't understand a legal system without knowing the language ... To me my ignorance is a great hindrance, I feel like an illiterate person, an ignoramus ... it's a real obstacle, because knowing English doesn't always suffice.

Further to that, researchers' language preferences are not only information availability-dictated, but need-driven. Indeed, as is more often than not the case where scholarly information behaviour is concerned, needs inherent to the nature of the research endeavour shape the requirements for information, which, in result, tend to be very much discipline-specific. In fact, here again the needs of researchers in the various disciplines along the 'hard' to 'soft' continuum seem to be associated with the previously noted differences in the utilisation of information for generating new knowledge. Thus, at the 'soft' end of the continuum, where the primary evidence used is the product of a specific place and time, shaped by the distinctive personality of its creator (Wiberley and Jones, 1994), and where the new contribution to the corpus of knowledge actually 'happens' in the research article, inheres in the way the scholar analyses, extracts and develops insights about the material (Bates, 1996), reading the original-language publication can be absolutely crucial. For the social scientists, with their aforementioned parochial information needs, it must be even more so than for their humanities colleagues.

It is very different indeed at the 'hard' end of the continuum, where, as has already been noted, the new discovery is reported in the research article, not contained in it (Stoan, 1984, 1991). As researchers in the 'harder' knowledge domains only need to learn the results of the progress made by their peers, without attempting to get inside their thought processes, they can more easily afford to save the time, effort and money costs of mastering any other language, bar English. Anyhow, precisely because they only need to know 'the bottom line' of new contributions to the corpus of knowledge in their fields, they can put translations to very good use indeed. Thus, their need for information exchange across linguistic barriers can be met these days via a host of convenient translation journals at their disposal. Another possible solution are the many English-language international state-of-the-art reviews in existence, which, as we have already seen, may not be considered adequate substitutes for reading the original publications, but can definitely help at a pinch.

Processing and packaging

These two aspects of an information need, concerned with the different ways and formats in which the same ideas and data can be represented and presented to potential users, are intertwined and overlapping to such an extent that they are best treated together. Indeed, the vast literature of recent years on the subject rarely separates the two. Vast literature it is, too, for the processing and packaging of information have been the focus of untold studies, articles and books ever since the first attempts to harness novel electronic technologies to information management wrought irrevocable changes to our information environments. Unavoidably so, of course: with information figuring higher and higher on our inventories of 'bare necessities', its processing and packaging could not but come to the fore; after all, the way a piece of information is geared up for consumption is a crucial factor in its accessibility and usability, although with so much talk centring on the mechanisms of information use and management, it does look from time to time as if it is the tail wagging the dog … In any case, let us take a closer look at this two-pronged characteristic of an information need.

Processing refers to the different ways that can be utilised to convey the very same information. Thus, for the same topic a researcher might want raw data with as little manipulation and interpretation as possible (unprocessed data), whereas a practitioner or somebody from outside the field might want the bare bones of data, with really only the significance of the information being spelt out (highly processed data). In fact, and this happens all the time, a single scientific discovery, social survey, government inquiry can be processed for a whole range of audiences and purposes. Take a piece of research undertaken on the effect of increased lighting on crime in a housing estate in East London. The work was originally published as a Home Office research report. As a research report it was typically densely and closely argued, full of data, descriptions of research methods and statistical appendices and, as a matter of fact, only accessible to other researchers. However, the topic itself was of interest to a much wider audience. Consequently, it was then condensed and fashioned for an article in a professional journal and, after that, it was picked up by the newspapers before, finally, being featured as a one-minute item on the local television news. At every stage in this chain detail was removed, interpretation featured more strongly and the information content was reduced. Thus, at each stage of processing the information was further compacted and simplified, resulting in a progressive reduction in the quantity, as well as a lowering of the intellectual level of the information. Processing does indeed often aim at achieving both these aims, although this need not be so, for condensation may not involve simplification and vice versa.

The reason processing, nevertheless, frequently does end up doing both is because it is quite typically all about popularisation. The newspapers, the radio, the TV and the internet are all purveyors of heavily processed information. Indeed, specialist correspondents spend a good deal of their time simplifying, popularising and explaining government reports, research studies and major surveys – and they are generally very good at this, making all kinds of difficult topics accessible to the uninitiated. By the same token, professionally written book reviews – together with the 'blurbs' – provide those concise summaries that, allegedly, are often the only part of a book that is ever read. Unfortunately, some of these popular reports can be so highly processed that they probably pass through the system without ever being absorbed by the brain. So, maybe the process can be taken too far?

There are, of course, other forms of presenting highly processed information, and not necessarily at a popular level, either. These include, most notably, abstracts, state-of-the-art reviews, executive summaries and interpretations. The best-known among them (and probably the one dearest to the information professionals' heart) is the abstract. Still, it has been long held that with the exception of academics, users do not much like the abstract, short and pithy as it is, possibly because, in many cases, abstracting results in too much loss of information. Even students did not use them, we were told (Keene,

2004). Thus, it was somewhat unexpected to find in a CIBER study of an e-journal database (Blackwell Synergy), reported in Nicholas et al. (2005), that undergraduates were the biggest users of abstracts (by a 5% margin over all other groups), and the population surveyed were all subscribers, so it cannot be simply put down to poorer access to full-text versions!

Perhaps more predictably, the abstract has remained popular among academics in the digital scholarly environment, too, as findings of the Virtual Scholar Research Programme clearly demonstrate (Nicholas et al., 2007d). Still, it is more of a surprise to see just how popular abstracts are, which is all the more interesting in today's information environment, rich as it is in full-text documents. The popularity of abstracts stems in part from technical reasons: search engines and gateways tend to point seekers of information to abstracts in the first instance and, obviously, viewing the abstract, typically free for all users, is the only option for the non-subscribers or the 'disenfranchised'. Also, as Pinto and Lancaster (1999) point out, abstracts may still be most advantageous for retrieval purposes, because the searching of full text will frequently cause an unacceptable level of irrelevancy.

However, there seems to be much more to it: abstracts are very important indeed in helping scholars deal with the information flood. First of all, abstracts allow for determining fairly quickly whether an article is of interest and of the appropriate quality and level, as one researcher explains: 'When I scan the literature, I do a very quick screen on the titles first. For the rare articles (from many journals) that make that cut, I then read through the abstracts to see if I wish to read more. I then pull down the full article only for a select few'. Further to that, present-day academics, working under unprecedented time pressures, may use the abstract as a substitute for the article itself: 'In some cases the abstract even provides me enough information and I don't need to read the full paper. Given the amount of papers published, good scientists only rarely can afford reading a full paper'. Apparently, at times the abstract is quite sufficient to fulfil an information need, as, for example, in the case of setting out to learn of new developments in one's field. True, this is very much field-dependent: as it has already been noted, at the 'hard' end of the continuum of disciplines, where the new discovery is reported in the research article, not contained in it (Stoan, 1984, 1991), it is probably fairly clear from the abstract how the results or conclusions of a paper fit with one's own research programme. However, at the 'soft' end, where the new contribution to the corpus of knowledge actually 'happens' in the research article, inheres in the way the scholar analyses, extracts and develops insights about the material (Bates, 1996), achieving the same end may often necessitate reading (or more likely skimming) the whole paper. Indeed, the conclusions of Nicholas et al. (2009) in their Research Information Network (RIN)-funded investigation of the impact of scholarly e-journals on the UK research community underscore this suggestion. The evaluation of the usage logs of the Oxford Journals in regard to use by 10 major UK research institutions and three representative subjects (life sciences, economics and history) indicated that despite the fact that a good proportion of history journals had abstracts, very few historians viewed an abstract during their visit. Three times as many life science and economics sessions viewed an abstract.

In any case, using the abstracts in lieu of reading the article in its entirety fits in very well with the 'power browsing' form of information behaviour, which, as it has repeatedly been noted, is endemic in the digital environment. Today's information consumers Hoover through titles, contents pages and abstracts at a huge rate of knots to help them stride across the digital information universe. They feed for information horizontally rather than vertically, looking for 'bite-size' information chunks and, in result, seldom delve deeply into a website or even return to it. It is not difficult to see how abstracts are suited to this style of behaviour; in fact, they may even encourage it: after all, abstracts and contents pages are made for that, they are the motorways by which users drive through content.

Another way to process information in order to make it more palatable is in the form of a review article. Such subject-specific synopses of the recent major research advances made ideally add up to a coherent view of the 'state of the art' in a given knowledge area. When such a review article bears the signature of an influential scholar, which, in point of fact, it often does, for the authority figures in the various knowledge areas frequently function as gatekeepers, the information to be found therein is greatly enhanced by the expert interpretation of its compiler. Therefore, review articles understandably carry a lot of weight. Actually, the mere inclusion of a work in a review article serves as warranty of its excellence. Indeed, this highly processed form of scholarly information can serve as a great starting point for people who want to master the up-to-date basics of a topic.

Carrying the notion of the subject-specific synopsis of the knowledge attained on a topic to its very extreme, managerial information is often condensed into one page listing bullet points. With very little time to spend on any one problem from among the many awaiting their attention, senior management and busy professionals generally have support staff to provide them with the highly processed information they require: brief and focused pointers on possible solutions and actions, as well as warnings concerning the obstacles that may crop up.

Proceeding to the second component in the processing and packaging aspect of an information need, we now come to the external presentation or physical form of the information – the form in which it is stored and communicated. However, first, a word on the relationship between processing and packaging. It is, obviously, a very close one, because certain information packages are designed for the storage and dissemination of specific levels of processed data. Thus, dissertations and theses are packages that convey a good deal of data and detail, as do research reports and statistical series. Almost inevitably then, there is a limited audience for these information packages. Conversely, the internet, newspapers, television and leaflets – all purveyors of highly processed information – have vast and popular audiences. Of course, it is not always as simple as that, for theses have abstracts and broadsheet newspapers have their heavy articles, and it is almost impossible to typecast books.

However, it is not the level of processing alone that attracts users to various forms of information package. There is a lot more to it than that, for, as we have already seen, some packages are more current than others (the web, news wires); some are far more exclusive (oral sources); some demand much less of the individual in digesting their messages (television); some are simply more 'in', and as such, have much greater appeal (mobile phones); others are very accessible (newspapers); and some are just plainly more familiar (books). The personality of the individual comes into it too – for instance, there are those who are more comfortable with oral sources, say, with having something explained to them, as opposed to fans of reading, who need to absorb information through their eyes.

In the same vein, the purpose for which information is sought can have quite some effect on the packaging required. That is, people quite consistently match the information task they are facing with the appropriate source. Factual information may be obtained easily enough via written sources, whether computer-mediated or hard copy, but when the need is for information that conveys complex ideas and thoughts, it is best attained via face-to-face interaction with human experts. The following account of an academic amply illustrates the point:

> If you write an article with a colleague, first you have to solve the problem you're working on ... Now ... this solution finding usually involves a face-to-face encounter, since you have to explain yourself, you have to use abstract arguments; it's not entirely trivial getting all that across to somebody, so it has got to be done verbally, it is truly essential to do it face-to-face.

Indeed, people unanimously appreciate the need for face-to-face communication for some purposes, as a historian contends:

> There's no substitute for the human touch, no substitute whatsoever ... The electronic devices can help to decrease the need for human touch, but they are no substitute for it ... After all, you wouldn't consider e-mailing your kids or even talking to them over the phone the equivalent of hugging them ... You can't join forces with somebody you don't know, haven't met, haven't had coffee with.

No wonder, then, that the aforementioned survey of the use and impact of key digital health platforms and services in the UK (Nicholas et al., 2007a) found that where information was needed for solving medical problems, which, of course, often necessitates some give and take of possibly sensitive and/or vital information, the two most important sources were a person's own doctor and the practice nurse. Similarly, Garvey et al. (1974), pointing out the intra-individual variations in scholarly information use, came to the conclusion that journals may be the most useful for providing information needed to place a scientist's work in proper context and to integrate his or her findings into current scientific knowledge, but informal channels, such as local colleagues were essential as sources of ideas, opinions and creative solutions to technical problems.

It seems then that a person's preference for a certain package is likely to be a result of an amalgamation of factors. Indeed, different user populations consistently want their information presented in specific packages, often to the exclusion of others. Thus, scientists have a love affair with journals and humanities researchers with monographs, students cannot get enough of the web, newspaper cuttings similarly smite journalists, and community workers revel in grey literature. It goes without saying, then, that information consumers are very much inclined to opt for the forms in which they regularly communicate, the forms to which they are accustomed. This is, of course, such a well-known phenomenon that people rarely stop to consider that it can lead to tunnel vision, as the media correspondent of the *Evening Standard* points out: 'We [journalists] do not know enough about the world. We rely too much on other newspapers [for information] ... ' (Glover, 1994). Not that anybody seems to be overly bothered about the possibility; people happily remain tradition-bound where the packaging of their information is concerned.

Still, nothing is set in concrete, as the massive uptake of electronic packaging of information amply proves. To be sure, the foundation-laying years of the digital revolution passed to the tune of heartfelt laments regarding 'the sluggishness of human nature and its superstitious cleavage to old habits' (Harnad, 1999). Yet, with all that not so long ago IT-based sources and services were a huge novelty for everybody, now we all seem to have joined the vast ranks of consumers of digital information. Generally speaking, today's information users seem to be quite at peace with the novel technologies, although some are undoubtedly more enthusiastic about it all than others. A philosopher's earnest diatribe against electronic texts, which, he says, 'lack the vitality of the printed word just the same as the canned music accompanying your purchase of a pair of underpants lacks the vitality of a live concert', undoubtedly attests to the soft spot many people still have for the erudite tradition of the book and the library. His colleague, a professor of literature, who readily admits to being a 'dinosaur' of sorts where anything electronic is concerned ('I have finally mastered the art of searching the computerised catalogue, but it has taken me fifteen years', he says), blames the ephemeral qualities of IT-based sources for his lingering wariness of them:

> There's a transient feeling about it all; when you hold in your hand a piece of paper, it has presence ... however, when you encounter the information on the computer screen, it is not only that your eyes and your brain are not accustomed to it, but it is also somehow of a temporary, insubstantial nature ... When you find your information in a book, it's something tangible, standing on a shelf, but if it's on the internet, today it's here, tomorrow it's gone, so how can you trust it?

However, most people seem to be of a rather more pragmatic mindset: the often reserved, sometimes outright reluctant attitude towards electronic information, so frequently encountered in the past, has now mostly been replaced by the matter-of-fact approach usually reserved for the rudimentary conditions and routine practices of life and living.

Interestingly, though, whether a specific electronic information form or practice is adopted at all, and if it is, to what extent and how fast, may vary greatly among different populations. Originally, it was widely held that all people would eventually flock as one to all of the promising-looking solutions to the need for information. After all, the novel technologies did afford easy and quick access to more and better information! Indeed, or so the reasoning went, it was only a matter of time before all information seekers would 'see the light', perhaps simply a matter of waiting for children, who were born into the realities of a digital world, to grow up. The technologising force sweeping over society was bound to culminate in an ultimate, unreserved conversion to a wholly electronic way of life; it was an inescapable imperative, even, and information work was no exception. Arguing strongly against this technological determinism, subsequent thinking, taking into consideration the many idiosyncratic factors governing the needs of different populations, posited that as all technological changes are weighed against a normative order, new technologies are either not adopted by some groups of people, or modified to fit in with the existing social structure of these groups.

A prime example, amply proving the validity of this way of reasoning, is the integration of electronic media into academic work. Many of the studies into the impact of IT-based resources on scholarly work practices (see, for example, Bruce, 1998; Erens, 1996; Lazinger et al., 1997; Liebscher et al., 1997; Pullinger, 1999; Starkweather and Wallin, 1999) proceed from the notion that the move to electronic scholarship is indeed just a matter of time across all disciplines. Proponents of this view, as Kling and McKim (2000) explicate, typically conceptualise their vision in either one of two ways. Those who focus on the technical features of the various media maintain that all the novel electronic channels are essentially equally valuable in all disciplines; they all are said to reduce the costs of communication, expand the range of people and locations from which materials are accessible, and generally speed communications. As scholars in all scientific fields work with data, and communicate both formally and informally with other scholars, all of the electronic media should be adopted and used fairly uniformly. Others of the same mindset employ an evolutionary approach: since various fields, through somewhat random experimentation, have developed a series of electronic communication forums, soon we should expect scholars of all fields to adapt these successful discoveries to enhance their communications. Thus, it is simply a matter of time – perhaps simply a matter of waiting for today's internet-savvy students to become working scientists – before academics of various fields will catch up with those among their colleagues who are already on the leading edge of an inexorable trend. True, so the logic of such analyses goes, first some basic problems need to be resolved, from lack of access, lack of awareness to the existence of electronic sources, lack of computer skills, lack of user friendliness of some IT-based systems, to the especially knotty issue of academics' conservative attitudes. Also, humanists, popularly assumed to be technophobes, might take longer before they, too, are persuaded that it is 'good for them'. Still, for those proceeding from this standpoint there seems to be little doubt as to the final outcome: all are bound to realise sooner or later that the advantages of electronic information work (ease, speed, convenience, etc.) are well-worth the effort of converting to IT-based practices.

However, other experts studying the phenomenon put forward an alternative scenario, maintaining that it is more likely that we will see field-specific or even sub-field-specific variations in the adoption of electronic research work practices (Covi, 1999; Covi, 2000; Fry, 2004; Kling and Covi, 1997; Kling and McKim, 2000; Mahe, 2003; Mahe et al., 2000; Talja and Maula, 2003; Walsh and Bayma, 1996). They suggest that it is the idiosyncratic nature of the scholarly undertaking in the different knowledge domains which determines the extent to which electronic resources are utilised and the rate of their adoption, remonstrating that the move to novel information work practices is not just a matter of time. Thus, the shaping of technology is highly specific to and emerges in reaction to the dynamic needs of particular communities. Therefore, as Kling and McKim (2000) maintain, field differences in the willingness to convert to electronic scholarship stem from the social practices that support trustworthy communications in each field. Take, for example, the much-debated uptake of e-print repositories. In some fields productive scholars are more aware of the work of their fellow researchers than in others. If the ongoing work is thus relatively transparent, the risks associated with sharing reports prior to their formal publications are fewer, and the willingness to base the scholarly communication on e-prints will be correspondingly higher.

Having thus looked in some detail at the specific point of electronic packaging of information, we now return to another of the more general aspects of the topic of our discussion here, focusing this time on the information professional's point of view. Plainly, information professionals, most notably librarians, are very well acquainted with this characteristic of need: after all, they do spend a good deal of their time organising and storing the physical embodiment of information – hard-copy and digital. So much so, that they are probably guilty of giving the processing and packaging aspect of an information need too much prominence. All too often it is a package and not the information that is given in answer to a question, an attitude that might explain why librarians tend to present to their clients the electronic version of some material, even when the hard-copy alternative is available and, if it were only given some consideration, more fitting to the enquirer's circumstances.

In addition, librarians seem to show marked bias towards some packages, in result of which the traditional library is full of books and journals. Newspapers, leaflets, CDs, unpublished information and personal contacts are generally neglected, even when they would appear to be more appropriate in dealing with an enquiry. However, in the case of the academic librarian, the manifest disregard for some sources could be a case of responding to the wishes of their users. As has already been noted, scholars may hold their colleagues to be excellent sources for news about pertinent work underway and for detailed information about apparatus and procedures, but they certainly would rather not rely on them for obtaining the knowledge base accumulated on a subject (Herman, 2005). Thus, they have a preference for authoritative, published sources – sources that in turn can be cited as acceptable evidence (e.g. Einstein *wrote* ranks ahead of Einstein *said*).

Information professionals' many practical concerns with form tend to result in their building information systems for certain publication packages – and so fragment and complicate the search for information. Thus the online public access catalogues (OPACs) in most of our college libraries provide access to content to be found in books only (something of which students are often totally unaware). The periodicals – often a far more suitable and certainly a much more expensive resource – are largely left to a scattered and mismatched set of abstracting/indexing services. No wonder 'Google Scholar' enjoys the degree of popularity it does – it offers a rather more convenient, one-stop option for the retrieval of scholarly literature: 'from one place, you can search across many disciplines and sources: peer-reviewed papers, theses, books, abstracts and articles, from academic publishers, professional societies, preprint repositories, universities and other scholarly organizations'. This is, of course, much more in line with our expectations these days: as Featherstone and Venn (2006) point out, thanks to the internet we can now think beyond the desktop covered with piles of opened books, journals and photocopies. Our resource base is now the screen with its own virtual desktop, on which we are offered new layout and graphics for text along with images, pop-ups and video-clips, as well as mobility between sites and, perhaps most importantly, the possibility of to-ing and fro-ing between the two modalities. Undoubtedly, there is a lesson here for information professionals, which should send them scurrying to rethink the still prevalent ghettoisation of information packages. The recent efforts made towards the implementation of federated searching at university libraries certainly represent a step in the right direction.

This is all the more important for, as Williams and Rowlands (CIBER, 2008, I, 22–3) find in their examination of the literature on the myths surrounding the digital information behaviour of the 'Google Generation', the prevalent belief that today's young people are format agnostic and have little interest in the containers that provide the context and wrapping for information, is yet to be proven and grounded in reality. Rather, they contend, future developments may turn out to be quite different: presentation will still be important, for it is expected in an online environment, in which the technology offers potentially more diverse and interesting styles of content presentation. Thus,

> ... the idea, often referred to in the online news context as shovelware, of migrating offline content online in a form as close as possible to its

original offline design will not generally work. The online world promises more and must deliver to be successful.

With this we conclude our review of the 11 characteristics of information need and the holistic approach to information needs analysis it represents. We hope that the implications from all this are crystal clear by now: only if most, preferably all relevant aspects of a need situation are considered, be it on the collective or on the individual level, can the call for effective information provision be appropriately met. However, for attaining a full understanding of an information need, it is also important that we look at the host of factors that may come into play when people set out to look for data in response to a problem perceived as calling for additional information.

4 The determinants of information needs and practices

Where information needs and practices are concerned, the rather worn-out cliché 'not everyone is the same' assumes new proportions, for the huge population of today's digital consumers demonstrates truly massive diversity. Indeed, CIBER's research programmes have all found substantial differences between consumers and their information-seeking activities in cyberspace (Nicholas et al., 2006a; Nicholas et al., 2007a; Nicholas et al., 2008b; Nicholas et al., 2008c; Nicholas et al., 2008e). Students do not behave like staff, women do not behave like men, chemists do not behave like historians and Germans do not behave like Italians, even when using exactly the same resource. Unfortunately, the availability of large amounts of usage data generated by the logs of digital libraries and resource discovery tools has made it all too easy for LIS researchers to come up with seemingly universal trends and patterns of information behaviour. After all, we are talking here of many hundreds of millions of people, for we are all ardent seekers and users of information. Inevitably, then, the population we are looking at is bound to be anything but a homogenous body. Generalising on the back of data coming from such a varied population can prove to be very misleading, not to say meaningless, even outright dangerous. Can you really clump together in an analysis, say, Nobel Prize winners with first year undergraduate students and get anything meaningful?

Obviously not, especially given that whether or not people actually get down to gathering data in response to a problem perceived as calling for additional information, and the ways and means they choose for the purpose when they do, are contingent on an amalgam of factors. Indeed, in each and every information-need situation, the idiosyncratic cognitive and emotional/ affective attributes of the person concerned combine with his/her individual perceptions of the dictates of the specific circumstances on hand to form a unique problem recognition and resolution process. The most prominent among the host of factors, which may thus come into play in an information-need situation, are related to: (1) work-roles and tasks; (2) personality traits; (3) gender; (4) age; (5) country of origin and cultural background; (6) information availability and accessibility; (7) information appetite and threshold; (8) time availability; (9) resources availability and costs.

Work-roles and tasks

As Huvila (2008) points out, basing his assertion on the mainstream research on the subject, work-roles and professional tasks have long been considered almost a standard framework for information seeking and information retrieval. Quite predictably, of course, for, as he states, work comprises a host of tightly interlinked human activities with explicitly or implicitly understood purposes, meanings and values, where individual tasks link together to form larger tasks, work flows, processes and, finally, the complete fabric of a human life-world. Indeed, people often find themselves in need of information as they tackle the vast variety of their work-role dictated goals, although the centrality of information does vary considerably for different occupations.

First of all, some jobs are simply more information demanding than others; journalism is an example of a very information-hungry profession. Second, the penalties that result from acting in the absence of information are greater in certain lines of work than in others. In fields like medicine, the consequences of acting without the benefit of the best information can indeed be grave, and in law and finance it could be incredibly costly. In research science, too, ignorance of the latest developments in a given field can lead to serious problems, perhaps not life-threatening ones, though that might happen too, but at least of the kind liable to slow down progress as well as to waste time, money and energy. Luckily, the very open, peer-evaluated information communication system of academe makes it somewhat easier to spot that a researcher has not kept up to date. A psycho-oncologist, for instance, said that more than once she had been 'called to order' by colleagues who remarked on her neglecting to cite a new article of relevance to her work 'despite its having been out for as much as three months'.

In any case, today's rushed workers, being the efficient managers of time that they now have to be, seem to have mastered the art of juggling the effort needed for obtaining information with the penalties that may result from doing without it. Not that this strategy is a novel one; rather the contrary – it is all too familiar for any parent or teacher, for we are talking here of a tactic dear to the heart of students when they have to face up to their academic information needs (Leckie, 1996; Fister, 1992). Plainly, students operate in an especially tightly regulated information environment, controlled as it is by their tutors, who give them lists of readings or websites in an attempt to make sure that they familiarise themselves with the topic being taught. This, you would think, should guarantee a certain measure of success, should it not? However, despite being told that the more reading they do, the better their grade will be, students frequently fail to read enough. They have made a trade-off between effort and risk, which must be reasonably well thought-out, because most succeed in their studies. Still, when students are asked to read in order to give a seminar presentation, they will – the penalties for ignorance now outweigh the expenditure of effort involved. Interestingly, this form of behaviour, which has long been associated mostly with young people, seems to have become the norm for everyone these days. Perhaps inevitably, for, as Williams et al. (2008) note, all in all the information behaviour of today's youngsters is basically no different from that of their elders.

The extent to which this 'cost-effective' approach to information needs is prevalent amongst today's information consumers can be demonstrated by the specific example of the academic community's differential utilisation of internet-based repositories of research results. Gaining access to the most recent research findings has been a prime concern of academics from time immemorial. In fact, as Kling and Covi (1997) observe, if scholars at times dismiss the value of journals for communicating the results of their investigations, it is because the publishing delays of one-to-three years between the time that an article is accepted and it appears in print render them purveyors of 'old news'. No wonder, then, that in many specialties, but in particular in the fast-moving fields, there is a clearly discernible preprint culture, which in the past amounted to no more than ' ... a fairly large scale, semi-private circulation of photocopies of papers in typescript before they appear in orthodox journal form ... ' (Becher, 1989, 80). These days, though, there is a much more opportune and convenient solution to the problem: e-print repositories, either discipline-focused and field-wide, of which the most visible is Ginsparg's ArXiv.org, or institutionally organised, for example, the website of BRIE – the Berkeley Roundtable on the International Economy (Kling et al., 2002; Kling, 2004).

The advantages of these electronic e-print systems are, of course, indisputable: rapid and inexpensive dissemination of research results to a broad audience, greater visibility among fellow academics, which is said to bring about greater research impact, speedy input from peers from all over the world, and enhanced features of communication, such as the inclusion of large data sets in research reports (Garner et al., 2001; Gorman, 2001; Harnad, 2003). True, authors cite a host of obstacles (excuses?) which prevent the massive migration to unrefereed publishing on the web, from fear that publishing an e-print will preclude later publication in a peer-reviewed journal, thereby jeopardising their prospects for promotions and grants, to wariness of exposing raw, unvetted work to the research community at large (Garner et al., 2001; Harnad, 2006; Kling, 2004; Nicholas et al., 2006b). However, there is really just one major point of contention concerning the dissemination of research results as e-prints posted on the internet: the scholarly value of the information to be had. After all, anyone can post research to electronic servers, which, unlike most scholarly journals, disseminate information without pre-publication, peer-review contingent selection. Lucky (2000, 263) voices the concern felt by many academics with regard to the lack of rigorous expert review of the information posted in e-print repositories when he says that in a world increasingly filled with questionable and irrelevant material, the guidance of peers regarding what is genuinely worth their time to read and examine has become more critical than ever.

Yet, if academics, quite understandably, do not as one flock to this promising-looking solution to the communication of the very latest research information, some nevertheless most definitely do; in fact, there are clearly discernible field-specific or even sub-field-specific variations in the adoption of e-print-based information dissemination systems (Cronin, 2000; Hurd, 2000; Kling, 2004; Kling and McKim, 2000). Apparently, researchers weigh up the realities of the scholarly enterprise in their particular specialisations and balance the advantages of having the information immediately available against the disadvantages of using unvetted material. Hence the differential approaches to the information opportunities offered by e-print repositories: their widespread adoption seems to be reserved to those fields where a reliance on unrefereed work is almost unavoidable, since the scientific investigations, clustering as they do around the comparatively few salient topics at the forefront of the developments, dictate a truly hurried pace of developments (Gorman, 2001; Hurd, 2000). According to Kling and McKim (2000), the divide is, therefore, between fields where researchers share unrefereed articles freely ('open flow fields') and those where peer review creates a kind of chastity belt ('restricted flow fields'). Thus, where these electronic forums suit the practices of a field, they are embraced; otherwise, they are shunned (Cronin, 2000; Kling and McKim, 2000).

Having seen how the very nature of a person's line of work can directly mould the meeting of his or her information needs, we now come to other work-related factors that may also come into play, among which experience in the job is certainly one of the first to come to mind. Obviously, the more experienced people are, the more knowledge they will have picked up in result and the less need they will have to go chasing it, although, as we have already seen, change, so characteristic of our fast-paced world, often brings about the rapid obsolescence of information. Thus, new discoveries, new technologies, political and economic factors, and legislation can render valueless – at times even dangerous – anything we hold to be true, which is the reason why people constantly need to supplement their individual base of expert knowledge by new information. Still, even when they do, the experienced among them are bound to set about locating new material and putting it to good use more competently. This, as Klahr and Simon (2001) point out, because an important method underlying all human problem-solving processes is that of analogy, which attempts to map a new problem onto one previously encountered, so that the new problem can be solved by a known procedure. Therefore, people in possession of an extensive portfolio of methods, techniques and knowledge pertaining to their professional domain can more easily recognise the best fit between a given problem and the possible alternatives for its solution.

Indeed, Herman's (2005) study of the information needs and information behaviour of university-based researchers lends support to the notion that experience does matter, precisely because of the reason just cited. Take just one example: that of the viewpoint aspect of scholars' information needs. As it has already been noted, in the social sciences and the humanities, where diverse interpretations of facts and data are possible and expected, detecting treatment of a subject from a particular viewpoint or perspective, not to mention any biased or one-sided approach, is considered by the majority of scholars a rather undemanding task. This, because academic researchers develop such a close familiarity with the literature of their areas of interest that they easily recognise the point of departure of the information under consideration: their pre-existing knowledge of their fields enables them to match the features of the source they are examining with those long known to represent various schools of thought, viewpoints, approaches and perspectives. However, considerably more of the seasoned researchers, whatever their disciplinary affiliation, find this task of critically assessing information sources easy, in all probability because with the passing of the years they grow to be more knowledgeable in their chosen fields and, at the same time, more practised in research work. By the same token, the veteran researchers are also far more inclined to seek out information presented from a certain point of view than their novice counterparts. Again, the reason seems to be the very same: as they get more and more experienced in research work, academics are bound to feel more confident that they would be able to determine whether some one-sided or biased information source represents a scientifically legitimate appreciation of the problem being considered.

Another work-related factor that may have an impact on a person's information needs and practices is seniority. First of all, senior people are simply more likely to have better resources at their disposal for acquiring and maintaining the personal information infrastructure appropriate to their needs. Thus, for example, CIBER's investigation into the information-seeking behaviour of hundreds of thousands of virtual scholars has shown that students demonstrate a much greater tendency to read online than staff, something which is partly to do with personal and generational preference, but also with the print charges students are faced with in many institutions (Nicholas et al., 2008b). However, people holding senior posts do not often enjoy at first hand the enhanced information options their position affords to them, for they show a marked inclination to delegate their information work, citing the time pressures of their position as justification. Still, the low status associated with (formal) information seeking is probably not inconsequential to their considerations, either.

No less importantly, senior people are also likely to have better access to the very latest information, which normally comes into an organisation/professional community from the top, perhaps a little less so in these disintermediated digital times. In addition, they have probably developed over the years a good informal communication network to keep them up to date, as well as to help them find information when they need it. Thus, for example, findings of the CIBER study into the information-seeking behaviour of the virtual scholar (Nicholas et al., 2008b) indicate that overall, usage of e-journals declines as academic status increases, a phenomenon which is probably traceable to the tighter professional ties seniority seems to bring about almost as a rule. After all, there really is no reason for senior people to wait for the formal publication, when getting the information much earlier, and straight from the horse's mouth, too, so to say, necessitates no more than an e-mail to a long-standing professional acquaintance.

Indeed, the importance of seniority is nowhere more apparent than in academia, where, as Cronin and McKim (1996) remind us, scholarship depends in no small measure on debating and sharing ideas, that is on the conduct of conversations amongst disciplinary peers. Thus, when scholars say 'peers' they mean just that, in the literal sense of the word! They insist on having access to their academic equals, forming for the purpose 'invisible colleges', those informal 'small societies of everybody who is anybody in each little particular specialty' (Price, 1975, 126). This may look like nothing but academic snobbery, pure and simple, but in point of fact they have very good reasons for behaving as they do. It is not that these 'invisible colleges' do not confer prestige and give their members status in the form of approbation from their peers; they certainly do. However, above all, they also effectively solve the problem of communication among scholars by reducing a large group to a small, select one of academic equals (Price, 1963), with the operative word being here 'equals'. Indeed, keeping in mind that researchers' purpose is the effective advancing of knowledge, it is crucial that they have convenient access to their professional counterparts, for information originating with seasoned people may quite often comprise considerable 'added value'. This is how a political scientist puts it:

> If you compare an article written by a well-known expert in the field with that of say, a graduate student, the latter may be more fastidious in his treatment of the subject, with the literature survey up to the very latest word on the topic, the methodology really impeccable, but it lacks the inspiration and the wide-perspective of the former ... if you're looking for originality of judgment, possibly controversial, but definitely thought provoking, you'd better choose the article written by the experienced, senior scholar.

Given this state of affairs, it is hardly surprising to find that the optimistic notion of the invisible college opening up to a much wider circle of peers, although by now technically quite unproblematic, is not accorded too enthusiastic a reception in academe, to put it mildly. In fact, as Matzat (2004) shows in his investigation of internet discussion groups, the inequalities concerning the access to unofficial academic forums have not been reduced. Thus, the hoped-for emergence of 'cyberspace colleges' (Gresham, 1994), envisaged as informal communication networks functioning as scholarly in-groups within specialisations, with crosscutting ties between academic researchers, be they low-status or high-status, from the core or the periphery, established or novice, is yet to materialise.

We come now to the last of the work-related factors, which may play a role in determining a person's information needs and practices: whether it is a solitary or team-based occupation. Workplaces, being in essence communities of similarly interested colleagues, provide plenty of opportunities for the exchange of information and ideas even for people whose job is essentially individualistic in nature, much more so for those who work in teams. Indeed, be the team formally appointed to form an official organisational unit or informally organised for *ad hoc* purposes, be it comprising equals from different areas with each contributing his/her expert knowledge, or a more opportunistic alliance of a person who comes up with an innovative idea with a knowledgeable colleague, its great advantage seems to lie to a considerable extent in the information sharing involved. The words of a biologist, an expert on animal eco-physiology, manage to capture the quintessence of it all:

> When I collaborate with a colleague, we each tackle one aspect of the problem and take responsibility for the information concerning that aspect ... Nowadays it's very difficult to work alone, to be a lone wolf. Wolves hunt in packs; that's why they succeed, because they combine forces, each contributing towards snaring their prey. That's the right way to work.

This joining of forces, at all times an apt solution for the need to bridge over the information gaps inherent to people's branching out beyond the boundaries of their own core areas of specialisation, has been assuming greater importance as professional knowledge gradually becomes limited to ever-narrowing, ever-more specialised subject areas. After all, expertise pooling, that is, depending on the knowledge of co-workers rather than seeking out the recorded information on a subject and learning new material independently, does allow for the multifaceted approach to a problem which one person cannot always offer. An archaeologist, a fervent supporter of co-operative undertakings, explains the logic behind it all:

> If I need information on a topic, which is not exactly in my line of expertise, I go to the experts and suggest that we collaborate. That's why I look for material in my own area only. I don't search for information in the subjects of the people I collaborate with, as I don't presume to have become all of a sudden an expert in their fields.

No wonder, then, that this synergetic approach to the information component of work performance has apparently been gaining a strong foothold in many organisations.

Having taken an admittedly longish look at the impact of people's work-role and job-related tasks on their information needs and behaviour (which in itself serves to underscore the centrality of this variable in information-need situations), we now proceed to another important factor which shapes a person's information consumption practices, their psychological makeup.

Personality traits

An in-depth exploration of the psychological reasons that send a person in pursuit of information, and the ways and means he/she opts for when doing so, is beyond the scope of the present undertaking. However, the influence of personality on the perception of an information need and the choice of the measures deemed necessary to meet these needs cannot possibly be ignored if we are to form a holistic picture of how information needs and practices are shaped. This, for the simple reason, pointed out by Heinström (2006): much depends on the situation, but also, to a considerable extent, on the individual concerned, for each individual is distinguished by unique and consistent patterns of thoughts, feelings and behaviour. It is perhaps best put by Wilson (2006, 666), who sums it all up in saying that people should be perceived 'not merely as driven to seek information for cognitive ends, but as living and working in social settings which create their own motivations to seek information to help satisfy largely affective needs'.

Indeed, since personality is a stable set of characteristics that manifest themselves in a consistent manner in an individual's behaviour in various situations and contexts, personality differences can lead to habitual information preferences and distinctive styles of information seeking. Therefore, personality traits are instrumental in moulding information behaviour, inasmuch as they create the possibilities, but also the boundaries, for meeting information needs (Heinström, 2005; Heinström, 2006). Thus, for example, Palmer's (1991) findings concerning the information behaviour of scientists demonstrate how dissimilarities in people's psychological attributes can account for inter-personal differences in information seeking. Those among the scientists, who fit more closely the psychological profile of innovators (open to experiences, intent on going their own way and doing their own thing) seek information widely and enthusiastically and use many different sources of information. In comparison, others, whose personality is more in line with the psychological profile of adaptors (conservative, accepting of prevalent theories, policies and paradigms, even if striving to improve them) are more controlled, methodical and systematic in their information seeking.

No wonder, then, that the role people's psychological make-up plays in determining their individual style of information seeking and gathering has been widely studied (see, for instance, Bellardo, 1985; Borgman, 1989; Heinström, 2005; Heinström, 2006; Kernan and Mojena, 1973; Palmer, 1991; Wang et al., 2000). A prime example of the insights thus gained into the matter is Heinström's (2005) exploration of the information behaviour of MA students, which, having set out to investigate the determinants of information-seeking behaviour, links information-seeking patterns to personality traits. According to her findings, the students' individual way of responding to their information need falls into three patterns – fast surfing, broad scanning and deep diving – each of which can be linked to different personality traits and approaches to studying. Thus, fast surfing, the neither very thorough, nor too arduous search mode of skimming the surface of the information wave, was found to be related to emotionality, as well as to low openness to experience and low conscientiousness. Broad scanning, the search mode characterised by the exhaustive and flexible exploration of a wide range of information sources, was found to be related to extroversion, openness and competitiveness. Deep diving, the search mode best described as diving far beneath the surface of the information flow in a controlled and structured effort to find information of the highest quality, was found to be related to a rigorous and analytical study approach as well as to openness to experience.

Information-seeking styles are indeed firmly grounded in personality traits, which cannot but bring us to the inevitable conclusion that some people are inherently better suited to efficient information work than others. Take, for example, persistence, which, in the context of information work, translates into the willingness to continue the hunt for information over a (reasonable) period of time, as well as into the readiness to try again with a new approach or strategy when initial forays have proved unsuccessful or unrewarding. By the same token, being thorough by nature is a bonus for anybody in need of information, for it brings about an inclination to search both deeply and painstakingly, truly to leave no stone unturned when searching for or evaluating information. Orderliness, too, is a quality that comes in very handy indeed where the retrieval and the storage of information are concerned, for it can aid greatly the systematic planning and execution of information tasks, from the preparation of inquiries to the keeping of records. One final example, receptiveness, the willingness to accept information from others, friends, colleagues or information officers, can also be quite influential a trait for seekers of information, inasmuch as it may be a key determinant in whether the information search is delegated or not.

Unfortunately, though, there is precious little that information professionals can do about their clients' possession or non-possession of such characteristics, for, as Heinström (2005, 244) maintains, 'the core personality is likely to remain the same across situations'. True, she does go on to say that the way the core personality,

> Is expressed and how much it influences behaviour varies according to context. We may thus perhaps be broad scanners at heart, but at times when we are stressed out and face a deadline, fast surfing is the only way out, while at other occasions a strong personal interest momentarily makes us deep divers.

Still, exerting a significant influence on personal-disposition contingent information behaviour patterns can hardly come into the province of the information professional, although effective training (especially when coupled with motivation), may obviously help in altering, at least to some extent, even deep-seated information practices.

If personality traits are thus among the least malleable determinants of information consumption, the next two factors – gender and age – are patently even less so, with all that this implies as to the extent of our ability as information professionals to change, rather than accommodate, user preferences.

Gender

The not so long ago still widely held image of the 'typical' digital information consumer as a young, IT-obsessed man is fast fading into oblivion, simply because it has little to do with reality today. Hardly an unexpected development, though, as Ono and Zavodny (2003) suggest, basing their contention on a host of studies into trends in computer and internet usage. It seems that when a new technology emerges, there are, as a rule, differences between initial users and those who wait until the technology is well established before using it. These initial adopters of new technologies are more likely to be young, male, urban, better educated and more affluent than the population as a whole, as well as not members of a racial or ethnic minority group. However, such inter-group dissimilarities tend to diminish eventually, even if not disappear altogether, as a technology spreads over time.

A case in point is gender disparity in the adoption of new information technologies, surely one of the more frequently noted dimensions of the phenomenon. The inequality between men and women in this respect has been traced to differences in their socioeconomic status (education, income and employment), which influence computer and internet accessibility; to the greater interest in computers more characteristic of men; to gender-stereotyped views about technology (men are better-able to comprehend the internet, possess more self-efficacy toward the computer and have lower levels of computer anxiety), communicated by parents, peers and teachers in the form of diverse expectations from boys and girls; and even to the possibility that the technology may be 'gendered by design', that is, embedded from its inception with a cultural association with masculine identity (Bimber, 2000; Morahan-Martin, 1998; Ono and Zavodny, 2003; Vekiri and Chronaki, 2008; Wasserman and Richmond-Abbott, 2005). Indeed, men, especially North-American, young, white, educated and fairly affluent men were the earliest to convert to electronic information-seeking practices, using the internet more frequently than females and making use of a greater variety of internet applications (Bimber, 2000; Katz and Aspden, 1997; Morahan-Martin, 1998).

No longer, though, as the substantial evidence (based on more than 6,000 interviews) gathered by the Pew Internet & American Life Project indicates. If in the mid-1990s males still accounted for 58% of the American online population, by 2000 and continuing on to today, 68% of men are internet users, compared to 66% of women. Furthermore, it is not only that these days roughly the same percentage of men and women are digital information consumers, but the total number of women in the internet population is in point of fact even slightly higher, because there are more women than men in the general US population (Fallows, 2005). In the UK, too, as Russell (2008) notes, the internet, initially a male-dominated domain, now reflects more closely the gender balance of the general population. Thus, for example, shoppers visiting e-commerce sites have increasingly moved towards the current UK population gender split of 49% males: 51% females, with a 56% male: 44%

female split in 2007. What is more, these trends seem to prevail almost universally, but at least in the so-called 'developed countries', for, as Haythornthwaite and Wellman (2002, 6) point out, by now the internet is being used ' ... by more people, in more countries ... access and use has diffused to the rest of the population and the rest of the world'.

Evidently, then, the gender gap in the use of electronically mediated information (which, in today's realities, is more often than not the kind of information we have at our disposal and, indeed, look for) is closing. Men and women alike seem to value greatly the many obvious appeals of easy, convenient and efficient access to an internet-based, borderless and almost limitless world of digital information. However, whilst women are indisputably catching up with men in their overall engagement with the online environment, once online they remain less frequent and less intense users of the internet, although this tendency appears to be decreasing over time (Ford et al., 2001; Ono and Zavodny, 2003; Wasserman and Richmond-Abbott, 2005). Moreover, their approach to the digital world remains quite distinctively 'feminine', that is, reminiscent of familiar 'womanly' traits in offline life. As Fallows (2005) finds, they seem to value more those of the internet-afforded opportunities that allow for the making and maintaining of human connections, rather than the ones, so dear to the hearts of their male counterparts, which aim at the execution of routine, everyday tasks in novel, different, more efficient, or at least more interesting ways. If and when possible, they prefer to gather information through e-mail exchanges with individuals and support groups, leaving it to men to opt, as their first choice, for searching the web. No wonder women have been found to be more satisfied and less critical with regard to such features of online information seeking as speed of delivery and navigation ease (Nicholas et al., 2007a); from their point of view, these are the more negligible features of the internet.

These gender-related differences in the ways the internet is used for acquiring information hardly come as much of a surprise: after all, common psychological knowledge holds that women cherish the sharing of information, regarding it as the key to interpersonal relationships, while, in stark contrast, men prefer to withhold information, perceiving their behaviour as holding tight the reins of power. Take, for example, the following story, related and analysed by Tannen (1991) in a *Guardian* article, which, almost 20 years after its publication, is clearly just as relevant as ever. It is the story of a couple driving to friends for dinner and having some trouble finding their way en route. The woman asks the man to stop and ask a passer-by for guidance. He refuses, insisting on finding the way without help. He persists in this manner until they are hopelessly lost. Sound familiar? Of course it does ... According to Tannen, the man does not ask for directions because that would be a sign of weakness, an admission of failure, whereas, for the woman, asking for information has no such connotations.

If the choice of the 'right' approach to the meeting of information needs thus seems to vary considerably with gender, so do, apparently, the topics of these needs. Indeed, the findings of the Pew Internet & American Life Project (Fallows, 2005) leave little room for doubt: men and women quite consistently differ as to the subject of their information queries. This is obviously a reflection, first and foremost, of the idiosyncratic interests of each group, which is why it comes as little surprise that according to Fallows (2005), sports, for example, are more likely to attract men, and cookery, women.

However, there seems to be more to it: the different life roles traditionally assigned to men and women must also play a part in bringing about a gender-specific focus in information seeking. Thus, for instance, men, responsible as they characteristically are for household maintenance, go online in greater numbers than women for getting do-it-yourself information, financial information and rating information on a product/person/service. By the same token, women, in their traditional role as the family's guardian of health and well-being, are more likely than men to use the internet to look for health and medical information, or to turn to websites to get support for health or personal problems. Thus, for example, in the aforementioned CIBER study into the use and impact of key digital health platforms and services in the UK (Nicholas et al., 2007a) women, and especially housewives/mothers, were found to be more intensive users of digital health services than men, searching for health-related information often for themselves, but also on behalf of their children and even friends. Similarly, according to a Pew Internet & American Life Project report on the use of internet health resources, 59% of online women have read up on nutrition information on the internet, compared with 43% of online men (Fox, 2005).

Having noted how the internet, reflecting, as it does, people's broader social roles and interests in the 'offline' world, perpetuates gender-related variations in the meeting of information needs, we now come to information seekers' actual behaviour in cyberspace. This, as Morahan-Martin (1998) suggests, seems to be fraught with more difficulties for women than for men. Apparently, women do indeed have problems using the internet: they do not use it effectively, testifying to problems in finding their way around the internet to the point of getting lost, in result of which they feel less competent and comfortable online (Ford and Miller, 1996; Li et al., 2001; Ybarra and Suman, 2008). Indeed, re-affirming this state of affairs, Ford et al. (2001) find a direct link between female gender and poor information retrieval performance. It is not inconceivable that even the higher use of PDFs among men compared to that among women, 37% versus 22%, found in the CIBER study into the use of scholarly journals (Nicholas et al., 2008b), can be accounted for by the latter's more hesitant utilisation of technologies: after all, HTML articles are so much easier to copy and paste.

However, as Wasserman and Richmond-Abbott (2005) point out, other studies present a more refined picture: when males and females habitually use the web for the same purpose, for example, in classrooms or workplaces, both groups are equally proficient in its use (see, for example, Aduwa-Ogiegbaen and Isah, 2005; Johnson, 2006; Martin, 1998). It is possible then, Wasserman and Richmond-Abbott (2005) argue, to attribute the variation in information-retrieval skills to historical differences between men and women with regard to the use of technology. Thus, if in the past the longer experience men have had with computers and the internet may have resulted in their possessing more IT-related know-how than women, this should change over time: the influence of gender on the skillful use of the internet should peter out. Indeed, according to the data gathered in the Pew Internet & American Life Project, 34% of men aged 65 and older are online, compared with 21% of women of that age, as opposed to 86% of women ages 18–29 who are online, compared with 80% of men that age (Fallows, 2005). Perhaps, then, change in this direction is underway as these words are written. Still, the above-noted female preference for acquiring information via social (preferably face-to-face) interaction may continue to influence adversely women's competence in the use of electronically mediated communication technologies.

Having thus attempted to unravel myth from reality as to the part played by gender in the meeting of information needs, we will now proceed to take a careful look at another item on our list of factors impacting on information consumption, which is just as much the focus of stereotyped views: age.

Age

Age is clearly seen as a major determinant of people's information needs and practices: many of the vast number of academic studies devoted to the roles accorded to information in the knowledge society explore the possibility of differential requirements and usage patterns characterising people of different ages. Not that it comes as much of a surprise: after all, given that people of different ages are at different psychosocial points in their lives, their needs, inclusive of information needs, are bound to vary. Thus, for example, as Ybarra and Suman (2008) point out, age-specific health-status and disease-risk changes give rise to typical information needs among people of a particular age-cohort, as do distinctive generational lifestyle trends (for instance, the information needs brought about by becoming care-givers for one's older parents as well as one's children obviously typify middle-aged adults only).

However, beyond the almost self-evident notion that the subject matter of people's information needs is bound to be frequently age-contingent, age also appears to be a significant factor in the decision whether a need for information is to be pursued at all and, if it is, how best to go about it. Inevitably so, of course, for the possession of the appropriate motor and cognitive abilities and skills, so many of which are age-related, is a crucial prerequisite of people's availing themselves of information. It is hardly by accident that neither the very young, nor the very old are held to be effective information searchers, not having developed yet (in the case of the former) or having lost (in the case of the latter) some of the cognitive and motor skills necessary for the purpose.

Take, for instance, the so called 'grey gap', that is, the difficulties the elderly may have with today's electronically mediated information systems, conveniently accessible and 'user friendly' as these are popularly held to be. First of all, people may become less mobile as they grow older, possibly because of physical disability, which, in the context of information seeking, can lead to their using only what is physically easy to get to. By the same token, the declining vision or loss of manual dexterity, so often afflicting aging people, can make for problems in the use of computers, keyboards or mice (Hoot and Hayslip 1983; Williamson et al., 1997). Also, since people's cognitive capabilities, response time and attention span can all be adversely affected with age, the elderly may encounter more difficulties in retrieving information (Marwick, 1999). Indeed, in the aforementioned CIBER study into the use of digital health platforms and services in the UK (Nicholas et al., 2007a) elderly people have been shown to be low users, whatever the platform (the internet, touchscreen kiosks and even digital interactive television). This state of affairs was undoubtedly brought about at least in part by age-associated difficulties: thus, for instance, kiosks, having been built for 'standing' use, did not serve very well many of the elderly, who were too frail to stand for the period of time necessary for profitable use. However, questionnaire returns suggested that there were other factors exacerbating these age inequalities. Older people were not used to living in an 'information age', in which it was common for the young to seek out their own information, and did not consider themselves to be competent in using new technology. This impacted on their use of the different systems at their disposal: on the whole, they were rather reluctant to set out to obtain information or to use available information, and even when they did, their usage was restricted – they viewed fewer web sources of health information and opened fewer kiosk pages.

Age, then, is a significant factor to contend with in the meeting of information needs, especially today, when information work is so often inextricably intertwined with the use of novel technologies. Obviously, young people, born into the realities of an electronic information world, are likely to feel more at home with innovative practices. Indeed, the data on both the USA and the UK clearly indicate that they dominate the online population, with 87% of those aged 12–17 and 46% of those aged 18–44 in the USA, as well as 97% of UK-based students aged 14–22 now using the internet (Dutton and Helsper, 2007; Jones and Fox, 2009; Lenhart et al., 2005). Still, technologically literate graduates increasingly filter through the age bands. Indeed, the biggest increase in internet use of any age group in the period between 2003 and 2005 in the UK was among those aged 55–65 and, similarly, in the USA, between 2004 and 2006, among those aged 50–64 (Fox, 2004; Dutton and Helsper, 2007).

True, as the previous research indicates, for the time being people in the older age groups are still likely to be less familiar with internet technology, less adept at the use of information technologies and to have more fears about the security of online communication and shopping. However, information seekers' age-related difficulties are not invariably insurmountable. Thus, for example, older people can take to information technology, particularly if it is relevant to their own personal needs (Blake, 1998). Academe is certainly a case in point: in areas where IT is perceived as a way of augmenting research, researchers hailing from the pre-internet era have been shown to be just as energised about the move to electronic scholarly practices as their younger colleagues (Herman, 2005). No wonder, then, that according to the Pew Internet & American Life Project surveys taken from 2006–08, larger percentages of older generations are online now than in the past, and they are doing more activities online, with the biggest increase in internet use since 2005 seen in the 70–75 year-old age group (Jones and Fox, 2009).

Indeed, electronically mediated information seeking is becoming more and more conventional, even normative among people of all ages, a process Mahe (2003) so aptly refers to as 'banalisation'. In point of fact, the reserved, if not blatantly averse attitude towards IT-based information practices, frequently encountered in the past, seems to be growingly replaced by a rather matter-of-fact approach: present-day seekers of information no longer seem to give the new technologies too much thought; but then, nobody glories in being able to breathe either, at least until something goes amiss. Unfortunately, as we have already noted, and will take up again further on, this omnipresent, increasingly skilled use of technology by no means guarantees the success of today's information seekers in their endeavours, for computer skills and information literacy are hardly one and the same. Meanwhile, we will proceed to take a look at other factors that frequently play a part in the emergence and resolution of information problems: country of origin and cultural background.

Country of origin and cultural background

People clearly display characteristics of a collective identity, which identify them as belonging to a particular place or culture. Thus, just as some individuals possess psychological characteristics that are beneficial to information seeking and gathering, the same, too, can be said about nations or cultures. A good example of this was given on the BBC TV's Business Breakfast programme. The supervisor of a computer telephone help-line, based in Milton Keynes, but servicing the whole of Europe, was asked whether the different European nations had different problems and asked different questions. She said they did, and mentioned the Germans versus the British as an example. Apparently the Germans always ask very specific questions, after having studied the manual in some detail beforehand. In comparison, the British never read their manuals and, in result, their questions are broad and unfocused. Much along the same lines, the CIBER study into digital health platforms and services in the UK (Nicholas et al., 2007a) indicates that people's geographical origins and associated cultural background may influence their information behaviour. Thus, for instance, males belonging to certain ethnic minority groups were found to be particularly reluctant to seek health information for fear of appearing vulnerable.

Indeed, Wilson (1997) puts forward the notion that differences in national cultures may affect the way members of different cultures view information acquisition and transfer. In this he builds on the work of Hofstede (1980, 1991), who proposed and tested five dimensions in which cultures might differ: *power distance,* or the acceptance of unequal distribution of power in organisations; *uncertainty avoidance,* or the extent to which a society feels threatened by uncertain situations and so tends to avoid such situations; *individualism-collectivism*; *masculinity-femininity,* or the prevalence of masculine values of materials things, etc., versus that of feminine values such as caring for others; and *long-term/short-term orientation to life.* Wilson argues that we could expect to find differences in information-seeking behaviour and information use across cultures correlating with these five dimensions. Thus, for example, cultures that score high on uncertainty avoidance, which has been shown to be associated with information seeking in individual behaviour, will be likely to foster information-seeking behaviour. To be sure, cultures that scored high on this factor in Hofstede's analysis across 50 countries, such as Norway, Sweden, Denmark, the UK, Australia, New Zealand, the USA, Canada and the Netherlands, are those with a tradition of library development.

Underscoring the theme of national culture-associated differences in information practices, a recurrent finding in the various CIBER projects evaluating the information-seeking behaviour of a number of information communities is that users hailing from different countries seek information in very different ways (Nicholas et al., 2000, Nicholas et al., 2007a and Nicholas et al., 2008b). This is what one might have expected in view of previous anecdotal evidence to this effect, but the scale of the diversity is really surprising. Take, for example, the data on the information-searching characteristics of users from different countries, as these come to light in a study of Elsevier's ScienceDirect website (www.sciencedirect.com), conducted as part of CIBER's Virtual Scholar research programme (2001–08). Thus, Germans proved to be the most 'successful' searchers in that they obtained more hits, had fewer searches resulting in zero returns and viewed the greatest number of pages in a session. In comparison, Eastern Europeans appeared to be the least 'successful' in their information seeking, recording a high percentage of zero searches and being the most likely both to view only one item in a session and to visit the site once only, something which clearly wins them the distinction of being the archetypical bouncers (Nicholas et al., 2007c; Nicholas et al., 2008b).

Where information needs and practices are concerned, the best-known national trait is probably the purported insular nature of the information seeking of US academics. Indeed, the national citation bias of American science has long been one of the more widely-held and well-documented features of academe (see, for example Møller, 1990; Braun et al., 1996; Narin and Hamilton, 1996). Apparently, American scientists have been found to be particularly prone to citing each other, hardly ever using the literature of other countries, even when the topic being studied is located in these other countries. However, very interestingly indeed, this long-established feature of scholarly information behaviour seems to be changing, at least amongst certain groups, as the CIBER studies of the British Library's learning site for young scholars and of Intute, a JISC-sponsored scholarly gateway site, amply illustrate (Nicholas et al., 2008b). In both cases US scholars were the majority user group, larger even than that of local, UK-based users, amounting, for example, to more than a third of all searches on the Intute site. Where UK education brands are concerned, there is a high demand from overseas users. This might not be surprising in itself, because, as there are no geographical boundaries in the virtual information space, scholars seek out information (and brands) internationally and the UK has a particularly good brand when it comes to education and, therefore, scholarly information. Still, the high percentage of US-registered users of British scholarly sources does seem to run counter to the time-honoured notions concerning scholarly information practices.

Thus, people's country of origin and cultural background is another factor that can and does influence the meeting of their information needs. However, the diversity does not stop here, as we are about to see.

Information availability and accessibility

These two situational factors, both of which obviously play a vital part in the shaping of information needs and practices, are inextricably intertwined. Admittedly, availability is particularly crucial: if there are no information sources or systems available it is highly unlikely that people will be able to meet their information needs; in fact, they may not attempt to do so at all. Still, availability in itself is not enough. If the information required is inaccessible, or even just a long way off, then you might as well not have it in the first place, as one participant in the JISC-funded UK National E-Books Observatory put it: 'Getting access to e-material has so far been a nightmare ... So I have not used e-books as much as I might in the future if access is easier for the user'. Thus, when we set out to explore the factors involved in the meeting of information needs, we need to consider simultaneously whether in fact a source/system is to be had at all and, if it is, how easily obtainable or reachable it is.

In our information-saturated and -centred world the availability of information rarely, if ever, poses any problems: there is an enormous array of formal and informal information resources to be had on virtually any subject under the sun, and a host of channels on hand to deliver them. Furthermore, not only does this huge body of information grow incessantly, but so do the ways and means of communicating it, with no new mode of information transmission supplanting earlier ones; indeed, the new ones actually appear to energise the old ones! Books were going to lose out to computers/video/television, but instead each piece of computer software comes with its manual, while videos and television programmes generate big publishing opportunities and a book shop (Amazon.com) is clearly one of the greatest success stories of the internet.

Neither is the accessibility of information fraught with too many difficulties in today's realities, thanks to the widespread availability of electronic and computerised means of communication and retrieval. True, the accessibility of digital information is contingent on the availability and accessibility of possibly costly resources (which, of course, is another factor to contend with where information needs and practices are concerned, a point to be taken up further on in the section on resources and costs). However, once the appropriate hardware/software/database necessary for your purposes is on hand, accessibility to information is pretty much ensured.

In ample proof of our contention that these days the accessibility of information no longer poses much of a problem, take, for example, its physical proximity aspect, which has been found to be a major factor influencing use (Allen, 1977; Zwemer, 1963). Indeed, information use and proximity go hand-in-glove; so much so that the probability of use of an information source or channel actually declines as distance increases (Allen, 1969; Slater, 1963), as *The Guardian* library discovered when they were relocated within the Farringdon Road building. Previously, the library had been situated close to Home News reporters – its biggest users. The Sports department people were on another floor and never used the library, something which was chalked up to a lack of need, as their field was very narrow and they were all enthusiasts (remembering all they needed to know). However, when the library moved to the floor on which Sports was located, they all turned into heavy users. Plainly then, proximity to sources/channels is very important indeed for seekers of information, primarily because it enables them to get information more easily and quickly, but also in view of the fact that seeing the information resource must stimulate the information appetite or jog the mind. Luckily, whereas not so long ago the only way of remaining instantly informed on a whole range of topics was to live next to the British Museum or the Bodleian Library, this no longer holds, for proximity to information is inherent to a networked environment. In fact, geographical distances have shrunk to a point where by now they have no significance at all. It is far quicker to search, say, the Library of Congress in Washington, DC, than go up a floor to the library.

Still, even in a digital environment, where you undoubtedly have your information much closer to you, it is all relative. Thus, if results of a study conducted a decade or so ago indicated that the adoption and use of electronic networks and network services by university faculty could be maximised by providing them with networked workstations as close as possible to their work area (Abels et al., 1996), in our times of laptop computers and mobile phones this would hardly suffice. People do still painstakingly build up office collections and have telephones and computers on their desks, but by now they also expect to be able to get hold of the information they need at home or even on the move, at airports, on trains and in cafés.

However, there is another aspect to accessibility: gaining access to the system once you have established physical (digital) contact with it. We have already discussed in some detail the problems of choosing the right terms with which to interrogate the system and the difficulties of grappling with soft subject vocabularies. In addition, coming to grips with the search interfaces can be quite challenging too – and allegedly user-friendly, menu-driven services can create as many difficulties as command-driven ones. True, if the will is there and the drive for information sufficiently strong, people will find a way to overcome any external and internal access problems they encounter. They will conquer unfriendly search interfaces, keep trying to go online when they get 'invalid password' messages, even leave their desks and stand in queues. MPs' Research Assistants at the House of Commons were subject to all this and yet they still searched the systems with some alacrity (Nicholas, 1995).

Forunately, it seems that extending such an effort is rarely perceived as necessary any more. Indeed, as the CIBER studies into the use of various e-information platforms, most notably in the areas of health (Nicholas et al., 2007a), scholarly journals (Nicholas et al., 2008b) and scholarly books (Rowlands et al., 2007) find time and time again, today's information seekers baulk at site menus, complicated interfaces and myriad search options. After all, they have a much 'better' option: search engines, seen (whether rightly or wrongly) as offering the prospect of trouble-free, targeted and direct access to a massive choice of material, and all this at the price of keying in a word or two.

Although it can still happen that a person has no access to a source or system. Obviously, lack of the funds required to pay for information may create an almost insurmountable obstacle, a point we will return to later on. Also, with open-access publishing still to be fully realised, there are people, labelled the disenfranchised (by librarians) and turn-aways or noise (by publishers), who can access subscription services, but do not have full-text access to the infor-mation therein. However, at times the inability to gain access to information is not so much superimposed on a person as perceived to be such. Thus, for example, feeling uncomfortable about approaching an individual higher on the totem pole in some organisation or community can erect a very real stumbling block for an individual intent on meeting an information need, as one fledgling academic researcher puts it:

> … you can't just write an e-mail to an expert and ask him! Even if you can locate his e-mail, you can't just land on him out of the blue, can you? He may not answer you at all, but even if he does, you can't be sure that you'll understand his reply and then, will you go on nagging him? It's not as if you know him personally, is it?

Add to this the fact that today's 'managerial cultures' often try to prevent information reaching subordinates and it becomes crystal clear that gaining access to information may occasionally take more than overcoming technical or even financial hitches.

By the same token, people may refrain from attempting to meet their information needs because they feel humbled and intimidated by an impress-ive information source or system. A case in point is the way some people go about tackling their health problems, as results of the study into the use and impact of key digital health platforms and services in the UK (Nicholas et al., 2007a) clearly indicate. There are patients, predominantly, but not exclusively, elderly and lower socio-economically grouped women, who seem to regard the health professional as the keeper of health information. Thus, holding the view that their GP or nurse will tell them all they need to know, they demonstrate a marked reluctance to seek additional information on their own. Another manifestation of information search avoidance behaviour, which stems from conceiving information services as threatening, is the phenomenon of library anxiety (Mellon, 1986; 1988). Thus, subjective perceptions of the huge size of the library, its complicated organisation and, perhaps primarily, its preoccupied, rude, inconsiderate and discourteous staff, add up to anxiety-inducing feelings of embarrassing incompetence, which is very likely indeed to prevent use.

All in all, though, these days neither the availability nor the accessibility of information present too challenging problems for seekers of information. Indeed, we seem to have reached the ultimate pinnacle of availability and accessibility in that nowadays information chases the consumer, rather than vice versa. As Noam (1997) observes, when information was scarce and hard to move, and reproduction expensive and restricted, people had to go to the information, wherever it was located. However, now that electronic information channels are increasingly powerful in storage, broad ranging in content and efficient in delivery, more often than not it is the other way round; plainly, the information flow has changed its direction. Indeed, Sack (1986) and Lancaster and Sandore (1997), thinking along the same lines, suggest we change our perspective: instead of viewing the universe in terms of libraries centrally located for users, we need to think in terms of each user being surrounded by information and information-accessing opportunities. The question is, of course, how this easily obtainable abundance of information affects the way we go about meeting our information needs, a point we will look into next.

Information appetite and threshold

With more information thus being delivered, more quickly, from more platforms, at more potential consumers, obviously even the most insatiable of information consumers cannot complain. True, the flow of information is more regulated than it would seem at first glance, for, as McCreadie and Rice (1999) point out, information is truly accessible only if it is intelligible to the potential user. Since this intelligibility necessitates mastery to the relevant degree of the contextual subject domain, on the one hand, and an appropriate level of intelligence, on the other, the extent of people's ability to take on-board information is necessarily kept under control. Indeed, their information threshold varies considerably with their cognitive capacity and individual knowledge base. Still, as we have already seen, these days people are far more likely to have a surfeit of information than to find themselves short of it, a state of affairs they regard as unproblematic (Nicholas et al., 2008b), if not eminently satisfactory (Herman, 2005).

However, this information affluence does have its downsides, although the much-cited danger of getting buried in the information mire is not one of them. As we noted in the section on the quantity aspect of an information need, the menace of 'information explosion', and its dreaded consequence, 'information overload' simply never materialised. People may very well be confronted still by the all-too-familiar situation described by a City of London worker:

> I come into the office in the morning and there are reams of fax paper from all over the world. I go to my answering machine to pick up my calls, and then I turn to my computer and find 72 messages in my electronic mail.
>
> (Williams, 1993)

Nevertheless, far from being beleaguered by a threat of an information avalanche swamping them, today's information consumers know very well indeed how to protect themselves from the information tidal wave. Having masterminded the intricacies of coping with the ever-growing abundance of information all around them, they sample and select, usually using what is easiest and what is closest to hand, and not what is necessarily best or most appropriate; in any case, satisficers that they are (Savolainen, 2007), they stop their information seeking after finding material that seems 'good enough'. They also deliberately ignore what they do not deem to be strictly necessary or relevant, frequently make do with reading information surrogates – book blurbs and reviews, abstracts and summaries of documents (Nicholas et al., 2007d) – and even information gamble, taking a chance on what comes to hand (say, the first item among thousands of search engine-generated items).

If 'drowning in a sea of information' is no longer the sword of Damocles forever hanging over our heads, then what can possibly be seen as a drawback of today's information opulence? First of all, to reiterate a point we have already discussed in some detail, people find it quite hard to curb their information appetites. At best, just like children let loose in a sweet shop, they will gorge themselves far beyond the true limits of their actual needs at the sight of so much free information of potential interest. At worst, the notion of an almost unlimited availability and accessibility of information tempts their information palates to an extent that it renders the possibility of effective information consumption unrealistic. Thus, rather than reading, users manifest the aforementioned squirreling behaviour, storing information for a later date, which never comes because of a shortage of time and the amount of squirreling that has been done.

Another negative aspect of living in our lavish digital information environment is that the ability to enjoy its benefits is reserved for the 'information haves', those who are in possession of three basic prerequisites, all of which we have already noted and will return to further on: accessibility to ICT-based infrastructures, computer prowess and information competencies. Unfortunately, although, as we have seen, ever-wider segments of the population do indeed have convenient internet access and diligently hone their expertise in skilled use of technology through constant use, it does not mean that they are proficient in information work, too. True, since so much of the information that reaches us is electronically mediated, computer literacy and information literacy do go hand in hand, but they are definitely not one and the same (although frequently taken to be). Indeed, with all that nowadays it is commonly held that we have all become librarians (as long as we have Google at our disposal), it is far from being the case, as the recent extensive study into the information behaviour of the Google Generation (Williams et al., 2008) amply proves.

Whilst much popular writing extols young people's ostensible competence with ITCs, in fact their information literacy has not improved with their constant exposure to technology. Rather the contrary: their apparent facility with computers disguises some worrying underlying problems. They search the web with a speed that can only mean that little time is spent in evaluating information, either for relevance, accuracy or authority; they have a poor understanding of their information needs and, therefore, find it difficult to develop effective search strategies, exhibiting instead a strong preference for expressing themselves in natural language; and, when faced with a long list of search hits, they find it difficult to assess the relevance of the materials presented and often print off pages with no more than a perfunctory glance at them. As Williams et al. (2008) conclude, if people are to really avail themselves of the benefits of living in an information-rich world, information literacy must appear much higher on society's list of priorities.

It seems, then, that in the electronic age concerns over information availability and accessibility have been replaced by concerns over our ability to take on board the wealth of information surrounding us. This ability of ours is greatly dependent, in its turn, on time – the time it takes to access and deal with the information at our disposal (this is where the constraints of time and availability/accessibility merge). Time availability must be, then, the next point on the agenda in our discussion of the factors shaping information needs and practices.

Time availability

As Savolainen (2006) points out, time is one of the main contextual factors of information seeking, in that it usually posits a major constraint to information consumption. This is all the more so today, when most people live in a hothouse environment, working and playing harder and faster, in an attempt to do more within the unalterable time framework of the 24 hours-long day. In direct consequence, more often than not time is in short supply for accomplishing any undertaking, inclusive of the information seeking evermore frequently required for its successful conclusion. It all depends on the deadline for which a given task has to be completed or the time for which a pursuit remains relevant; this sets the time limit within which information has to be gathered and used. Thus, for example, in his study of the information-seeking habits of humanities graduate student researchers, Barrett (2005) found that their decisions to concentrate more on writing up projects than researching them were often triggered by the appearance of defence deadlines on the horizon. 'The clock ran out', as one of his interviewees put it, and another added: 'a lot of the time we start writing it up when the deadline approaches, whether we're finished or not'.

Still, availability and scarcity of time are relative concepts, very much contingent on people's idiosyncratic circumstances. So much so that, as Savolainen (2006) contends, the experience of information overload may be seen as based on the almost wholly subjective judgment that there is too much potentially useful information to be accessed within too short a period of time. Thus, for example, journalists may have as much time in the day as academics, but the information seeking of the former, unlike that of the latter, is limited by – and presses up against – the daily deadlines of the newspaper. Not that time pressures are foreign to research work, either; rather to the contrary, as we have seen in the course of our discussion here.

Obviously not, for even those scholars who already boast the much-coveted professional reputation essential to survival in academe are still anxious to do everything in their power to safeguard, maintain and enhance their achievement by publishing as much as possible, as quickly as possible. It is all too easy to become a 'has been' in one's field. In result, as one seasoned academic put it: ' ... there's always an element of immediacy in research work ... we too work in an emergency room, only it's a virtual one, existing only in our heads'. However, academics, too, vary as to the extent to which time constraints affect their daily work. In fact, they demonstrate perceptible discipline- and seniority-associated differences regarding the matter.

It is easily understood how this comes about, for when the sought-after rapid pace of progress is of overriding importance, time is much more at the forefront of a researcher's concerns. Thus, in the fast-moving, competitive fields, where there is high mutual visibility of work conducted by one's peers (Kling, 2004), researchers, anxious 'to win first place in a sprint to the finishing post', as Becher (1989, 84) so aptly phrases it, work under considerable time pressure. This is far from being the case in those specialties where competition tends to be less prevalent, because there is not as much of an overlap of topics and little consequent concern with priority: the need for a brisk work tempo is, therefore, nowhere near as vital and, in direct consequence, the scarcity of time is less anxiety-inducing. By the same token, the stage of career a scholar has reached influences his or her perceptions of the time pressures involved in achieving demonstrable results (Wiberley and Jones, 2000). Indeed, Herman's (2005) findings re-affirm one of the better-known features of academic life, according to which across all disciplines the novice researchers, for whom the struggle to attain promotion or tenure is a prime consideration, are more inclined than their senior colleagues to see time constraints as significant factors in shaping and focusing their research projects.

In any case, with time being such a scarce resource, people are quite intent on accomplishing their goals as effectively as possible, and information seeking is no exception. No wonder, then, that today's consumers look above all for efficiency and time-saving qualities in their information practices: busy people that they are, they are not very inclined to spend a minute longer than absolutely necessary on the meeting of their information needs. It is, of course, the very reason why they appreciate so greatly the host of electronic information technologies at their disposal: the searchability of digital databases, the speed of word processing and the convenience of remote access to full-text material add up to greater effectiveness of information work and, therefore, of almost everything we do, for, as we have repeatedly emphasised, information is now an inseparable component of every aspect of life and living. Thus, for example, the massive growth in e-retail sales only came about when better utilisation of technology made the process of e-shopping slicker, more efficient and less time-consuming (Russell, 2008). If further proof is necessary that IT is seen as the key to efficiency, suffice to remember that even the fast-disappearing breed of technophobes was receptive enough to technology, as long as it meant savings in time or effort. Indeed, even humanities researchers, who took much longer to warm up to the wonders of technology, nevertheless made productive use of those new tools that were deemed the most appropriate for meeting an information need (Wiberley and Jones, 1989; 2000; Lehman and Renfro, 1992).

Unfortunately, although computerised systems undoubtedly aid seekers of information in overcoming the time barrier, the gain is soon lost, for people relentlessly clamour for ever-quicker solutions to their information problems. They want (or are perceived to want) 'better' systems or channels, which respond even more rapidly and provide information 'bites' that can be consumed even more swiftly (Twitter.com – the latest manifestation of a current awareness service, limits the messages to 140 characters each). Since the only systems or channels that will be used are those that measure up to people's expectations, everything moves relentlessly faster and faster. This, in its turn, serves to perpetuate, if not accelerate the above-noted endemic form of information seeking we have dubbed 'power browsing'. As it emerges again and again from CIBER's various research projects, people 'feed for information' horizontally through sites, titles, contents pages and abstracts in pursuit of quick wins, with scarcely any opportunity to digest the information encountered. Thus, courtesy of today's faster-than-fast information opportunities, consumers, smitten with the prospect of meeting their information needs quickly and easily, happily exchange knee-jerk reactions for considered ones in their information-seeking practices. Still, whichever way they choose to go about their information seeking, it is greatly dependent on the last factor on our list of the determinants of information consumption: resources availability and costs.

Resources availability and costs

The central role played by information in today's knowledge-based world has brought to the fore the threat of potential inequalities among people, communities, organisations and states unable to afford the acquisition of the technologies through which information and knowledge are generated and disseminated (Burkett, 2000). Indeed, a salient feature of contemporary developed nations is a strong commitment to narrowing the digital divide in society. Thus, as

Macgregor (2005) points out, governments across the globe inject vast funds directly, or indirectly, into large information creation and digitisation projects and make freely available web-based value-added reports, documents, legislation, health advice, community information and news coverage. The afore-mentioned roll-out of the UK digital health services programme is a case in point (Nicholas et al., 2007a). Aimed at making health information accessible to the general public, large segments of which had been generally starved of such information, the Department of Health (DoH)'s initiative was meant to result in the provision of widely accessible digital health information and advice services, this through various platforms utilising the rapidly emerging ICTs: the web, touch-screen kiosks and digital interactive television.

Concurrently, governments, at least in the developed countries, make every effort to ensure that every citizen has the resources and skills necessary to access and use digital information. Thus, for example, one of US President Barack Obama's first initiatives upon taking office was the extension of broad-band internet service to rural and underserved areas at a cost of billions, with the express purpose of expanding the information superhighway to every corner of the land. This, according to the *New York Times*, will 'give local businesses an electronic edge' and offer residents 'a dazzling array of services like online health care and virtual college courses' (Herszenhorn, 2009). Much along the same lines, the Israeli Government, explicitly seeking 'to improve the quality of life in the country's outlying communities', has started and strongly supports the 'computer for every child' project (www.maly.co.il), which, in point of fact, is directed at a far wider range of population groups, from early childhood to golden-agers. These are but a few random examples, for municipalities through-out the world provide free wireless access to promote information-seeking behaviour.

The developments in this direction are obviously of great benefit for today's information-hungry people, although, as Burkett (2000) suggests, telecommunica-tions may be able to overcome all the major technical barriers preventing access to information, but technology will never address the human psycho-social, emotional and cultural dimensions of communication and interaction, without which the challenges of equity cannot be fully met. Be that as it may, what is more of our concern here is that today's information-enfranchised general public have at their disposal a host of information systems and channels at a considerably lower cost than ever before. Gone are the days when the fat information pipes were reserved for academe or for undertakings where infor-mation was seen as having a direct and immediate financial return, such as stockbroking. Indeed, if in the past organisations were quite likely to demon-strate an aversion to spending money on information, this is clearly no longer the case. Thus, for example, up until a few years ago UK Social Services departments went without libraries and information systems, despite having budgets – admittedly tight ones – stretching into millions of pounds. Not any more, though: it may have been political and economic pressures, or perhaps a real ongoing need for information for successful work performance, but the culture has completely changed. These days putting new field social workers on the streets is no longer held to be a higher priority than providing the existing ones with facilities for improving their access to information.

True, where the financial aspects of information provision are concerned, we find ourselves in wholly new (and rather absurd) circumstances, as Nicholas et al. (2003b, 30) point out: ' ... it is not the information or content providers that are making anything out of digital information provision but the telecoms companies ... ' (of course, it is the ISPs now). 'Could you imagine a world in which supermarkets gave their produce away for free and the councils charged you for access to the roads that led to the supermarkets? No, well that is the situation we have in cyberspace.' It is hardly surprising, then, that as Macgregor (2005, 18) contends,

> ... the expansion of information over the past decade or so has entirely extricated information from the concept of value ... [the] existing user perception [is] that the creation of information incurs no costs and that high-quality information should always be available for free.

Indeed so. Take, for example, the case of academics: as Herman's (2005) findings indicate, with all that researchers expect very swift and prompt delivery of information, only a scant minority of them (one-fifth of the participants in her study) are prepared to spend any of their hard-to-come-by research money on speeding up the process of obtaining some necessary information.

It may thus run contrary to expectations, but while the web offers a vast array of information sources at no direct cost, and even in academic publishing there is an Open Access crusade (Suber, 2007), information does not invariably come free, especially since computers, printers, modems, telephone lines and rental charges cost money. Still, from the point of view of the individual information consumer, circumstances have clearly changed considerably for the better. First of all, the expenses involved in computerisation and networking have been steadily and markedly declining for quite a few years now. Also, as we have just seen, the expenditure required for the acquisition of both equipment and content is often subsidised. All in all, then, not only do seekers of information now have at their disposal mobile, real-time and interactive systems in the home, instead of yesteryear's static, archival systems in public or work places, but these systems are also much more affordable, compared with their predecessors.

As this chapter has highlighted, each and every information need situation is shaped by an amalgam of personal and situational factors, which coalesce to form a unique problem recognition and resolution process. This, obviously, makes for the great variability and dynamic nature of the data, which sent the information professionals of yore scurrying to the safe haven of traditional need (user) survey-generated stereotypes of user behaviour. True, it is questionable whether, outside research science, any of these stereotypes existed, but they certainly made librarians' lives so much easier. Fortunately, today there is no reason to go on shying away from studying need and information-seeking behaviour. First of all, as people's information-seeking activities mostly take place in cyberspace, we are able to follow their footsteps more closely than ever before, gaining in the process unprecedented insights into the ways in which their needs and coping tactics differ. No less importantly, we have at our disposal the know-how, as well as the ways and means to bring about a fundamental transformation in the defunct 'one size fits all' policy of the past, providing instead custom-made, personal information infrastructures, tailored to the distinctive needs of individuals.

5   Collecting the data

Having seen the conceptual perspective-driven, but very much field-work based tenets of the individual centred approach to the assessment of an information need offered here, we now turn to the practicalities of its application. More specifically, to the various data-capture methods available, for methods determine results, and this is never truer than in the case of information needs assessments, which probe beneath the visible surface of people's actual behaviour. Indeed, the methods utilised for collecting the data are a crucial measure of the quality and worth of the picture of need with which we are presented. Therefore, a basic understanding of these methods is of considerable benefit to anyone interested in the significance of a particular information needs exploration: it provides the ability to judge some information on the merits of the validity and reliability of the process by which it was obtained. In today's information-conscious world, developing this ability is, of course, absolutely crucial, which is why it is, as it should be, at the heart of any information literacy or digital literacy instruction programme. Obviously, where information professionals are concerned, the importance of familiarising themselves with the available data-collection methods and techniques goes beyond that: after all, being the ones who take decisions, determine policies and act on the basis of information needs studies, they have to be well aware of the value of the data they build upon. As they are also the ones who initiate and plan, at times even carry out, needs/consumer studies, understanding the ins and outs of the methods and techniques appropriate for the purpose enables them to choose wisely when they embark on such ventures.

True, it must be noted here, deciding on the appropriate data-collection method is not always a straightforward process of weighing up the inherent advantages and disadvantages of a method for addressing a given research question. Other considerations inevitably come into play, too: costs, obviously, but also the information community to be investigated (there is little chance of getting, say, busy practitioners like journalists, politicians or lawyers to subject themselves to the kind of examination that students may agree to – diaries, for instance). Thus, sometimes there is little choice but to accept what is to hand and/or what is cheap. To complicate things even further, the use of different methodological approaches (methods triangulation) is, as we have already noted, an inescapable imperative if we are to achieve the powerful, holistic and comprehensive portrayal of people's information needs for which we aim. This, because such methodological pluralism is the only way to counterbalance the flaws and weaknesses inherent to any given method with the strengths of others. It is particularly important to combine both qualitative and quantitative methods when setting out to determine people's information needs: the former serves exceptionally well for capturing what individuals' information-related experiences mean to them, in their own terms and on their home turf, too, whilst the latter makes it possible to establish the extent to which the insights thus derived are generalisable to a wider population.

All this clearly adds up to a very real need for professionals to acquire a good understanding of the various data-collection methods available for use, although, as we have seen, a basic appreciation of these methods should not come amiss to lay people either, seeing that we are all librarians now ... This chapter sets out, then, to lay the foundations for a working knowledge of the key data-collection methods: (1) interviews, which, held as they are to be the most appropriate for unearthing data on information needs, are given a considerably more expansive treatment; (2) observation; (3) diaries; (4) questionnaires; (5) citation analyses; (6) web log analyses.

Interviews

Considered the 'bread and butter' of qualitative evaluation and an important source of qualitative data, interviews are uniquely suitable for probing beneath the surface in order to solicit detail and provide a holistic understanding of individual points of view (Bawden, 1990). As such, they are particularly suited to gathering data on information needs, which, by definition, refer to imprecise, far from concrete and not easily definable notions. They can probe for both qualitative and quantitative data, throw up unexpected findings, which were not asked about, and, unlike other methods, allow for studying not only users, but also non-users. Indeed, where information need investigation methods are concerned, the interview is undeniably the real star. It is very much a case of horses for courses. If need is the horse then the interview is the course, offering, as it does, a fuller, richer and possibly more trustworthy source of data than all the rest. With the people interviewed given the opportunity for musing out loud on needs, wants, requirements, practices and routines, as well as for voicing concerns, the evidence gathered certainly holds the potential for providing a true-to-life, multifaceted snapshot of information needs and their role in triggering information behaviour.

Another great advantage of interviews, at least from the point of view of researchers needing to procure data from people, is that with interviews high response rates can be obtained. In fact, it may be the only method for getting information from some people, especially high-status ones. To be sure, if persuading people to participate in surveys is far from being an easy task in general, getting VIPs or even busy practitioners to fill in questionnaires is often simply doomed to failure. There can be, however, much less of a problem obtaining their agreement to be interviewed, especially if it is over lunch or coffee. A student of one of the authors, interested in soap operas, discovered this for herself when she managed to obtain interviews with the editors of Neighbours, Coronation Street and Brookside. The only problem that remains, then, is pinning people down to a time to interview them, something which sounds easy, but frequently, as it turns out, is not.

There are many types of interview: the street/shopping mall interview, so liked by polling organisations and market research companies, which is really nothing more than a spoken questionnaire; the telephone interview; the group interview, including the very fashionable focus group; and the one best-suited for our purpose here – the face-to-face, open-ended, in-depth interview.

The face-to-face, open-ended, in-depth interview

Characterised by their open, wide-ranging questions and their loose, flexible and unstructured format, interviews belonging to this category are particularly useful for information needs evaluation, affording as they do plenty of opportunities to question, explain and reflect. Indeed, they often yield genuinely new and authentic data: facts, certainly, but also attitudes, opinions and examples. The observational opportunities, which are, of course, part and parcel of the face-to-face interview situation, serve to further enhance the rich data thus obtained. This is especially the case when the interview takes place in the interviewee's natural surroundings, as it should. Stepping into someone's office, workspace or home can double the researcher's information, treble his/her insight. The non-verbal communication component of interviews can also serve to complement the picture, indicating, for instance, how strongly people believe in what they are saying.

Crucially, too, the data come in the interviewees' own words. This is quite an advantage over other research techniques, most notably questionnaires, which too often shoehorn individuals into forms of words devised by the researcher. It is not only that users might never have expressed themselves as they do in reply to the questions posed to them, but, all too often, the researcher puts words in the mouths of the people being interrogated and then proceeds to describe what 'they' said; that is just a little incestuous. Not so here: with the interviewees allowed to express freely, and in their own terms, what they consider to be the important issues, the intrusion of an unwanted or unwarranted bias is avoided. Indeed, the real gems to be quarried by the method are forms of words, expressions and quotes. They are the diamonds in this methodological mine.

Thus, the greatest plus of the open-ended, in-depth interview is the space people are given to air their views as they see fit, without the constraints characterising other, more rigidly structured data-collection methods. However, this should not be taken to mean that there are no real rules to interviewing. Quite the opposite, in fact: not only are there rules, but they have to be adhered to meticulously if the interview is not to become stilted, boring, uncomfortable and, inevitably, unproductive. True, there are no prescribed or familiar lines of questioning – certainly not the sort that lend themselves to the satisfied/unsatisfied formula so beloved of quantitative researchers. In fact, whilst the structured interview, with a long list of quite specific questions, provides a high degree of security and confidence (a methodological comfort blanket), the open-ended interview poses the challenge of sustaining a long conversation around a very general opening line, with the momentum kept going with the use of gentle prompts. Indeed, the ratio of interviewer-to-interviewee contribution should be 10:90, at most 20:80 in the case of reticent interviewees or non-users, where more prompting might be needed.

Obviously, then, much depends on the interviewer, for although with all interviews the presence of the researcher of necessity affects what is said and done, in the open-ended, unstructured interview, it must be tenfold so. The interviewer, required to probe for data in unfamiliar territory outside his/her control, asking (often personal) questions for which there are no stereotypical responses and relying on the dynamics of the interview process to reveal as much as possible, has to tread particularly carefully – hence the need for playing by the rules.

First of all, since the researcher is going into the fray with a small number of broad questions and relying on the dynamics of the interview process to reveal as much as possible, it is absolutely essential that the people being interviewed should feel free to offer any observations and talk in general terms about the subject under discussion. This is contingent on creating a relaxed atmosphere throughout the interview, although that is clearly easier said than done. Undesirable formality and artificiality can creep in despite the interviewer's best efforts, especially when the interviewee is reserved or simply taciturn. Also, the need for some sort of recording apparatus, whether visible or not, may serve as an unfortunate reminder of the formalities involved, as does the fact that interviewees are well aware that they have been invited for a purpose. Still, small talk at the beginning of the interview usually helps to establish rapport and if the interviewer is genuinely interested, curious and understanding, the coveted easy mood is attainable.

Sometimes, though, the hoped-for relaxed, informal atmosphere cannot be established because of a presumed shortage of time on the part of the interviewee. Now, time is an important part of the method's success; so much so that reducing the interview length is, as a rule, quite inadvisable. Needs interviews are typically of around 30–60 minutes long, but they can last 90 minutes if the interviewee is particularly talkative, or is known to the interviewer. Conversely, they can be completed in 15–20 minutes, if a person's time or patience is limited, or where the interview pertains to a single search query. Thus, where there is a shortage of time (real or assumed), the interviewer may have to forgo the use of the customary techniques for enlisting the interviewee's good will and readiness to co-operate. A valuable 'shortcut' then would be to pose a neutral, balloon-type question, such as: 'The authority/

validity of information has merited a lot of discussion recently; what is your opinion on this?' This has an obvious value of 'helping' those for whom information plays a small part in their priorities to declare as much, while still permitting enthusiasts to put their case with relish. A similar approach is to place before the user an item of relevance in the news, say, an article on 'dumbing down', and build a line of questioning around it. This requires some preparation, but newspapers provide an excellent source of questions. However, when the normal preliminaries do indeed have to be dispensed with and the points be made very quickly, the interviewer sometimes resorts to an involuntary adoption of a question and answer-type formal interview, in an attempt to avoid interviewees thinking the exercise is a mere 'chat' and, as such, something of a time waster. This, obviously, may come at the expense of the stress-free atmosphere so vital for the success of the interview.

Another imperative of interviewing is the onus on the researchers never to convey, whether intentionally or unintentionally, the impression that they are promoting the commodity, system or idea (information in our case) about which they are enquiring. If they do, they will be typecast and the interviewee might well try to please, or, in the case of non-users, either lie or shut-up completely. One tried and proven way of overcoming the problem is starting by questioning the interviewees about a relevant aspect of their lives, their job, for instance, and the problems they are experiencing in this context. Once users find out the questions are about them and not about the researcher (or his/her systems), profitable lines of communication open out.

Moreover, setting things in motion by requesting people to recount their experiences in the context of a specific activity – on a typical day, perhaps – inclusive of the problems or difficulties involved, often spontaneously leads to a discussion of past and present information needs and behaviour. Thus, although statements concerning information need are seldom on the tip of the tongue or crafted with well-chosen prose, the information component of an activity, largely of an implicit nature as it is, becomes more easily retrievable to consciousness. In fact, virtually everything turns out to have information needs and information-seeking connotations. Sources of information and systems are mentioned as a natural part of the discussion, with anecdotes, cases and examples alerting the interviewer to characteristics of information needs and practices. True, the flow of information may at times be staunched by problems of privacy and confidentiality. Thus, discussing e-mail (to whom? how often? why?) may appear intrusive, as it would with 'conventional' mail. Also, in some lines of work people are often quite reluctant to discuss what they are doing. For example, journalists, analysts or politicians are not noted for their openness concerning the material on which they are currently working. Fortunately, reassuring participants that their privacy would be scrupulously safeguarded often suffices to solve the problem and it also goes a long way towards setting the tone of the interview.

Even when the discussion ignites readily and flows without restraint throughout the interview, with the interviewees coming forward with information willingly enough, probing remains an essential part of an open-ended interview. How else can the researcher encourage further communication, show interest and make a direct bid for more information? Probing questions are particularly important for following up an interviewee's responses, for getting to the depth and detail of information required. Obviously, they are also instrumental for overcoming the problem of incomplete replies, for participants are understandably unable always to give complete accounts of their information need. It is noticeable how many interviewees apologise for not remembering more, saying something like: 'I use the internet much more than I've described ... I can't remember any examples ... I'm afraid I've got a poor short term memory'.

A vital component of the interview situation such probing questions may be, then, but they must be asked sensitively to avoid discomforting the interviewee. What is required from the interviewer is motivation and direction, but without giving any signs that some responses are more acceptable than others (otherwise it is back to the pitfalls of conveying the impression that the researcher is promoting the commodity, system or idea under consideration). Postural signs of interest and acceptance – like nodding of the head – have a big role to play, especially in noisy workplaces. Brief assertions of understanding and interest, assenting comments like, 'I see', 'um-hm', can also help things along, especially for indicating that the answer is on the right lines, but has not been answered fully. It is quite possible, however, to go further and be rather more directional, whilst still retaining neutrality, as in: 'In what way were your needs not met?' Silence can also be an effective – though sometimes disconcerting – probe, encouraging the interviewee to contribute more. Mirroring the thoughts of the interviewee can be very useful too. The process allows interviewees to see what they said more clearly and to make modifications if their words were interpreted mistakenly or if they were hurried into saying the wrong thing.

Apparently, then, no detail concerning the interview is small enough or marginal enough to safely go unnoticed. Take, for example, the appropriate method for capturing the data. The technique used for the purpose – notebook or recording device (or both) – can prove to be central for the success of the open-ended interview.

Obviously, if the real data diamonds – the quotes – are to be captured, then some recording is necessary. Also, if an interview session is being recorded, then the interviewee is freer to think about the next question or interact with the interviewee. However, the technique does not come without some drawbacks. First of all, interviews are intrusive anyway; recording them may make them seem doubly so (an interviewee of one of the authors was so wary of being recorded, that he recorded the interview too). Also, when people are conscious of the fact that every word they utter is being captured for further use, they might feel very uncomfortable indeed and, in consequence, their responses might become stilted or evasive. In fact, some interviewees – especially non-users – might not respond at all, in the case of the latter, frequently because of a sense of failure, which they are not keen to 'broadcast'. Moreover, although this is certainly the least of the problems that may arise, recording can prove a distraction in an interview situation (especially if a tape needs changing). A pocket memo recorder, with a lapel microphone, which could also be detached and placed on a holder on a table, can make recording rather more discreet. A final point related to recording, which, however, is bound to be of real concern for the researcher, is that transcription times can be horrendous (four-to-six hours for each one-hour interview). This is especially problematic when several hundred interviews are being conducted. However, with rapid developments in voice-recognition software, this last problem will, one hopes, fade away.

The big advantage of a notebook, as opposed to a recording device, is that it is not so obtrusive. Also, it can be taken out quickly (for the impromptu interview) and, since the researcher tends to do some editing as he/she goes along, less typing is involved later. People are also generally impressed by the fact that something they said was so important as to warrant the interviewer taking it down. So much so, that it is advisable to take notes even during recorded interviews, to add a degree of authority to the respondents' answers; notes come in very handy indeed as a back-up in case of poor-quality recording, too.

Very interestingly indeed, with all the difficulties that may present themselves in an interview situation, interviewees often see it as an enjoyable experience. They find the questioning – and the periods of reflection that go with it – intriguing and stimulating, and often come out of the interview feeling that they have been involved in an (information) counselling session. Wanting to know how they did or talk about the interview afterwards is a typical reaction. Indeed, when the pressure of being recorded and being 'formally' interviewed comes to an end, many interviewees open up and provide additional valuable information, generally about the wider issues – the way information technology has changed their workplace, for instance.

However, this, no less than the quality of the evidence obtained, depends to a considerable measure on the interviewer's conduct of the interview. Indeed, with all that the researcher should take a back seat in the course of the interview, allowing the interviewees to lead the way and go wherever they want to, he/she needs to be very much in control of the data-mining process underway. This is best done through the use of the need framework proposed here, not so much as an interview schedule, but more as a template through which data can be fed and evaluated. The framework draws the interviewer's attention to the data he/she needs and the relevance of the data being volunteered; it acts as a filter, a place to collect and classify data. The researcher can simply take each comment made, mentally run it through the analytical framework and tick it off. During a well-run interview, data are likely to be volunteered on most, if not all, of the needs topics, as the following example amply illustrates.

This is what an interviewee said in result of a question concerning information overload, which followed on from his mentioning the information inputs that came into a newspaper:

The presence of such vast quantities of information can lead to problems other than trying to digest/process it. Indeed, it can lead also to an unbalanced view on events. For the danger is to rely on the incoming paper flood and in so doing obtaining a far too institutional viewpoint on events. Take the example of *The Guardian*'s education correspondent. For a start he would get about a metre and a half of post a day. Masses will be coming from educational institutions, from pressure groups, trade unions. It is all institutional, it's all about providing education – little of it is consumer oriented. It is not about what is going on in the classrooms, it's not about what parents are wanting, etc. To get that information you must leave the office. But that takes a tremendous act of will, for the pressure is to stay in the office and read the post and take the phone calls.

Apart from the graphical description provided, the answer also discloses an unexpected connection between information overload and the viewpoint of information sources.

In any case, the framework can alert the researcher to topics which may not have been covered in the course of the interview. These can be swept up at the end, via direct questioning. By this time, when a bridge has already been built and an understanding achieved, the interviewees should be so immersed in talking about their work or problem (and its information requirements) that they lose their inhibitions and are sure enough of their ground not to be easily led. Also, returning to the interviewees full transcripts of their interviews can provide much help with obtaining more complete and richer data.

Once the necessary evidence has been gathered, with the researcher taking good care to ensure that the interview approach remains consistent between interviewers and across different interviewees, the information needs analysis framework proposed here can be put to good use again. Used at this stage as a template for identifying and classifying the central themes recurring in the data at hand, the framework enables the systematic performance of cross-case analysis, aimed at disaggregating the accumulated evidence into its thematic components according to the 11 aspects of an information need.

The group interview

Group interviews embody many of the qualities and virtues of the open-ended, face-to-face interview. Similarly characterised by a free range and high levels of interaction, they come in especially useful when time and funds are restricted. Also, and this is perhaps their greatest advantage over the one-to-one interviews, group interviews tend to have legs and can run on irrespective of the intervention of the interviewer. The interviewer can sit back, observe and note the interaction between interviewees. Indeed, in many respects the interviewer takes on the role of referee. As the role of the interviewer is thus diminished and less instrumental in the proceedings, the opportunities for spoon-feeding and bias are reduced. Also, group interviewing provides for triangulation: it is clear by looking at the rest of the group whether the others accept a view that is being expounded. Consequently, group interviews yield reliable data for establishing frames of reference for interview schedules and questionnaires.

Moreover, and this is another considerable plus of the method, people like group interviews because, bolstered as they are by their friends and colleagues, they feel less threatened. Participants who might feel intimidated in a tête-à-tête situation, especially when the interviewer is older or perceived as more senior, soon lose their inhibitions in a group. Children, though less likely to subscribe to the perceived expectations of the interviewer anyway, are a case in point. By the same token, a lot of help can be expected in the clarification of the issues being considered: participants rephrase and explain questions on behalf of other members of the group who might not have understood the crux or objective of the question.

There are, though, two main technical problems associated with group interviews: firstly, it is far from easy scheduling things so that you can get six or more busy people together; secondly, transcribing a recording on which many people are speaking, sometimes all at once, is not easy and takes a long time.

The very fashionable focus groups, courtesy of the media publicity that has arisen in result of their use by political parties in taking the political pulse of the voting public, are a form of group interview: discussions set up to explore a specific range of issues, most notably consumers' views and experiences with regard to a particular hot topic. They may be made up of people from a pre-existing group (students, for instance) or of complete strangers to one another. It can be advantageous to recruit participants who do know each other – that way they can relate more easily.

Focus groups differ from the generic group interviews in that they have a moderator or facilitator, rather than an interviewer. The role of the moderator is to keep things flowing, encourage interaction and ensure that things emerge spontaneously. The question and answer format is jettisoned and the participants replace the interviewer as the dynamic. In result, the data generated are said to be richer and more authentic, and with good reason, too: after all, the spontaneous responses of the participants are bound to reflect more directly the workings of their minds. The key to success, then, is to ensure that everybody participates, feels relaxed and a momentum is established. This is best done via ice-breaking, autobiographical introductions and/or the handing out of some material to serve as the springboard for discussion. The timing of moderator interventions is, plainly, important too.

Telephone interviews

Telephone interviews have been gaining popularity for quite some time now. As people feel more and more comfortable about conducting business over the phone, they increasingly tend to treat phone interviews as a conventional way of giving out information. Nonetheless, such interviews do not sit well with everyone, because there is still a sense of double glazing-selling about them, although probably less so where the questions concern information needs. In any case, setting the interview up for a specific pre-scheduled time lends an air of seriousness to it all, which often solves the problem.

From the point of view of the researcher, conducting interviews over the phone is certainly an attractive option, for the spontaneity of face-to-face interviews comes here at a much lower price: there is no need to travel. All it takes for the technique to succeed, at least according to telesales people, is an assertive attitude on the part of the interviewer and giving the interviewee a sense of the importance of the exercise. However, the opportunity to take note of messages conveyed via body language is lacking in these interviews and, as phone calls are bound to be shorter, the possibility of obtaining evidence is more limited. Also, talking on the phone and taking notes at the same time is not easy.

Having seen the considerable benefits of interviews for capturing data on information needs, we now come to a method that often plays an important preparatory part in their implementation: observation.

Observation

Observation is best suited for preparing the ground for an interview or a questionnaire study, as it provides the investigator/question framer with an understanding of the circumstances surrounding the objects being studied. The evidence obtainable is a direct and unfiltered/unedited portrayal of the situation – along the lines of watching a play rather than asking the actor what happened. Indeed, since people are not being asked questions, formalised language does not impede the reliability of the emerging data.

In the context of information needs and practices, observation is a particularly suitable method for gathering basic evidence as to how, when and why information is used in a specific setting. Plainly, the need to witness the whole information process unfolding and to see the live interaction between an individual and system, source (human or documentary) or intermediary means that consumers have to be observed in a situation in which a lot of information is being transmitted and received. The great attraction of the method is that the people being surveyed do not have to do anything other than give their permission to be observed – not always forthcoming, of course.

There are, though, problems with the method. First of all, the very act of observation changes the nature of what is being observed. It may interfere with normal behaviour and provide a false, 'on my best behaviour' picture. Anyone who has been visited by the numerous panels of inspectors that inhabit all levels of education these days will know that it does change things: lectures start on time and lecturers turn up in suits. Proponents of the method argue that while there is indeed an initial period of unreality, this soon goes as the subject gets used to the shadow.

Beyond that, observation does not work very effectively when subjects are inactive or if they spend long times at a single activity, which is not directly related to the behaviour being observed, say, in our case, writing, when the focus of the investigation is information seeking. It works best in busy environments, where the observer is easily forgotten, for example, in the open-plan newsrooms of newspapers.

Observation will not be very effective either if the status of the observer imposes a threat to the subjects under scrutiny. Imagine being observed by your boss – there is an implicit judgement being taken about your performance. More than one observer, and the feeling of threat increases considerably.

There is also the problem of accurately describing and interpreting an event. So much is likely to happen while an observation is taking place that there is a need to focus only on the things that pertain directly to the observation brief. This cannot be easy when studying communication, because much of what happens could be of value – something which cannot always be foreseen. Also, interpreting behaviour is inevitably subjective and contingent on the investigator's perceptions. Take intent as an example: a group member is asking a question concerning the implications of a proposed solution to a problem. An observer ignoring intent might classify this as information seeking, but one who takes intent into consideration might code it as attacking the solution.

Finally, observation is extremely time-consuming. So much so, that it can only be undertaken on a small-scale basis, which renders the method quite unsuitable for collecting data for any purpose other than laying the foundations of an interview or questionnaire survey; it is certainly not the appropriate technique for collecting generalisable data.

Diaries

In a methodological sense diaries are simply self-recorded observations of events, activities and thoughts, recorded either in a structured format or in a free-flowing account. Hardly surprisingly, then, the two methods, diaries and observations, have many advantages and disadvantages in common, although diaries have their idiosyncratic features, too.

For the researcher, the main attraction of diaries is the opportunity the technique affords to collect a lot of data over a relatively short period of time. Moreover, the return for the truly little effort involved (at least on the part of the investigator) is ample: the data yielded are very specific and very close to the point of action. Indeed, actions and reactions to events can be recorded at the time of occurrence, something which allows for getting at people's actual intentions in order to compare these to the eventual information outcomes.

Still, there are some quite significant problems associated with the use of diaries. There is the issue of authenticity and bias – the editing of events by the diarists at a conscious and subconscious level. There is also a question mark over the accuracy and completeness of diaries. To what extent can people, busy as they are, be expected to maintain them diligently?

The successful utilisation of this technique requires a particularly high degree of co-operation, which renders the recruitment of participants, tricky at all times, even more difficult. Volunteers thus tend to be a small, self-selecting group and, in result, obtaining a representative sample can be even more of a problem here. What is more, since maintaining motivation and interest over time is difficult, and there can be a big drop-out rate, these groups tend to become progressively smaller and even more self-selecting. One solution is to use a large sample over a relatively short time period. Another solution is to pay people for their co-operation (on completion, of course).

Apparently, then, the various quantitative methods – interviews, observation and diaries – have considerable benefits for information needs analysis, either for pathfinding, that is, for pinning down tentative patterns of information needs, usages and problems, or for rounding out, enhancing and bringing into sharper focus the picture obtained via other methods. However, since these techniques can only yield restricted-scope data, the need for generalisable quantitative evidence inevitably brings about the use of other methods as well.

Questionnaires

Any attempt at capturing a broad and valid picture of information needs thus clearly necessitates surveying large numbers of people, who are also often geographically scattered. Questionnaires are perhaps the best-known technique for doing so; indeed, time and resources often dictate that questionnaires should be used for the purpose, especially nowadays, given the internet's ability to reach out to a huge population with ease – and with little cost. However, this tried and proven method has other, quite significant advantages as well.

First of all, if we look at questionnaires from the researcher's angle, when large numbers of participants are recruited (a not too easily accomplished feat in itself, as we are about to see), questionnaires can provide copious amounts of quantitative and outwardly impressive data, which then serve to generate numerous tables, graphs and figures. Also, at least some of the work is done by the people canvassed.

Questionnaires have their benefits for the people being questioned, too. Obviously, the method is a boon for the shy and timid, but it can appeal to almost everybody because the personal factors are largely removed from the questioning process and there is no rush to it – people are usually given time to consider the questions and to collect the necessary data.

However, there are also quite a few problems associated with the method. The chief among them is that it is extremely difficult to produce a good questionnaire. More specifically, it is very difficult to formulate questions that are completely free from excess verbiage, unclear or ambiguous wording, emotional charge, leading or biased phrasing and unnecessary jargon. In any case, it is very difficult to be certain that people understand the line of questioning taken; however, when a conscious attempt is made to simplify, questions can become lightweight – sometimes not really worth asking. In particular, attempts to obtain use/needs data can descend into vague categorisation, along the lines of 'satisfactory, very satisfactory'. Still, being well aware of the likelihood of such problems cropping up in a survey makes it possible to take appropriate measures to prevent them.

One solution for the problem is piloting the questionnaires in interviews, in an effort to identify potential difficulties. Ideally, the pre-testing procedure consists of two phases. In the first phase participants are requested to fill out the questionnaire while 'thinking aloud' and commenting on it. The recorded sessions of their musing aloud on the questions presented to them, deliberating the different options and voicing their doubts, serves as the basis for amending the survey instrument. In the second phase of the pre-testing procedure the last revised version of the questionnaire is filled out under realistic conditions, although the participants are asked to let the investigator know of any difficulties encountered. Thus, the questionnaire is revised and modified after each session, resulting in an incremental pre-testing process.

Another problem that often creeps into a questionnaire survey is that response rates can be notoriously low, especially where busy practitioners are concerned (bulging in-trays and long lists of unread e-mail messages tend to compete for attention and have a habit of burying questionnaires). Brevity, prizes (book tokens, for instance), offers of a copy of the survey findings, chasers, good timing and a promise of anonymity can all improve response rates. However, the best response rates come from a well-designed questionnaire that engenders interest on the part of the respondents and goes to a group that has not been targeted before, in particular if they feel that they will benefit directly from the exercise. Probably the most extensive questionnaire study on the topic of information needs was conducted as part of the Investigation of the Information Requirements of Social Sciences (INFROSS) research project (Line, 1971). During this project over a thousand individuals filled out questionnaires of nearly a hundred pages in length. This level of co-operation is highly unusual and is largely explained by the fact that the target group – social science academics, were experiencing big problems in coming to terms with an information explosion that resulted from the expansion in higher education, which occurred at the time, and felt that their answers might lead to an improvement in their condition. The fact that they were largely an uncanvassed group helped too.

Having looked at questionnaires, the one technique almost intuitively associated with the collection of quantitative data, we now come to another, perhaps somewhat less familiar method of data collection, at least outside academe: citation analyses.

Citation analyses

Citations provide large quantities of stark and bald evidence of information use. Interestingly, though, while citations are used as a surrogate for use data, they actually represent a qualified form of use. Documents may be consulted, that is, used, but not cited, because they are rejected on grounds of value or direct worth. It is not simply the poor papers that are rejected, either: those that have already gone into the general consciousness no longer have specific ideas, statements or quotes attributed to them. Plainly, there are also cases where items are not used, but still get cited – students might refer to items in the lecturer's reading list or authors might mention their own publications (self-citation) as a boost to their reputation and intellectual standing.

Generally speaking, though, someone who cites a work has read it (used it). What is more, the user has selected the cited paper from a group of other works, so there is a quality and relevance judgement operating here, too; indeed, citations are also taken to be indicators of value and worth.

From the researcher's angle, citations can be a real methodological boon, for they form a vast pool of evidence, which covers all subjects and all countries. What is more, the data can be collected easily and inexpensively, without any special equipment or permission. In fact, the work is done by the users themselves, for author-users leave behind a bibliographic fingerprint. To boot, the database is relatively easy to analyse: the bibliographic record is a standardised, highly structured and regulated piece of use data.

Still, citation analyses have their limitations.

The chief problems flow from the fact that citations only provide a limited view of use for a relatively narrow band of specialist users. Obviously so, for, as a rule, the publications that carry citations are academic in nature and the data on their use are based purely on the activities of authors; non-academics cannot, therefore, fully profit from the methodology. Also, citations do not contain too many details: typically only author, subject, journal name, date, publication form, country and language of publication can be discerned.

There are four major types of citation analyses: obsolescence/decay analyses, subject analyses, country/language analyses and ranked lists.

Obsolescence/decay analyses

One of the prime and most direct uses of citation studies is to determine how far back in time consumers search for scholarly material. This is important for publishers as well as for librarians, in helping them determine their policies. In the case of the former – the retaining and marketing policies of their back files, and in the case of the latter, the selection (and weeding) of the information they put at the disposal of their clients.

Just how important citation data can be emerges loud and clear from the widespread misconceptions concerning the decay of scholarly literature. It has long been thought that academics are more interested in the new, especially in science and practitioner disciplines, where research, innovation and technology render information obsolescent at a rapid rate. However, we now know that this popularly held notion has been exaggerated by a number of factors. First of all, the most recently published literature is subject to a much wider range of uses, from current awareness to retrospective searching, whereas the use of older items is much more restricted. There is also the problem of distinguishing between genuine decay and the appearance of decay given by a youthful, rapidly growing subject field. Perhaps above all, as long as older material was more difficult to access (back files are the last to go online), new material was indeed much more likely to be viewed. This has led to the most recent year (or two) of a journal accounting for the vast majority of uses. However, massive improvements in access to back files and search engines that prioritise relevance over age have increased the visibility of older material, bringing about a substantial use of back files.

Subject analyses

Subject analyses generate data of highly practical value for policy-makers in charge of information systems and services: what subjects are being used; the scatter of subject use – the extent to which scholarly consumers use a large/small number of subjects; the extent to which consumers are dependent on their own subject; and the subject fields most closely related to theirs. All this assists information providers in determining their information selection and organisation policies.

Country/language analyses

Country and language analyses can show how international the need is: whether information flows across frontiers (are we truly part of a global village?); the strengths of national relationships and how international a field is. However, international authorship and publishing can make it difficult to identify nationality.

Ranked lists

Ranked lists refer to journal titles. Here the interest largely lies in the scatter of citation over the journal population. Most analyses show a concentration of use on a relatively small number of journals: a minority of the literature accounts for the majority of use. This gives rise to the concept of a core literature. At one time this data was thought to be of enormous value, for it enabled librarians to cost their information provision on the basis of a library that would meet 75% or so of the demands (citations) made upon itself.

Having taken a look at the more traditional techniques of data collection, we now come to a more innovative method, web log analysis.

Web log analysis

With online searching having become a routine activity for millions and millions of people, our ability to capture data on information need-induced behaviour has moved into an entirely different league. This, because the digital footprints that people leave behind them when they visit the web are automatically recorded in log files, which can be collected to generate datasets of unparalleled magnitude in terms of size and detail. However, and this is a key point which must be made at the outset, whilst web logs provide us with very valuable evidence indeed as to what consumers actually do when they set out to meet their information needs online, they can alert us to only a few characteristics of people's information needs, and then only imperfectly. Hardly surprisingly, of course, for, as we have already noted, information use is by no means the ostensible clean, hard, direct manifestation of need that it is so readily assumed to be. Thus, it is the combination of methods appropriate for unearthing information needs with methods suitable for monitoring the actual meeting of those needs, which can yield the robust data for which we are looking. However, first things first: what exactly are web log files?

Web log files are a record of everything that people do online: requesting stored web page(s), viewing, searching, browsing and navigating. This information on client (computer) activity is recorded automatically and routinely on server computers and stored as a text file called a log file, where each line represents a single request by the client on the server. A typical, unresolved line from a log file would look something like this: 193.150.189.1. This is the Internet Protocol (IP) number, which identifies the client computer (the user). The number can be translated into a name, via a database of IP numbers and domain names called DNS (Domain Name Services). A resolved name looks like: hadrian.guardian.co.uk, where 'Hadrian' is the name of a computer, 'Guardian' is the name of the domain name organisation, 'co' is the organisation type and 'uk' is the country code.

The record made of client activity thus contains information first and foremost on users. The IP number, identifying the user, can be used to derive count statistics on users and use as well as user and use profiles by location and by type of organisation. Beyond that, the date and time (and its offset from Greenwich Mean Time) of the transaction are recorded, too, which makes it possible to identify approximately how long a given user has taken to read a page and how long he/she has remained logged on to the site. The aggregated data on this, that is, the total amount of use per hour, can serve to identify the time distribution of users logged on over hours, days and months. In addition, the record contains information on the type of request made, whether for a normal HTML page or for forms and programmes, and the page or URL viewed. A series of pages sorted by time can, then, give us an idea of how the user has jumped from one URL to another and, hence, some notion of how the user has moved and searched through the site. Finally, the log records the number of bytes downloaded to the client computer and the success or failure of the transaction.

All in all, then, web logs provide three types of data: on activity or use; on information-seeking characteristics; and on users. What makes the method unique, though, is its capability to yield data of truly enormous reach and detail, for logs record each use of everyone who happens to engage with the system. To researchers, generally starved of hard statistical data, the sheer volume and level of specification that can be attained is beguiling. Survey-based investigations can never hope to match log-based ones in this. To be able to describe activity characteristics in terms of many hundreds of thousands of incidences, rather than tens of them, gives log studies a certain weight and authority – not always warranted, of course. Still, with the population studied in its entirety, at least the thorny problem of representative samples is solved; although, of course, by definition non-users are not covered.

Indeed, the objectivity of the method is one of its strong points: logs tell it as it was, providing as they do a direct and immediately available record of people's activities in cyberspace: not what they say they might, or would do; not what they were prompted to say; not what they thought they did; not what they remember they did; what they actually did do. Of course, users' attitudes towards the investigator and/or the system he/she represents do not affect the results, either.

The technique is unobtrusive, too: the data are collected routinely, automatically and quite anonymously. There is no need to contact the users or obtain their co-operation because the 'users' under investigation are computers, not individuals.

Finally, a considerable attraction of web log-based data collection is that the method does not involve a lot of labour; in fact, it is simplicity itself. Unfortunately, though, the subsequent analysis of the data can be long, painstaking and frustrating.

All this is not to say that web log analysis is free from problems. Just like any other method, this one, too, has its drawbacks. Even the greatest attraction of logs – the unparalleled size and reach of the evidence – comes with a snag: web log-derived use counts are not completely accurate. First of all, there is the problem of proxy connections, where a number of computers are connected to the internet via a single IP number. Plainly, a single person or a group of people may use this computer, but all use appears to come from the same 'proxy' user, since users are identified by IP numbers. This, of course, leads to an underestimation of number of users and sessions. Exacerbating the problem is the widespread practice of allocating computers in an organisation with a floating IP address. With floating IP addresses, an IP address is allocated to a computer as required and will be allocated to another computer when it becomes available. If a computer is allocated a floating IP address, the IP number cannot be assumed to be associated with a particular computer; hence it is difficult to determine whether an IP address represents a single computer or many computers. Floating IP addresses make it particularly difficult to monitor/track a user over time, rendering calculations based on repeat use inherently unstable. The picture of use is further distorted by having a cache (the storage of previously viewed pages on the client's computer), because repeat in-session accesses to pages are made from the cache, rather than being requested from the website's server and, as such, they are not recorded in the logs. Similarly, if someone views a full-text document in HTML format and then goes on to view this item in PDF, proprietary software tends to count this as two views.

Logs also yield truly copious amounts of data, but of a rather superficial nature. Yes, big numbers are there, but what it all means is not always clear. Take the duration of a search session. What does it actually tell us? Does a slow search mean a poor search or a thorough search? Does a fast search mean an efficient search or a skimpy search? Indeed, even determining what actually constitutes 'use' presents some problems. With information seeking on the web typically more in the nature of surfing than searching, as well as characteristically imprecise, volatile and bouncing, many sites and pages are visited, but not, in fact, put to actual meaningful use. Thus, a 'hit' – a line in a log file, which represents a request by the client for a file on the server, page impressions or pages downloaded – presents a very crude, at times misleading picture of use. This is all the more so since a single page viewed on the client's machine can generate several transaction hits on the server because each image is downloaded as a separate request to the text. Another difficulty arises from the fact that, as far as the logs are concerned, nobody logs off on the web, they just depart anonymously. Therefore, session ends have to be estimated, as does the time spent online.

However, perhaps the biggest problem of them all is that web logs provide a record of computers interacting with computers, not an individual interacting with a computer. It is a user 'trace', really, a computer, an IP address, not a real user. Indeed, robots harvesting information on the World Wide Web for a wide variety of purposes – indexing and data-mining, for instance, account for a good deal of usage. This state of affairs makes it difficult to assign data to individual users or even categories of users. Even when websites have a subscriber database, it is rarely possible to relate this information to the logs. The database information itself, while useful, suffers from the fact that people provide false names (Tony Blair and Mickey Mouse are regular users of *The Times* website, it would seem) and, in any case, subscribers are not necessarily users. Thus, while it is relatively easy to translate the IP address into a domain name, typically all there is to work on is the location of the computer and the name and type of organisation to which it belongs, and even this is problematical, for an IP registration address need not have any bearing on the computer's actual location. For example, UK-based companies may (and often do) decide to register their IP address in the USA.

Fortunately, deep log analysis (Nicholas et al., 2000; Nicholas et al., 2005; Nicholas et al., 2007a), developed by CIBER researchers to combat the frustrations experienced in trying to employ proprietary log software to provide a nuanced, but at the same time very big picture of information behaviour, can add demographic data to the trace. Indeed, when enhanced by user demographic data, logs can tell us far more about the kinds of people who use a service/system and the outcomes resulting from its use. Still, although this way logs do plot particular forms of behaviour from which needs can be inferred, such as requirements for very current or huge amounts of information, they do not directly record users' needs, motives or intentions; nor do they measure satisfaction. Method triangulation is thus plainly the name of the game: what the logs are good at is highlighting patterns of use, identifying broad sweeps of information-seeking behaviour that can be further investigated for their validity and significance during interview or questionnaire surveys.

6 Information needs analysis

Ensuring the effective information enfranchisement of the digital consumer

The just-concluded review of information needs analysis, its purposes, importance, recommended manner of conduct and attendant difficulties, hopefully, leaves little room for doubt: only if people's information needs and their ways and means of coping with these needs are routinely monitored and evaluated, can today's vital requirement for effective information management and retrieval be appropriately met. This has direct implications for all of us in the present-day information environment, which sees us all fending for ourselves when it comes to sorting out our information needs. Indeed, this state of affairs has rendered the mastering of a basic comprehension of what information needs analysis is all about quite crucial for obtaining the positive outcomes we (and society) want. However, the need for taking a holistic approach to information needs concerns first and foremost information service providers. Expected to come up with up-to-date, swiftly delivered, custom-made, targeted, authoritative and qualitative solutions for meeting the constantly changing needs of information seekers, they have little choice but to collect and analyse information needs data as comprehensively as possible, and on an ongoing basis, too. Thus, keeping a watchful eye on individual information needs and practices should be an inescapable imperative for information professionals, a key management activity, the basis for all decision-making processes; hence the importance of their taking note of the needs analysis framework proposed here.

Indeed, information professionals all agree, and have done so for decades, that it is very, very important to understand their users, but have made almost no progress towards attaining their proclaimed goal. Rather the contrary, in fact: with the number of the ubiquitous (and anonymous) digital consumers amounting to many hundreds of millions in result of the information free-for-all, undoubtedly information professionals know far less about their user base than they ever did. The result of this wholesale neglect is leading to fatal consequences: information professions are increasingly being decoupled from their consumers, a process which threatens to culminate in professional Armageddon. The now disintermediated seekers of information have massive and unfettered choice and are quite happy to take matters into their own hands, simply doing it themselves, often badly, of course.

Unfortunately, although far too much is going on in the information world for complacency to reign, information professionals have been (and still are) complacent about their customers – real and potential. In the IT fog they seem to have lost their way, thinking all too readily that the solution, any solution, lies in the technology. Ironically, though, each new system and each new upgrade in point of fact takes them ever further from the consumers and their information needs. That is why the mission of this book is to get information professionals to re-affirm their professional vows with their customers: to connect and reach out in an era of disintermediation, disconnection and decoupling. The very personal nature of the information needs assessment process can, in itself, contribute to this, but, of course, it goes far beyond that: the close contact between information service provider and information consumer is the only way to ensure that the information service reflects the mainstream activities of the community it serves and provides truly personalised responses to information seekers' needs. Plainly then, information needs assessments should become a vital part of information professionals' armoury: the methodology is there, the technology is there, the opportunity is there; all it takes is their moving closer to their clients, the consumers.

It is to be hoped that information professionals will rise up to the challenge, but, in any case, this book sets out to show the information consumers how to connect effectively to information and best meet their needs by themselves (perhaps aided by teachers, call-centre managers, citizens' advisers and the like). Indeed, it is vital for everyone to take up the torch; otherwise, instead of capitalising on the information cornucopia available to us all at the touch of a button or click of a mouse, we shall, as a society and a world, be guilty of blowing one of the greatest gifts anyone could have, that of information.

References

Abels, E. G., Liebscher, P. and Denman, D. W. (1996) 'Factors That Influence the Use of Electronic Networks by Science and Engineering Faculty at Small Institutions: Part I: Queries', *Journal of the American Society for Information Science*, 47(2), 146–58.

Adams, A., Blandford, A. and Lunt, P. (2005) 'Social Empowerment and Exclusion: A Case Study on Digital Libraries', *ACM Transactions on Computer-Human Interaction*, 12(2), 174–200.

Aduwa-Ogiegbaen, S. E. O. and Isah, S. (2005) 'Extent of Faculty Members' Use of Internet in the University of Benin, Nigeria', *Journal of Instructional Psychology*, 32 (4), 269–76.

Allen, T. (1969) 'Information Flow in Research and Development Laboratories', *Administrative Science Quarterly*, 14(1), 12–19.

——(1977) *Managing the Flow of Technology: Technology Transfer and the Dissemination of Technological Information with the R&D Organization*. Cambridge, MA: MIT Press.

Arunachalam, S. (1999) 'Information and Knowledge in the Age of Electronic Communication: A Developing Country Perspective', *Journal of Information Science*, 25 (6), 465–76.

Arunachalam, S. and Singh, U. N. (1992) 'Access to Information and Scientific Output of India', *Journal of Scientific & Industrial Research*, 51(2), 99–119.

Baldwin, N. S. and Rice, R. E. (1997) 'Information-Seeking Behavior of Securities Analysts: Individual and Institutional Influences, Information Sources and Channels, and Outcomes', *Journal of the American Society for Information Science (JASIS)*, 48(8), 674–93.

Ball, D. (2004) 'What's the 'Big Deal', and Why Is It a Bad Deal for Universities?', *Interlending and Document Supply*, 32(2), 117–25.

Barrett, A. (2005) 'The Information-Seeking Habits of Graduate Student Researchers in the Humanities', *The Journal of Academic Librarianship*, 31(4), 324–31.

Bates, M. J. (1996) 'Document Familiarity, Relevance, and Bradford's Law: The Getty Online Searching Project Report no. 5', *Information Processing and Management*, 32 (6), 697–707.

——(1998) 'Indexing and Access for Digital Libraries and the Internet: Human, Database, and Domain Factors', *Journal of the American Society for Information Science and Technology*, 49 (13), 1185–205.

Bath University Library (1971a) *Investigation into Information Requirements of the Social Sciences*, Research Report no. 5: 'The Research Procedures of Social Scientists', Bath: Bath University.

——(1971b) *Investigation of Information Requirements of the Social Sciences*, Research Report no. 1: 'Information Requirements of Researchers in the Social Sciences', Bath: Bath University.

Bawden, D. (1990) *User-Oriented Evaluation of Information Systems and Services*. Aldershot: Gower.

Bawden, D., Holtham, C. and Courtney, N. (1999) 'Perspectives on Information Overload', *Aslib Proceedings*, 51(8), 249–55.

Becher, T. (1989) *Academic Tribes and Territories: Intellectual Enquiry and the Cultures of Disciplines*, Stony Stratford: The Society for Research into Higher Education & Open University Press.

Belkin, N. J. and Vickery, A. (1989) *Interaction in Information Systems: A Review of Research from Document Retrieval to Knowledge-Based Systems*, London: British Library.

Bellardo, T. (1985) 'An Investigation of Online Searcher Traits and Their Relationship to Search Outcome', *Journal of the American Society for Information Science (JASIS)*, 36(4), 241–50.

Bernal, J. D. (1959) 'The Transmission of Scientific Information: A User's Analysis', in *Proceedings of the International Conference on Scientific Information, Washington, D.C., 1958*, Washington, DC: National Academy of Sciences – National Research Council, V. 1, 77–95.

Bernstam, E. V., Walji, M. F., Sagaram, S., Sagaram, D., Johnson, C. W. and Meric-Bernstam, F. (2008) 'Commonly Cited Website Quality Criteria are Not Effective at Identifying Inaccurate Online Information about Breast Cancer', *Cancer*, 112(6), 1206–13.

Biggs, M. (1981) 'Sources of Tension between Librarians and Faculty', *The Journal of Higher Education*, 52(2), 182–201.

Bimber, B. (2000) 'Measuring the Gender Gap on the Internet', *Social Science Quarterly*, 81(3), 868–76.

Blake, M. (1998) 'Internet Access for Older People', *Aslib Proceedings*, 50(10), 308–315.

Borgman, C. (1989) 'All Users of Information Retrieval Systems are Not Created Equal: An Exploration into Individual Differences', *Information Processing and Management*, 25(3), 237–51.

Braun, T., Glänzel, W., Grupp, H. (1995) 'The Scientometric Weight of 50 Nations in 27 Science Areas, 1989–93. Part II. Life Sciences', *Scientometrics*, 34(2), 207–37.

Brittain, J. M. (1984) 'Internationality of the Social Sciences: Implications for Information Transfer', *Journal of the American Society for Information Science (JASIS)*, 35(1), 11–18.

Brockman, W. S., Neumann, L., Palmer, C. L. and Tidline, T. J. (2001) *Scholarly Work in the Humanities and the Evolving Information Environment*, Digital Library Federation and Council on Library and Information Resources. Available at: www. clir.org/pubs/reports/pub104/pub104.pdf (last accessed April 2008).

Bruce, H. (1998) 'User Satisfaction with Information Seeking on the Internet', *Journal of the American Society for Information Science* (JASIS), 49(6), 541–56.

Burkett, I. (2000) 'Beyond The 'Information Rich and Poor': Futures Understandings of Inequality in Globalising Informational Economies', *Futures*, 32(7), 679–94.

Buschman, J. and Brosio, R. A. (2006) 'A Critical Primer on Postmodernism: Lessons from Educational Scholarship for Librarians', *The Journal of Academic Librarianship*, 32(4), 408–18.

Calas, M. B. and Smircich, L. (2001) 'Introduction: Does the House of Knowledge Have a Future?', *Organization*, 8(2), Special Issue on Re-Organizing Knowledge,

Transforming Institutions: Knowing, Knowledge, and the University of the 21st Century, 147–8.

CIBER (2008) *The Behaviour of the Researcher of the Future ('Google Generation' Project')*, University College London. Available at: www.publishing.ucl.ac.uk/download/GoogleGeneration.pdf (last accessed March 2008).

Coulter, A., Entwistle, V. and Gilbert, D. (1999) 'Sharing Decisions with Patients: Is the Information Good Enough?', *British Medical Journal*, 318(7179), 318–22.

Covi, L. M. (1999) 'Material Mastery: Situating Digital Library Use in University Research Practices', *Information Processing and Management*, 35(3), 293–316.

——(2000) 'Debunking the Myth of the Nintendo Generation: How Doctoral Students Introduce New Electronic Communication Practices into University Research', *Journal of the American Society for Information Science*, 51(14), 1284–94.

Cox, C. (2006) 'An Analysis of the Impact of Federated Search Products on Library Instruction Using the ACRL Standards', *Portal: Libraries and the Academy*, 6(3), 253–7.

Cronin, B. (1981) 'Assessing User Needs', *Aslib Proceedings*, 33(2), 37–47.

——(2000) 'Bibliometrics and Beyond: Some Thoughts on Webometrics and Influmetrics', in *Proceedings of the Freedom of Information Conference 2000*. Available at: www.biomedcentral.com/meetings/2000/foi/transcripts/cronin (last accessed July 2007).

Cronin, B. and McKim, G. (1996) 'Science and Scholarship on the World Wide Web: A North American Perspective', *Journal of Documentation*, 52(2), 163–71.

Crotty, M. (1998) *The Foundations of Social Research: Meaning and Perspective in the Research Process*, London: Sage.

Das, S., Echambadi, R., McCardle, M. and Luckett, M. (2003) 'The Effect of Interpersonal Trust, Need for Cognition, and Social Loneliness on Shopping, Information Seeking and Surfing on the Web', *Marketing Letters*, 14(3), 185–202.

Delanty, G. (1998) 'The Idea of the University in the Global Era: From Knowledge as an End to the End of Knowledge?', *Social Epistemology*, 12(1), 3–25.

Dervin, B. and Nilan, M. (1986) 'Information Needs and Uses', in Williams, M. E., ed., *Annual Review of Information Science and Technology (ARIST)*, 21, Medford, NJ: ASIS, 3–33.

Duderstadt, J. (1997) 'Revolutionary Changes: Understanding the Challenges and the Possibilities', *Business Officer*, 1–15.

Dutton, W. H. and Helsper, E. J. (2007) *The Internet in Britain: 2007*. Oxford: Oxford Internet Institute, University of Oxford. Available at: www.oii.ox.ac.uk/microsites/oxis (last accessed February 2009).

Egan, M. and Henkle, H. H. (1956) 'Ways and Means in Which Research Workers, Executives, and Others Use Information', in Shera, J. H., Kent, A. and Perry, J. W., eds, *Documentation in Action*, New York: Reinhold.

Elayyan, R. M. (1988) 'The Use of Information by Physicians', *International Library Review*, 20(2), 247–65.

Ellis, D. (1989) 'A Behavioural Approach to Information Retrieval System Design', *Journal of Documentation*, 45(3), 171–212.

Ellis, D., Cox, D. and Hall, C. (1993) 'A Comparison of the Information Seeking Patterns of Researchers in Physical and Social Sciences', *Journal of Documentation*, 49(4), 356–69.

Ellis, D. and Haugan, M. (1997) 'Modelling the Information-Seeking Patterns of Engineers and Research Scientists in an Industrial Environment', *Journal of Documentation,* 53 (4), 384–403.

Erens, B. (1996) *Modernizing Research Libraries: The Effect of Recent Developments in University Libraries on the Research Process*, London: Bowker-Saur.

Eysenbach, G. and Diepgen, T. L. (1999) 'Patients Looking for Information on the Internet and Seeking Teleadvice: Motivation, Expectations, and Misconceptions as Expressed in e-Mails Sent to Physicians', *Archives of Dermatology*, 135(2), 151–6.

Fallows, D. (2005) *How Women and Men Use the Internet*, Washington, DC: Pew Internet & American Life Project. Available at: www.pewinternet.org/pdfs/PIP_Women_and_Men_online.pdf (last accessed December 2008).

——(2006) *Browsing the Web for Fun*, Washington, DC: Pew Internet & American Life Project. Available at: www.pewinternet.org/pdfs/PIP_Surfforfun_Feb06.pdf (last accessed May 2008).

Featherstone, M. and Venn, C. (2006) 'Problematizing Global Knowledge and the New Encyclopaedia Project: An Introduction', *Theory, Culture & Society*, 23(2–3), 1–20.

Fister, B. (1992) 'The Research Process of Undergraduate Students', *Journal of Academic Librarianship*, 18(3), 163–9.

Ford, N. and Miller, D. (1996) 'Gender Differences in Internet Perception and Use', in Collier, M. and Arnold, K., eds, *Electronic Library and Visual Information Research. ELVIRA 3: Papers from the Third ELVIRA Conference, 30 April–2 May 1996*, London: ASLIB, 87–100.

Ford, N., Miller, D. and Moss, N. (2001) 'The Role of Individual Differences in Internet Searching: An Empirical Study', *Journal of the American Society for Information Science and Technology*, 52(12), 1049–66.

Fox, S. (2004) *Older Americans and the Internet*, Washington, DC: Pew Internet & American Life Project. Available at: www.pewinternet.org/PPF/r/117/report_display. asp (last accessed July 2008).

——(2005) *Health Information Online: Eight in Ten Internet Users Have Looked for Health Information Online, with Increased Interest in Diet, Fitness, Drugs, Health Insurance, Experimental Treatments, and Particular Doctors and Hospitals*, Washington, DC: Pew Internet & American Life Project. Available at: www.pewinternet.org/pdfs/ PIP_Healthtopics_May05.pdf (last accessed January 2009).

Friedewald, V. E., Jr (2000) 'The Internet's Influence on the Doctor-Patient Relationship', *Health Management Technology Online*, 21(11), 79–80.

Fry, J. (2004) 'The Cultural Shaping of ICTs within Academic Fields: Corpus-based Linguistics as a Case Study', *Literary and Linguistic Computing*, 19(3), 303–19.

Fulton, C. (1991) 'Humanities as Information Users: A Review of the Literature', *Australian Academic and Research Libraries*, 22(3), 188–97.

Gaines, B. R. (1995) *An Agenda for Digital Journals: The Socio-Technical Infrastructure of Knowledge Dissemination*. Available at: pages.cpsc.ucalgary.ca/~gaines/reports/ HM/DigitalJ/DigitalJ.pdf (last accessed September 2008).

Garner, J., Horwood, L. and Sullivan, S. (2001) 'The Place of E-Prints in Scholarly Information Delivery', *Online Information Review*, 25(4), 250–6.

Garvey, W. D., ed. (1979) *Communication: The Essence of Science: Facilitating Information Exchange among Librarians, Scientists, Engineers and Students*, Oxford: Pergamon Press.

Garvey, W. D., Lin, N. and Nelson, C. (1970) 'Communication in the Physical and Social Sciences', *Science*, 170, 1166–73.

Garvey, W. D., Tomita, K. and Woolf, P. (1974) 'The Dynamic Scientific Information User', *Information Storage and Retrieval*, 10, 115–31.

Glover, S. (1994) 'Media: Mystery of Mariella', *Evening Standard*, 8 June 1994, 43.

Gorman, G. E. and Corbitt, B. J. (2002) 'Core Competencies in Information Management Education', *New Library World,* 103(11/12), 436–45.

Gorman, J. (2001) 'The End of Good Science?' *Science News,* 159, 76–8.

Green, A. (1990) 'What Do We Mean by User Needs?' *British Journal of Librarianship,* 5 (2), 65–78.

Greene, J. C. and Caracelli, V. J. (1997) *Advances in Mixed-Method Evaluation: The Challenges and Benefits of Integrating Diverse Paradigms,* San-Francisco: Jossey-Bass.

Gresham, J. L. (1994) 'From Invisible College to Cyberspace College: Computer Conferencing and the Transformation of Informal Scholarly Communication Networks', *Interpersonal Computing and Technology,* 4, 37–52.

Griffith, M. and Fox, S. (2007) *Hobbyists Online,* Washington, DC: Pew Internet & American Life Project. Available at: www.pewinternet.org/pdfs/PIP_Hobbies_2007. pdf (last accessed June 2008).

Gunter, B. (2008) 'Trends in Digital Information Consumption and the Future', in Nicholas, D. and Rowlands, I., eds, *Digital Consumers: Reshaping the Information Professions,* London: Facet Publishing, 193–212.

Hammersley, M. (1981) 'Using Qualitative Methods', *Social Science Information Studies,* 1, 209–20.

Harnad, S. (1990) 'Scholarly Skywriting and the Prepublication Continuum of Scientific Inquiry', *Psychological Science,* 1, 342–43. Available at: www.ecs.soton.ac.uk/~harnad/ Papers/Harnad/harnad90.skywriting.html (last accessed September 2008).

——(1999) 'Free at Last: The Future of Peer-Reviewed Journals', *D-Lib Magazine,* 5 (12), no page numbers. Available at: www.dlib.org/dlib/december99/12harnad.html (last accessed January 2008).

——(2003) 'Open Access to Peer-Reviewed Research through Author/Institution Self-Archiving: Maximizing Research Impact by Maximizing Online Access', in Law, D. and Andrew, J., eds, *Digital Libraries: Policy Planning and Practice,* Aldershot: Ashgate.

——(2006) 'Opening Access by Overcoming Zeno's Paralysis', in Jacobs, N., ed., *Open Access: Key Strategic, Technical and Economic Aspects,* Chandos. Available at: eprints. ecs.soton.ac.uk/12094 (last accessed May 2008).

Harvie, D. (2000) 'Alienation, Class and Enclosure in UK Universities', *Capital & Class,* 71 (Summer), 103–32.

Haythornthwaite, C. and Wellman, B. (2002) 'The Internet in Everyday Life: An Introduction', in Wellman, B. and Haythornthwaite, C., eds, *The Internet in Everyday Life,* Malden, MA: Blackwell, 3–44.

Heinström, J. (2005) 'Fast Surfing, Broad Scanning and Deep Diving', *Journal of Documentation,* 61(2), 228–47.

——(2006) 'Broad Exploration or Precise Specificity: Two Basic Information Seeking Patterns among Students', *Journal of the American Society for Information Science and Technology,* 57(11), 1440–50.

Herman, E. A. (2005) *The Information Needs of Contemporary Academic Researchers,* PhD Dissertation, London: Department of Information Science, City University.

Hernon, P. and Pastine, M. (1977) 'Student Perceptions of Academic Librarians', *College and Research Libraries,* 38(2), 129–39.

Herszenhorn, D. (2009) 'Internet Money in Fiscal Plan: Wise or Waste?', *The New York Times,* 3 February 2009.

Hewins, E. T. (1990) 'Information Need and Use Studies', in Williams, M. E., ed., *Annual Review of Information Science and Technology (ARIST),* 25, Medford, NJ: ASIS, 145–72.

Hjorland, B. (2005) 'Empiricism, Rationalism and Positivism in Library and Information Science', *Journal of Documentation*, 61(1), 130–55.

Hofstede, G. (1980) *Culture's Consequences: International Differences in Work-Related Values*, Beverly Hills, CA: Sage.

——(1991) *Cultures and Organizations: Software of the Mind. Intercultural Cooperation and Its Importance for Survival*, London: McGraw-Hill International.

Hoot, J. L. and Hayslip, B. (1983) 'Microcomputers and the Elderly: New Directions for Self-Sufficiency and Lifelong Learning', *Educational Gerontology*, 9(5/6), 493–9.

Huitt, W. (2004) 'Maslow's Hierarchy of Needs', *Educational Psychology Interactive*, Valdosta, GA: Valdosta State University. Available at: chiron.valdosta.edu/whuitt/col/regsys/maslow.html (last accessed September 2008).

Huntington, P., Nicholas, D., Gunter, B., Russell, C., Withey, R. and Polydoratou, P. (2004) 'Consumer Trust in Health Information on the Web', *Aslib Proceedings*, 56(6), 373–82.

Huotari, M.-L. and Wilson, T. D. (2001) 'Determining Organizational Information Needs: The Critical Success Factors Approach', *Information Research*, 6(3)

Hurd, J. M. (2000) 'The Transformation of Scientific Communication: A Model for 2020', *Journal of the American Society for Information Science* (JASIS), 51(14), 1279–83.

Huvila, I. (2008) 'Work and Work Roles: A Context of Tasks', *Journal of Documentation*, 64(6), 797–815.

Jamali, H. R., Nicholas, D. and Huntington, P. (2005) 'The Use and Users of Scholarly E-journals: A Review of Log Analysis Studies', *Aslib Proceedings*, 57(6), 554–71.

Jeanneney, J. (2007) *Google and the Myth of Universal Knowledge: A View from Europe*, Chicago, IL: University of Chicago Press.

Jiao, Q. G. and Onwuegbuzie, A. J. (1997) 'The Antecedents of Library Anxiety', *The Library Quarterly*, 67(4), 372–89.

Johnson, N. F. (2006) 'Boys and Girls are the Same: Gender Perceptions in Using Computers in the Classroom', *Computers in New Zealand Schools*, 18(3), 5–11, 33, 41.

Jones, S. and Fox, S. (2009) *Generations Online in 2009*, Washington, DC: Pew Internet & American Life Project. Available from www.pewinternet.org/Reports/2009/Generations-Online-in-2009.aspx (last accessed July 2009).

Jorna, K. (2002) 'Educating Information Professionals in a Multicultural Information Society', *Library Review*, 51(3/4), 157–63.

Katz, J. and Aspden, P. (1997) 'Motivations for and Barriers to Internet Usage: Results of a National Public Opinion Survey', *Internet Research: Electronic Networking Applications and Policy*, 7(3), 170–88.

Kay, W. (1994) 'Streetwise: Profile Geoffrey Mulcahy', *InterCity Magazine*, June, 20–2.

Keene, J. (2004) 'From Abstract to Relevant: Encouraging Access to Journals', *Library and Information Research News*, 28(89), 2–12.

Kennan, M. A., Cole, F., Willard, P., Wilson, C. and Marion, L. (2006) 'Changing Workplace Demands: What Job Ads Tell Us', *Aslib Proceedings*, 58(3), 179–96.

Kernan, J. B., and Mojena, R. (1973) 'Information Utilization and Personality', *Journal of Communication*, 23(3), 315–27.

Kibirige, H. M. and DePalo, L. (2000) 'The Internet as a Source of Academic Research Information: Findings of Two Pilot Studies', *Information Technology and Libraries*, 19(1), 11–16.

King, D. W. and Tenopir, C. (1999) 'Using and Reading Scholarly Literature', in Williams, M. E., ed., *Annual Review of Information Science and Technology (ARIST)*, 34, Medford, NJ: ASIS, 423–77.

Kircz, J. G. (1998) 'Modularity: The Next Form of Scientific Presentation?', *Journal of Documentation*, 54(2), 210–35.

Klahr, D. and Simon, H. A. (2001) 'What Have Psychologists (And Others) Discovered About the Process of Scientific Discovery?', *Current Directions in Psychological Science*, 10(3), 75–9.

Kling, R. (2004) 'The Internet and Unrefereed Scholarly Publishing', in Cronin, B., ed., *Annual Review of Information Science and Technology (ARIST)*, 38, Medford, NJ: ASIS&T, 591–631.

Kling, R. and Covi, L. (1997) 'Digital Libraries and the Practices of Scholarly Communication: Report of a Project, October 1, 1994 – September 30, 1996', CSI Working Paper, No. WP–97–03. Available at: scholarworks.iu.edu/dspace/html/2022/179/wp97–03B.html (last accessed January 2009).

Kling, R. and McKim, G. (1999) 'Scholarly Communication and the Continuum of Electronic Publishing', *Journal of the American Society for Information Science*, 50 (10), 890–906.

——(2000) 'Not Just a Matter of Time: Field Differences and the Shaping of Electronic Media in Supporting Scientific Communication', *Journal of the American Society for Information Science* (JASIS), 51(14), 1306–20.

Kling, R., Spector, L. and McKim, G. (2002) 'Locally Controlled Scholarly Publishing Via the Internet: The Guild Model', *Journal of Electronic Publishing*, 8(1). Available at: www.preess.umich.edu/jep/08–01/kling.html (last accessed April 2008).

Kuhn, T. S. (1963) *The Structure of Scientific Revolutions*, Chicago: University of Chicago Press.

Kujala, S. (2003) 'User Involvement: A Review of the Benefits and Challenges', *Behaviour & Information Technology*, 22(1), 1–16.

Lancaster, F. W. and Sandore, B. A. (1997) *Technology and Management in Library and Information Services*, Urbana-Champaign: University of Illinois, Graduate School of Library and Information Science.

Lazinger, S. S., Bar-Ilan, J. and Peritz, B. C. (1997) 'Internet Use by Faculty Members in Various Disciplines: A Comparative Case Study', *Journal of the American Society for Information Science (JASIS)*, 48(6), 508–18.

Leckie, G. J. (1996) 'Desperately Seeking Citations: Uncovering Faculty Assumptions about the Undergraduate Research Process', *Journal of Academic Librarianship*, 22(3), 201–8.

Lehman, S. and Renfro, P. (1992) 'Humanists at the Keyboard: The RLIN Database as a Scholarly Resource', *Computers and the Humanities*, 26(3), 175–80.

Lenhart, A., Hitlin, P. and Madden, M. (2005) 'Teens and Technology', Washington, DC: Pew Internet & American Life Project. Available from www.pewinternet.org/Reports/2005/Teens-and-Technology.aspx (last accessed July 2009).

Levy, D. M. (2001) *Scrolling Forward – Making Sense of Documents in the Digital Age*, New York, NY: Arcade Publishing.

Li, N., Kirkup, G. and Hodgson, B. (2001) 'Cross-Cultural Comparison of Women Students' Attitudes Toward the Internet and Usage: China and the United Kingdom', Cyberpsychology & Behavior, 4(3), 415–26.

Liebscher, P., Abels, E. G. and Denman, D. W. (1997) 'Factors That Influence the Use of Electronic Networks by Science and Engineering Faculty at Small Institutions. Part II. Preliminary Use Indicators', *Journal of the American Society for Information Science (JASIS)*, 48(6), 496–507.

Line, M. B. (1969) 'Information Requirements in the Social Sciences: Some Preliminary Considerations', *Journal of Librarianship*, 1(1), 1–19.

——(1971) 'The Information Uses and Needs of Social Scientists: An Overview of INFROSS', *Aslib Proceedings*, 23, 412–34.

——(1973) 'Information Needs of the Social Sciences', *INSPEL, International Journal of Special Libraries*, 8(2), 29–39.

——(1974) 'Draft Definitions: Information and Library Needs, Wants, Demands and Uses', *Aslib Proceedings*, 26(2), 87.

Line, M. B. and Sandison, A. (1974) '"Obsolescence" and Changes in the Use of Literature with Time', (Progress in Documentation) *Journal of Documentation*, 30(3), 283–350.

Lippincott, J. K. (2005) 'Net Generation Students and Libraries', *Educause Review*, 40 (2), 56–66.

Liu, Z. (2004) 'Perceptions of Credibility of Scholarly Information on the Web', *Information Processing and Management*, 40(6), 1027–38.

London, J. (1999) 'Lay Public Use of Healthcare Websites', in Davidson, P. L., ed., *The Handbook of Healthcare Information Systems*, Boca Raton: CRC Press.

Lucky, R. (2000) 'The Quickening of Science Communication', *Science*, 289(5477), 259–64.

McCreadie, M. and Rice, R. E. (1999) 'Trends in Analyzing Access to Information. Part I: Cross-Disciplinary Conceptualizations of Access', *Information Processing and Management*, 35 (1), 45–76.

Macgregor, G. (2005) 'The Nature of Information in the Twenty-First Century: Conundrums for the Informatics Community?' *Library Review*, 54(1), 10–23.

Madden, M. (2003) *America's Online Pursuits: The Changing Picture of Who's Online and What They Do*, Washington, DC: Pew Internet & American Life Project. Available at: www.pewinternet.org/pdfs/PIP_Online_Pursuits_Final.PDF (last accessed May 2008).

Mahe, A. (2003) 'Beyond Usage: Understanding the Use of Electronic Journals on the Basis of Information Activity Analysis', *Information Research*, 9(4)

Mahe, A., Andrys, C. and Chartron, G. (2000) 'How French Research Scientists are Making Use of Electronic Journals: A Case Study Conducted at Pierre et Marie Curie University and Denis Diderot University', *Journal of Information Science*, 26 (5), 291–302.

Martell, C. (2008) 'The Absent User: Physical Use of Academic Library Collections and Services Continues to Decline 1995 – 2006', *The Journal of Academic Librarianship*, 34(5), 400–7.

Martin, S. (1998) 'Internet Use in the Classroom: The Impact of Gender', *Social Science Computer Review*, 16(4), 411–8.

Marwick, C. (1999) 'Cyberinformation for Seniors', *Journal of the American Medical Association*, 281(16), 1474–7.

Maslow, A. (1954) *Motivation and Personality*, New York: Harper.

Massey-Burzio, V. (1999) 'The Rush to Technology: A View from the Humanists', *Library Trends*, 47(4), 620–39.

Matzat, U. (2004) 'Academic Communication and Internet Discussion Groups: Transfer of Information or Creation of Social Contacts?', *Social Networks*, 26, 221–55.

Meadows, A. J. (1974) *Communication in Science*, London: Butterworths.

Meho, L. I. and Tibbo, H. R. (2003) 'Modelling the Information-Seeking Behavior of Social Scientists: Ellis's Study Revisited', *Journal of the American Society for Information Science and Technology* (JASIST), 54(6), 570–87.

Mellon, C. A. (1986) 'Library Anxiety: A Grounded Theory and Its Development', *College and Research Libraries*, 47(2), 160–5.

——(1988) 'Attitudes: The Forgotten Dimension in Library Instruction', *Library Journal*, 113(14), 137–9.

Menzel, H. (1964) 'The Information Needs of Current Scientific Research', *Library Quarterly*, 34, 4–19.

Meyer, J. B., Kaplan, D. and Charum, J. (2001) 'Scientific Nomadism and the New Geopolitics of Knowledge', *International Social Science Journal*, 53(2), 309–21.

Møller, A. P. (1990) 'National Citations', *Nature*, 348(6301), 480.

Morahan-Martin, J. (1998) 'Males, Females and the Internet', in Gackenback, J., ed., *Psychology and the Internet: Intrapersonal, Interpersonal and Transpersonal Applications*, San Diego, CA: Academic Press, 169–97.

Moss, M. (2008) 'The Library in the Digital Age', in Nicholas, D. and Rowlands, I., eds, *Digital Consumers: Reshaping the Information Professions*, London: Facet Publishing, 69–91.

Narin, F. and Hamilton, K. S. (1996) 'Bibliometric Performance Measures', *Scientometrics*, 36(3), 293–310.

Nicholas, D. (1995) *An Assessment of Stereotypical Models of On-Line Searching Behaviour: End-Users. Case Study Practitioners: Politicians and Journalists*, PhD Dissertation, London: City University.

Nicholas, D., Huntington, P., Lievesley, N. and Wasti, A. (2000) 'Evaluating Consumer Web Site Logs: Case Study, The Times/Sunday Times Website', *Journal of Information Science*, 26(6), 399–411.

Nicholas, D., Huntington, P. and Watkinson, A. (2003a) 'Digital Journals, Big Deals and Online Searching Behaviour: A Pilot Study', *Aslib Proceedings*, 55(1/2), 84–109.

Nicholas, D., Dobrowolski, T., Withey, R., Russell, C., Huntington, P. and Williams, P. (2003b) 'Digital Information Consumers, Players and Purchasers: Information Seeking Behaviour in the New Digital Interactive Environment', *Aslib Proceedings*, 55(1/2), 23–31.

Nicholas, D., Williams, P. and Dennis, K. (2004a) 'Improving Websites in the Voluntary Sector', *Library and Information, Update: The Magazine of the Chartered Institute of Library and Information Professionals*, 3(3), 35–7.

Nicholas, D., Huntington, P., Williams, P. and Dobrowolski, T. (2004b) 'Reappraising Information Seeking Behaviour in a Digital Environment: Bouncers, Checkers, Returnees and the Like', *Journal of Documentation*, 60(1), 24–43.

Nicholas, D. and Huntington, P. (2005) *Digital Health Information Consumers and the BBC Website*, (bbc.co.uk) London: UCL, SLAIS (unpublished report).

Nicholas, D., Huntington, P. and Watkinson, A. (2005) 'Scholarly Journal Usage: The Results of Deep Log Analysis', *Journal of Documentation*, 61(2), 248–80.

Nicholas, D. and Huntington, P. (2006) 'Digital Journals: Are They Really Used?', *Interlending and Document Supply*, 34(2), 74–7.

Nicholas, D., Huntington, P., Jamali, H. R. and Watkinson, A. (2006a) 'The Information Seeking Behaviour of the Users of Digital Scholarly Journals', *Information Processing and Management*, 42(5), 1345–65.

Nicholas, D., Jamali, H. R. and Rowlands, I. (2006b) 'On the Tips of their Tongues: Authors and Their Views on Scholarly Publishing', *Learned Publishing*, 19(3), 193–203.

Nicholas, D., Huntington, P. and Jamali, H. R. (2007a) *Digital Health Information for the Consumer: Evidence and Policy Implications*, London, England: Ashgate Publishing.

Nicholas, D., Huntington, P., Rowlands, I., Dobrowolski, T. and Jamali, H. R. (2007b) 'Superbook: An Action Research Project', *Online Information 2007 Proceedings*, 50–7.

Nicholas, D., Huntington, P., Jamali, H. R. and Dobrowolski, T. (2007c) 'Characterising and Evaluating Information Seeking Behaviour in a Digital Environment: Spotlight on the 'Bouncer'', *Information Processing and Management*, 43(4), 1085–102.

Nicholas, D., Huntington, P. and Jamali, H. R. (2007d) 'The Use, Users, and Role of Abstracts in the Digital Scholarly Environment', *The Journal of Academic Librarianship*, 33(4), 446–53.

Nicholas, D., Huntington, P., Jamali, H. R. (2007e) 'Open Access in Context: A User Study', *Journal of Documentation*, 63(6), 853–78.

Nicholas, D., Rowlands, I., Withey, R. and Dobrowolski, T. (2008a) 'The Digital Consumer: An Introduction and Philosophy', in Nicholas, D. and Rowlands, I., eds, *Digital Consumers: Reshaping the Information Professions*, London: Facet Publishing, 1–11.

Nicholas, D., Huntington, P., Jamali, H. R. and Dobrowolski, T. (2008b) 'The Information-Seeking Behaviour of the Digital Consumer: Case Study the Virtual Scholar', in Nicholas, D. and Rowlands, I., eds, *Digital Consumers: Reshaping the Information Professions*, London: Facet Publishing, 113–58.

Nicholas, D., Rowlands, I., Clark, D., Huntington, P., Jamali, H. R. and Olle, C. (2008c) 'UK Scholarly e-Book Usage: A Landmark Survey', *Aslib Proceedings*, 60 (4), 311–34.

Nicholas, D., Huntington, P. and Jamali, H. R. (2008d) 'Diversity in the Information Seeking Behaviour of the Virtual Scholar: Institutional Comparisons', *The Journal of Academic Librarianship*, 33(6), 629–38.

Nicholas, D., Huntington, P. and Jamali, H. R. (2008e) 'User Diversity: As Demonstrated by Deep Log Analysis', *The Electronic Library,* 26(1), 21–38.

Nicholas, D., Clark, D., Rowlands, I. and Jamali, H. R. (2009) 'Online Use and Information Seeking Behaviour: Institutional and Subject Comparisons of UK Researchers', *Journal of Information Science*, XX(X), 1–22.

Nielsen, J. (2000) *Designing Web Usability*, Indianapolis: New Riders Publishing.

Noam, E. M. (1997) 'Electronics and the Future of the Research Library', in *Proceedings of the 1997 ACRL National Conference: Choosing Our Futures.* Available at: www.ala.org/acrl/invited/noam.html (last accessed June 2007).

OCLC (2007) Sharing, Privacy and Trust in Our Networked World: A Report to the OCLC Membership, Dublin, OH: OCLC.

Odlyzko, A. M. (2000) 'The Rapid Evolution of Scholarly Communication', in *Conference on the Economics and Usage of Digital Library Collections, March 23–24, 2000.* Available at: www.si.umich.edu/PEAK-2000/program.htm (last accessed February 2008).

Ono, H. and Zavodny, M. (2003) 'Gender and the Internet', *Social Science Quarterly*, 84(1), 111–21.

Onwuegbuzie, A. J., Jiao, Q. G. and Bostick, S. L. (2004) *Library Anxiety: Theory, Research, and Applications*, Lanham, MD: Scarecrow.

Palmer, C. L. and Neumann, L. J. (2002) 'The Information Work of Interdisciplinary Humanities Scholars: Exploration and Translation', *Library Quarterly*, 72(1), 85–117.

Palmer, J. (1991) 'Scientists and Information: II. Personal Factors in Information Behavior', *Journal of Documentation*, 47(3), 254–75.

Park, T. K. (1993) 'The Nature of Relevance in Information Retrieval: An Empirical Study', *Library Quarterly*, 63(3), 318–51.

Pettigrew, K. E., Fidel, R. and Bruce, H. (2001) 'Conceptual Frameworks in Information Behavior', in Williams, M. E., ed., *Annual Review of Information Science and Technology (ARIST)*, 35, Medford, NJ: ASIS, 43–78.

Pew Center for the People & the Press (2008) *Continuing Partisan Divide in Cable TV News Audiences; Internet Now Major Source of Campaign News*, Pew Research Center

Biennial News Consumption Survey, 31 October 2008. Available at: people-press. org/reports/pdf/467.pdf (last accessed May 2009).

Pinto, M. and Lancaster, F. W. (1999) 'Abstracts and Abstracting in Knowledge Discovery', *Library Trends*, 48(1), 234–48.

Planck, M. (1968) *Scientific Autobiography and Other Papers*, New York: Greenwood.

Price, D. J. de Solla (1963) *Little Science, Big Science*, New York: Columbia University Press.

——(1975) *Science since Babylon*, New Haven, CT: Yale University Press.

——(1986) *Little Science, Big Science ... and Beyond*, New York: Columbia University Press.

Pullinger, D. (1999) 'Academics and the New Information Environment: The Impact of Local Factors in the Use of Electronic Journals', *Journal of Information Science*, 25(2), 164–72.

Rosenbaum, H., Davenport, E., Lievrouw, L. and Day, R. (2003) 'The Death of the User', in Todd, R. J., ed., *Humanizing Information Technology: From Ideas to Bits and Back,* Proceedings of the 66th ASIST Annual Meeting, 40, Medford, NJ: Information Today, 429–30.

Rothenberg, D. (1993) 'Changing Values in the Published Literature with Time', *Library Trends*, 41(4), 684–99.

Rowlands, I. and Nicholas, D. (2007) 'The Missing Link: Journal Usage Metrics', *Aslib Proceedings*, 59(3), 222–8.

Rowlands, I., Nicholas, D., Jamali, H. R. and Huntington, P. (2007) 'What Do Faculty and Students Really Think about e-Books?', *Aslib Proceedings*, 59(6), 489–511.

Russell, C. (2008) 'The e-Shopper: The Growth of the Informed Purchaser', in Nicholas, D. and Rowlands, I., eds, *Digital Consumers: Reshaping the Information Professions*, London: Facet Publishing, 35–67.

Russell, J. M. (2001) 'Scientific Communication at the Beginning of the Twenty-First Century', *International Social Science Journal*, 53(2), 271–82.

Sack, J. (1986) 'Open Systems for Open Minds: Building the Library without Walls', *College and Research Libraries,* 47(6), 535–44.

Saule, M. R. (1992) 'User Instruction Issues for Databases in the Humanities', *Library Trends*, 40(4), 596–613.

Savolainen, R. (2006) 'Time as a Context of Information Seeking', *Library and Information Science Research*, 28(1), 110–27.

——(2007) 'Filtering and Withdrawing: Strategies for Coping with Information Overload in Everyday Contexts', *Journal of Information Science*, 33(5), 611–21.

Schauder, D. (1994) 'Electronic Publishing of Professional Articles: Attitudes of Academics and Implications for the Scholarly Industry', *Journal of the American Society for Information Science (JASIS)*, 45(2), 73–100.

Schwartz, C. A. (1992) 'Research Significance: Behavioral Patterns and Outcome Characteristics', *Library Quarterly*, 62(2), 123–49.

Schwartz, H. and Jacobs, J. (1979) *Qualitative Sociology: A Method to the Madness*, New York: Free Press.

Schwartz, J. (2008) 'Logging On for a Second (or Third) Opinion', *The New York Times*, 30 September 2008.

Shenton, A. K. and Dixon, P. (2004) 'The Nature of Information Needs and Strategies for Their Investigation in Youngsters', *Library and Information Science Research*, 26 (3), 296–310.

Sherwin, A. (2008) 'Web Socialites Succumb to Facebook Fatigue', *The Times*, 22 February 2008, 10.

Shinebourne, J. (1980) 'User Needs, the New Technology and Traditional Approaches to Library Services', *Journal of Information Science*, 2(3/4), 135–40.

Simon, P. (2001) 'The Strange Online Death and Possible Rebirth of Brand Theory and Practice', *Aslib Proceedings*, 53(7), 245–9.

Slater, M. (1963) 'Types of Use and Users in Industrial Libraries: Some Impressions'. *Journal of Documentation*, 19(1), 12–18.

Smeby, J.-C. and Trondal, J. (2005) 'Globalisation or Europeanisation? International Contact among University Staff', *Higher Education*, 49(4), 449–66.

Smith, A. (2009) 'The Internet's Role in Campaign 2008', Washington, DC: Pew Internet & American Life Project. Available at: www.pewinternet.org/Reports/2009/6-The-Internets-Role-in-Campaign-2008.aspx (last accessed May 2009).

Starkweather, W. M. and Wallin, C. C. (1999) 'Faculty Response to Library Technology: Insights on Attitudes', *Library Trends,* 47(4), 640–68.

Stefl-Mabry, J., Belkin, N., Dillon, A. and Marchionini, G. (2003) 'User-Centered Design: Science or Window Dressing?', in Todd, R. J., ed., *Humanizing Information Technology: From Ideas to Bits and Back,* Proceedings of the 66th ASIST Annual Meeting, 40, Medford, NJ: Information Today, 441.

Stoan, S. K. (1984) 'Research and Library Skills: An Analysis and Interpretation', *College and Research Libraries*, 45(2), 99–109.

——(1991) 'Research and Information Retrieval among Academic Researchers: Implications for Library Instruction', *Library Trends*, 39(3), 238–58.

Stone, S. (1982) 'Humanities Scholars: Information Needs and Uses', *Journal of Documentation*, 38(4), 292–313.

Storer, N. W. (1967) 'The Hard Sciences and the Soft: Some Sociological Observations', *Bulletin of the Medical Library Association*, 55, 75–84.

Suber, P. (2007) 'Open Access Overview'. Available at: www.earlham.edu/~peters/fos/overview.htm (last accessed June 2008).

Swope, M. J. and Katzer, J. (1972) 'Why Don't They Ask Questions? The Silent Majority', *RQ*, 12(2), 161–6.

Talja, S. and Maula, H. (2003) 'Reasons for the Use and Non-use of Electronic Journals and Databases: A Domain-Analytic Study in Four Scholarly Disciplines', *Journal of Documentation*, 59(6), 673–91.

Tannen, D. (1991) 'War of Words', *The Guardian*, 27 April 1991.

Tenopir, C. and King, D. W. (2000) *Towards Electronic Journals: Realities for Scientists, Librarians, and Publishers*, Washington, DC: Special Libraries Association.

Thorsteinsdottir, O. H. (2000) 'External Research Collaboration in Two Small Science Systems', *Scientometrics*, 49(1), 145–60.

Tibbo, H. R. (1994) 'Indexing for the Humanities', *Journal of the American Society for Information Science (JASIS)*, 45(8), 607–19.

Vekiri, I. and Chronaki, A. (2008) 'Gender Issues in Technology Use: Perceived Social Support, Computer Self-Efficacy and Value Beliefs, and Computer Use Beyond School', Computers & Education, 51(3), 1392–404.

Voorbij, H. J. (1999) 'Searching Scientific Information on the Internet: A Dutch Academic User Survey', *Journal of the American Society for Information Science (JASIS)*, 50 (7), 598–615.

Walsh, J. P. and Bayma, T. (1996) 'Computer Networks and Scientific Work', *Social Studies of Science*, 26(3), 661–703.

Wang, P., Hawk, W. B. and Tenopir, C. (2000) 'Users' Interaction with World Wide Web Resources: An Exploratory Study Using a Holistic Approach', Information Processing & Management, 36(2), 229–51.

Wang, Y. and Cohen, A. (1998) 'University Faculty Use of the Internet', in *Proceedings of Selected Research and Development Presentations at the National Convention of the Association for Educational Communications and Technology (AECT)*, St Louis, MO, 18–22 February 1998.

Wasserman, I. M. and Richmond-Abbott, M. (2005) 'Gender and the Internet: Causes of Variation in Access, Level, and Scope of Use', *Social Science Quarterly*, 86(1), 252–70.

Weintraub, K. J. (1980) 'The Humanistic Scholar and the Library', in Proceedings of the Fortieth Conference of the Graduate Library School, The University of Chicago, 18–19 May 1979, *The Library Quarterly*, 50(1), 22–39.

Wiberley, S. E., Jr and Jones, W. G. (1989) 'Patterns of Information Seeking in the Humanities', *College and Research Libraries*, 50(6), 638–45.

——(1994) 'Humanists Revisited: A Longitudinal Look at the Adoption of Information Technology', *College and Research Libraries*, 55(6), 499–509.

——(2000) 'Time and Technology: A Decade-Long Look at Humanists' Use of Electronic Information Technology', *College and Research Libraries*, 61(5), 421–31.

Wildemuth, B. M. (1993) 'Post-Positivist Research: Two Examples of Methodological Pluralism', *Library Quarterly*, 63(4), 450–68.

Williams, P., Nicholas, D. and Huntington, P. (2003) 'Non-use of Health Information Kiosks Examined in an Information Needs Context', *Health Information and Libraries Journal*, 20(2), 95–103.

Williams, P., Rowlands, I. and Fieldhouse, M. (2008) 'The 'Google Generation' – Myths and Realities about Young People's Digital Information Behaviour', in Nicholas, D. and Rowlands, I., eds, *Digital Consumers: Reshaping the Information Professions*, London: Facet Publishing, 159–92.

Williams, R. (1993) 'Office Slaves Miss Out on the Office Revolution', *The Independent*, 4 July 1993, 5.

Williamson, K., Bow, A. and Wale, K. (1997) 'Older People and the Internet', *Link-Up*, 9–12 March. Available at: www.sims.monash.edu.au/research/itnr/papers/olderp2.html (last accessed December 2008).

Wilson, P. (1993a) 'Communication Efficiency in Research and Development', *Journal of the American Society for Information Science (JASIS)*, 44(7), 376–82.

——(1993b) 'The Value of Currency', *Library Trends*, 41(4), 632–43.

——(1995) 'Unused Relevant Information in Research and Development', *Journal of the American Society for Information Science (JASIS)*, 46(1), 45–51.

——(1996) 'Interdisciplinary Research and Information Overload', *Library Trends*, 45 (2), 192–203.

Wilson, T. D. (1981) 'On User Studies and Information Needs', *Journal of Documentation*, 37(1), 1981, 3–15.

——(1997) 'Information Behaviour: An Interdisciplinary Perspective', *Information Processing and Management*, 33(4), 551–72.

——(1999) 'Models in Information Seeking Behaviour Research', *Journal of Documentation*, 55 (3), 249–70.

——(2006) 'On User Studies and Information Needs', *Journal of Documentation*, 62 (6), 658–70.

Ybarra, M. and Suman, M. (2008) 'Reasons, Assessments and Actions Taken: Sex and Age Differences in Uses of Internet Health Information', *Health Education Research*, 23(3), 512–21.

Zhang, Y. (1999) 'Scholarly Use of Internet-Based Electronic Resources: A Survey Report', *Library Trends*, 47(4), 746–70.

Ziman, J. (1970) 'Ziman Plays Cassandra', *New Scientist*, 46, 318–24.

Zwemer, R. L. (1963) 'A Biological Information User Survey: Discussions and Observations', *Studies in Biological Literature and Communications*, 2, Philadelphia: Biological Abstracts, Inc.

Index

academic, researcher 9; citation 79–80,
151–52; 'cyberspace colleges' 116;
determinants of information needs
and practices (age 125; experience
114–15; resources availability and
costs 136; seniority 115–16, 133;
solitary/team-based occupation
116–17; time availability 133); Ellis's
'differentiating' information-seeking
patterns 62, 71; English 100–101;
e-print repositories 41, 108, 113–14;
'hard'/'soft' continuum of knowledge
domains 61, 86–87, 100, 101, 103;
health-related area 46, 59, 61, 86, 89,
112; information consumption 71
(selective reading 71); information
date/currency 39–41, 86–89;
information needs 22–23, 54, 58;
information point of view 61–67
(school of thought 61–64; subject
orientation 66–67); information
quality/authority 74, 76–77, 78–80,
89; information quantity 68, 69, 71;
information retrieval 109;
information-seeking behaviour 29, 30,
31, 33, 34–35, 37, 38, 41–42, 46, 71,
79, 92, 115, 132–33; information
speed of delivery 90, 91–92, 93;
information use 36, 38–39, 41, 87, 101
(briefing/background function 45–46;
current awareness function 38–42;
research function 42–44; stimulus
function 47–48); levels of information
58; librarian, library 9, 12, 13, 33, 34,
38, 93, 109; nature of information
53–54; place of publication/origin
95–98 (language proficiency 100–101;
practitioner/academic divide 95,
98–99); processing and packaging
102–8 (abstract 102–4; electronic
media 107–8; personal contact 105,
109, 112, 115–16; printed/electronic
information packaging 106–7; review
article 104); scholarly information
78–80, 92, 97, 98, 103, 104, 105, 113,
126, 127; scholarly journals/
publications 22, 34, 60, 78–81, 113,
115, 151 ('publish or perish' system
80–81, 92, 133); scholarly sites 69, 92;
United States 126; see also digital
consumer; humanist;
information-seeking behaviour;
scientist; social scientist
accountability, auditing 15–16, 21;
digital consumer 16
Amazon 5, 93, 127
archive, archiving 2, 41–42, 88;
accountability 16; archivist 2

bibliographic tools 31, 34, 64, 151; see
also information-seeking
browsing 22–23, 25, 30, 32, 40, 153;
abstracts 104; humanist 48; library 36;
'power browsing' 23, 50, 60, 73, 82,
92, 104, 134; recreational browsing
function 37, 48–49, 50, 55; search
engine 36; surfing 47, 48, 49, 55, 118,
119, 155; young people 50; see also
information-seeking;
information-seeking behaviour
British Broadcasting Corporation (BBC)
36, 77, 83, 125

catalogue 5, 31, 48, 51, 94, 106; online
public access catalogues (OPACs) 109
CIBER 22, 34, 36, 49, 50, 90, 98, 111,
129; British Library's learning site for
young scholars 98, 126–27; digital